BY THE SAME AUTHOR

Korea: *The First War We Lost*

The Strange Connection: *U.S. Intervention in China 1944–1972*

Lost Victories: *The Military Genius of Stonewall Jackson*

HOW
GREAT
GENERALS
WIN

 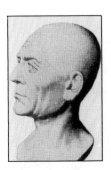

HANNIBAL BARCA   SCIPIO AFRICANUS

GENGHIS KHAN   NAPOLEON BONAPARTE   THOMAS J. JACKSON   WILLIAM T. SHERMAN

E. LAWRENCE   SIR EDMUND ALLENBY   MAO ZEDONG   HEINZ GUDERIAN

ERICH VON MANSTEIN   ERWIN ROMMEL   DOUGLAS MAC ARTHUR

NEW YORK · LONDON

HOW GREAT GENERALS WIN

BEVIN ALEXANDER

W · W · NORTON & COMPANY

First published as a Norton paperback 2002

*The text of this book is composed in Caledonia with the display set in Caslon
and Craw Modern. Composition and manufacturing by the Maple-Vail Book
Manufacturing Group. Book design by Marjorie J. Flock.*

Cartography by Jacques Chazaud

Library of Congress Cataloging-in-Publication Data
Alexander, Bevin.
    How great generals win/by Bevin Alexander
        p. cm.
    Includes index.
    1. Military art and science—History. 2. Battles. 3. Generals.
    I. Title.
    U27.A625 1993
    355'.009—dc20   92-40518
ISBN 0-393-03531-X
ISBN 0-393-32316-1 pbk.

W. W. Norton & Company, Inc.
500 Fifth Avenue, New York, N.Y. 10110
www.wwnorton.com

W. W. Norton & Company Ltd.
Castle House, 75/76 Wells Street, London W1T 3QT

1 2 3 4 5 6 7 8 9 0

Contents

Maps

Photographs

HOW GREAT GENERALS WIN

Introduction

THE RULES OF WAR ARE SIMPLE BUT SELDOM FOLLOWED

MY UNDERSTANDING of how great generals win commenced with realizing how not-so-great generals *don't* win. This learning process started on a hot day in August 1951, when, as commander of the U.S. Army's 5th Historical Detachment, I stood in a valley of the Taebaek Mountains of eastern Korea and watched American artillery pulverize Hill 983 about 1,000 yards in front of me.

This mountain and the similar one just to the north had not then attained the names—Bloody Ridge and Heartbreak Ridge— by which they would go down in history as the quintessential battles of the Korean War. But those of us standing there on that summer day watching the artillery shells methodically obliterate all traces of vegetation from 983 already knew what was in store.

The attack was to be direct—straight up the steep slopes of the mountain, climbing 3,200 feet above sea level. The attack was also to be without surprise: the assemblage of a dozen artillery battalions in the valley south of the mountain had told the North Korean defenders that the top American commander in Korea, Lieutenant General James A. Van Fleet, had singled out their bastion for assault.

Thus the gruesome battle that followed, and the even more gruesome battle to capture Heartbreak that came directly on its heels, were programmed from the outset, as if both sides had been handed a script and told to follow it precisely.

The American artillery destroyed all the vegetation but could damage only a tiny fraction of the dirt-, rock-, and timber-covered bunkers in which the Communist soldiers hid. Thereafter, American, South Korean, and, on Heartbreak, French infantrymen climbed the steep fingers leading up to the peaks, the only avenues available to root the enemy out of their bunkers and drive them away. The North Korean and Red Chinese soldiers knew these avenues of approach as well as the United Nations troops, and they carefully zeroed in their automatic weapons and mortars on them and created fields of fire to decimate the climbing United Nations infantry.

It all worked out as programmed—the superior UN firepower at last wrested the peaks from the Communists—but the cost was staggering. UN casualties, the vast bulk of them American, totaled 6,400, while Communist losses may have reached 40,000. Yet the UN command gained nothing. Its strategic position in Korea was not affected one iota, and there were almost no tactical gains: behind Heartbreak loomed another ridgeline equally pitted with bunkers. And behind this third ridge rose many more ridges that could have been armored with bunkers as well.

The only thing achieved by the battles of Bloody and Heartbreak ridges—and by all the numerous other battles for ridgelines that the 8th United States Army in Korea ordered during the fall of 1951—was that the American command finally realized the futility of frontal attacks against prepared positions. There was no great intellectual awakening to the foolhardiness of the policy. The reason was simply that the cost of further attacks was too high. The period between the start of the "peace talks" in July and the cessation of the ridgeline assaults at the end of October 1951 had produced 60,000 UN and an estimated 234,000 Communist casualties.

It is incredible that it took such bloodletting to teach an obvious lesson. From the beginning of organized warfare, frontal attacks against prepared defenses have usually failed, a fact written large in military history for all generals to see. Even more pertinent, because it was part of the active-service experience or training of the senior generals in Korea, was the trench warfare of World War I—which this phase of the Korean War copied almost exactly. World War I had showed conclusively that frontal attacks could not succeed, except at such an enormous human cost that the term "victor" became derisory, since no one emerged a winner from those rendezvous with death at the disputed barricades of the western front.

Yet the lesson had not been learned. The men who had seen or studied the trench warfare of World War I ordered it anew in the Korean War. And the results in Korea were identical to what they had been in Europe: enormous human losses and no appreciable tactical or strategic gains.

The lesson I learned from Bloody Ridge and Heartbreak Ridge was that great generals do not act as did the generals who ordered the ridgeline battles in Korea. Great generals do not repeat what has failed before. They do not send troops directly into a battle for which the enemy is prepared and waiting. On the contrary, great generals strike where they are least expected against opposition that is weak and disorganized.

The tremendous advances in military technology since the Korean War have not changed this fundamental truth. Technology governs only what methods we use to achieve military decisions. Advances in weaponry actually increase the need for generals to avoid the most heavily defended and dangerous positions and to seek decisions at points where the enemy does not anticipate strikes.

Especially since the Vietnam War, astonishing improvements have occurred in the accuracy and deadliness of rocketry and conventional (nonnuclear) weapons by use of satellites to navigate with precision and radar, infrared, laser, and other sounding devices to guide "smart" bombs and missiles onto targets. These advances have brought forth predictions of future "automated battlefields" where weapons will be so effective that human beings will be unable to survive on them and battles will be fought by robots and all sorts of unmanned aircraft, vehicles, and weapons.

But there is a significant countertrend that portends warfare depending less on overwhelming firepower and more on movements of small bodies of unobtrusive individuals who achieve their goals by surprise, ambushes, and unanticipated movements.

The reason war may be moving in this seemingly contradictory direction is that the technology that has produced main battle tanks, assault aircraft, warships, and rockets has also produced weapons that can destroy many of these offensive weapons. Defensive weapons are much cheaper than offensive weapons, and some can be held in the hands of a single defender. One such is the Stinger missile, which Afghan rebels used effectively to knock down helicopters during the Soviet Union's intervention in Afghanistan in the 1980s. The Patriot missile, which destroyed Iraqi Scud missiles in the Persian Gulf War of 1991 and can destroy attacking aircraft, costs only a fraction of a Scud's price and about 1 percent of a fighter-bomber's.

If, as a number of technologists believe, the tank is already obsolete and manned aircraft and large warships too expensive, complicated, and vulnerable to survive for long against defensive missiles, then future wars may be fought less by unmanned weapons and robots on an "automated battlefield" and more by small bodies of dispersed, well-trained, and well-armed troops who move deceptively and inconspicuously around obstacles, conducting war more like what we associate today with guerrilla or semiguerrilla forces. The Soviet Union lost such a war in Afghanistan.

It is unlikely that mankind will resort to nuclear war. Any use of a nuclear bomb would bring an instant nuclear reprisal, which could accelerate beyond human capacity to control and result in making most of the earth uninhabitable. No sane ruler wants to sentence his own people to death. Even if a mad dictator secures a nuclear device and uses it, sensible world leaders almost certainly will destroy him and his scientists with a surgical blow but will not succumb to nuclear holocaust.

The future is not ours to see. But it will probably bring to war the same challenges that have burdened generals since the beginning of armed conflict: how to avoid the enemy's main strength and how to strike a decisive blow against him. War will change, but the principles of war will remain the same.

The English strategist Basil H. Liddell Hart says the goal of the great captain is the same as that of Paris in the Trojan War of Greek legend 3,000 years ago. Paris avoided any obvious target on the foremost Greek champion, Achilles, but instead directed his arrow at Achilles' only vulnerable point, his heel.

The outstanding Confederate cavalry raider Nathan Bedford Forrest encapsulated the secret of great generals when he said that the key to victory is "to get there first with the most."

However, the true test of the great general is broader than this: it is to decide where "there" is, where the Achilles' heel can be located. For the point where the successful commander concentrates his forces must be a point that is vital or at least extremely important to the enemy. To get there first with the most, the military commander must understand and practice the aim of another great Confederate leader, Stonewall Jackson, to "mystify, mislead, and surprise" the enemy.

This is because no intelligent enemy commander will willingly uncover a point or place that is vital or important to him. He will do so only if forced or deceived. To achieve such force or deception, the great captain will nearly always act in one of two manners. He will move so as to make the opposing general think he is aiming at a point different from what he is actually aiming at. Or he will operate in such a way that the enemy commander must, in the words of the greatest Union general in the American Civil War, William Tecumseh Sherman, find himself "on the horns of a dilemma," unable to defend two or more points or objectives and thus forced to cede at least one in order to save another.

One of the remarkable facts about great generals throughout history is that—except in cases where they possessed overwhelming power—practically all their successful moves have been made against the enemy's flank or rear, either actual or psychological. Great generals realize that a rear attack distracts, dislocates, and often defeats an enemy physically by cutting him off from his supplies, communications, and reinforcements and mentally by undermining his confidence and sense of security. Great generals know a direct attack, on the other hand, consolidates an enemy's defenses and, even if he is defeated, merely forces him back on his reserves and his supplies.

These concepts have been accepted in principle in many armies for a long time. Against a weak or incompetent enemy they are easy to apply. In the 1991 Gulf War, for example, U.S. General H. Norman Schwarzkopf applied this classic doctrine to defeat the 500,000-man Iraqi army in a hundred hours. While "fixing" the main Iraqi force in Kuwait in place by threatening an amphibious invasion from the gulf and by launching two U.S. Marine divisions and other forces directly on Kuwait, he sent two mobile corps nearly 200 miles westward into the Arabian Desert. These corps then swept around behind the Iraqi army, cutting off its line of supply and retreat to Baghdad and pressing it into a tight corner between the Euphrates River, the gulf, and the marines advancing from the south. Iraqi soldiers surrendered by the thousands and resistance collapsed.

Not all wars are so one-sided as the 1991 Gulf War and not all opponents so ready to surrender. In war the one great incalculable is human resistance. Because enemy response is so unpredictable, commonplace or mediocre generals often do not understand the full significance of flank or rear attacks and, usually because of strong enemy resistance, find themselves drawn or provoked into a direct strategy and frontal attacks, which are rarely decisive.

One of the factors that make a general great, and therefore make him rare, is that he can withstand the urge of most men to rush headlong into direct engagements and can see instead how he can go around rather than through his opponent.

One reason such generals are few is that the military profession, like society as a whole, applauds direct solutions and is suspicious of personalities given to indirection and unfamiliar methods, labeling them as deceptive, dishonest, or underhanded. A big cause of American hatred of the Japanese in World War II was that they launched a "sneak" attack against an unexpected point, Pearl Harbor in Hawaii. The military profession and the public have idealized rather the "manly" virtues of the straightforward hero who confronts his opponent in the open, a type romanticized in the cowboy of the American West who never draws his six-shooter until his opponent has already reached for his gun.

Soldiers for generations have drawn analogies between war

and sports. The Duke of Wellington said the battle of Waterloo was won on the playing fields of Eton. It is common in the U.S. Army today to equate war with American football. This is no accident. Football—not baseball—has become a symbol of war because football consists primarily of a direct challenge by an attacker against a defender. Although football can have indirect aspects, it is decidedly less a game of subtle ploys, surprise, and deception than baseball. Until the mid-1970s, U.S. Army doctrine resembled the straightforward grind-it-out, pounding, "three-yards-and-a-cloud-of-dust" game played at Ohio State University in the Woody Hayes era in mid-century. Although teaching since then has emphasized maneuver, direct solutions and head-on attack are engrained in military psychology and will be difficult to eradicate.

The sincere, candid, unsecretive leader has always been an ideal. As a consequence, the successful great general must possess a Janus-faced personality, conveying honesty and openness to his troops and subordinate leaders while hiding or dissembling the parts of his character that permit him to "mystify, mislead, and surprise" the enemy.

Some great generals have found this a difficult assignment and have suffered for it. Stonewall Jackson was notorious for his secrecy and his reluctance to tell plans to subordinates. Although his men idolized him for bringing them victories, they looked on him as strange and unapproachable, and his major commanders found him difficult, demanding, and uncommunicative. His answer to the charges was enlightening: "If I can deceive my own friends I can make certain of deceiving the enemy."

Few individuals are able to assume the double-faceted, contradictory persona required of great captains. The military system, moreover, tends to promote the direct person over the indirect. Consequently, most generals are guileless, uncomplicated warriors who lead direct campaigns and order frontal assaults. The resulting heavy casualties and indecision that characterize most wars are therefore predictable.

Even some generals who enjoy high reputations or fame have actually been predominantly direct soldiers who brought disaster to their side. One such general was Robert E. Lee, the *beau ideal* of the Southern Confederacy, who possessed integrity, honor, and loyalty in the highest degree and who also possessed skills as a commander far in excess of those of the Union generals arrayed against him. But Lee was not, himself, a great general.

Lee generally and in decisively critical situations always chose the direct over the indirect approach. For example, when the 1862 invasion of Maryland proved to be abortive, Lee did not retreat quickly into Virginia but allowed himself to be drawn into a direct confrontation at Antietam, which he had no hope of winning and which proved to be the bloodiest single battle in American history. Since the Confederacy was greatly inferior to the North in manpower, any such expenditure of blood should have been made only for great strategic gains. Standing and fighting at Antietam offered no benefits, whereas a withdrawal into Virginia would have retained the South's offensive power. Antietam also gave Abraham Lincoln the Northern victory he needed to issue the Emancipation Proclamation, which ensured that Britain and France would not come to the aid of the Confederacy.

In 1863, Lee allowed himself to be drawn into an identical battle of attrition at Gettysburg. When his direct efforts to knock aside the Union forces failed, Lee compounded his error by destroying the last offensive power of the Army of Northern Virginia in Pickett's charge across nearly a mile of open, bullet-and-shell-torn ground. This frontal assault was doomed before it started. James Longstreet and other commanders recognized this, and Lee himself acknowledged the blunder at its disastrous end, when only half of the 15,000 men in the charge returned to Confederate lines.

Yet Lee was not in a dangerous position when he bumped into the Federal Army of the Potomac at Gettysburg. He was north of the Union forces, and since supplies were far more plentiful in this direction than back in Virginia, he could easily have swung past the Federal force blocking his path and swept on to Harrisburg or York, thereby putting the Union command on "the horns of a dilemma" by threatening Philadelphia in one direction, Baltimore in another, and Washington in a third. If the bulk of the Army of the Potomac had pulled back to defend the nation's capital, Lee could have moved southeast along the Susquehanna River, threatening Philadelphia or Baltimore. If George G. Meade, the Union commander, had kept his main army shielding Washington, Lee could have captured Baltimore, where all of the rail lines to the North met, thereby cutting Washington off from reinforcements and supplies. If Meade had moved his troops to defend Baltimore, Lee could have crossed the Susquehanna and seized Philadelphia, the second-largest American city and a point disastrous for the North to lose.

Another Civil War general who enjoys fame but who came close to losing the war, this time for the North, was Ulysses S. Grant. In his 1864 campaign in Virginia, Grant threw his army into one direct assault after another against emplaced Confederate forces. Grant's aim was to destroy Lee's army. But he nearly destroyed his own, losing half of his total strength between the Wilderness in the spring and the stalemate in front of Petersburg in midsummer. By the late stages of this campaign, Grant's troops no longer were willing to press their attacks, because they knew they would be defeated. Indeed, at Cold Harbor the Union soldiers were so certain of death that before the assault they pinned their names and addresses on the backs of their uniforms so their families could be notified after the battle.

Grant achieved his only strategic success not by battle but by maneuver. He got across the James River and close to the main railway supplying Richmond from the south because he elected not, once again, to attack Lee directly in another defensive emplacement, but to slip across the James and try to capture Petersburg before it could be defended. He barely failed, and the war in Virginia turned into a stalemate that Sherman, not Grant, broke by his move on the Confederate rear.

Direct moves intellectually similar to those of Lee and Grant contributed to German defeats in two world wars. In the opening stages of World War I, the German commander, Helmuth von Moltke, undermined the famous plan of Count Alfred von Schlieffen to send the great bulk of the German army on an "end run" to the west and then south of Paris. This main German "hammer" was to turn back north and shatter the French and British armies against the German "anvil" positioned in fortresses along the Franco-German border. Moltke turned the wide indirect sweep intended to cross the Seine River west of Paris into a direct attack to the north of the river and squarely on Paris. This permitted the French to block the army's path and achieve the "miracle of the Marne" by stopping the German offensive and creating the trench-war stalemate that lasted until 1918.

In late 1942, Adolf Hitler's insistence upon a direct assault on Stalingrad instead of withdrawing German forces while there was still time resulted in the destruction of a large German army and the loss of initiative in the east—and ultimately the war—to the Russians and other Allies.

This book is intended to show, by specific examples, how great generals in the past have applied long-standing rules or principles of war that nearly always will secure victory—if only because they have used them when their opponents have not. These rules are not rigid prescriptions, like algebraic formulas, but *concepts,* which must be applied artfully as circumstances call for. They are not esoteric abstractions understandable only to military experts and advanced students in command and general staff colleges. Rather, they are applications of common sense to the ever-present problems that emerge when two nations or groups of nations range against each other in mortal combat.

The purpose of every belligerent is to impose his will on his opponent. Trying to induce others to abide by one's wishes is a common human aim, applicable to individuals and groups as well as nations. The only distinction between ordinary human disputes and war is that war is an act of violence in which one side exerts *force* against the other side. If a side could attain its purpose without force, it would, of course, do so, since no nation will attack unless there is resistance. The nineteenth-century Prussian theorist Karl von Clausewitz defined war as the continuation of national policy by other means.

It may appear obvious that every individual, group, and nation engaged in any conflict should *always* apply the policy of Paris in the Trojan War and strike only at the Achilles' heel. Yet the history of human relations, as well as of war, shows conclusively that human beings more frequently ignore or do not see the opportunities for getting around an enemy or opponent and instead strike straight at the most obvious target they see.

It is uncommon for a person to achieve his goals by moving on his opponent's rear, either literally or figuratively. Human beings have been conditioned by a million years of culture to cooperate within a group. This conditioning makes us loyal to our group and bellicose to the enemy of our group. Our tendency in each case, whether cooperating with our friends or fighting our enemies, is to be direct, not devious or circuitous.

It is only the unusual person who can separate his primeval desire to confront his enemies directly from the need to disguise and hide his actions so as to catch the enemy off guard and vulnerable. Yet this is the only route to great generalship. Sun Tzu, the celebrated Chinese strategist, wrote about 400 B.C. that "all warfare is based on deception. Hence, when able to attack, we must seem unable; when using our forces, we must seem inactive; when we are near, we must make the enemy believe that we are away; when far away, we must make him believe we are near. Hold out baits to entice the enemy. Feign disorder and crush him." Sun Tzu also wrote that in war "the way to avoid what is strong is to strike what is weak."[1]

Many people misunderstand the true objective in war. It is *not*, as numerous military and civilian leaders alike believe, the destruction of the enemy's armed forces on the battlefield. This concept, generally rendered into shorthand as "Napoleonic doctrine," dominated the writing of military textbooks and regulations and the teaching in general staff colleges for well over a century.

Napoleon himself was not the author of this "doctrine," although, as Liddell Hart points out, it emerged from Napoleon's

1. Sun Tzu, 11, 29. (In notes throughout the book, some references give only the last name of the author or editor. Works referred to are cited in full in the Selected Bibliography. References not listed in the bibliography are cited in full where they appear in the notes. Numbers in notes refer to pages.)

practice after the battle of Jena in 1806 of relying on mass rather than mobility, which had governed his strategy until then. After Jena, Napoleon was concerned exclusively with battle, confident he could crush his opponent if brought to close grips.

Later Napoleonic campaigns based on sheer offensive power obscured the lessons of earlier campaigns in which Napoleon combined deception, mobility, and surprise to achieve tremendous results with great economy of force. Clausewitz was most impressed with Napoleon's later campaigns and became the "prophet of mass," focusing attention on great battles. This doctrine suited the Prussian system of mass conscription to create a "nation in arms." The concept achieved its triumph in the Franco-Prussian War of 1870–71, when superior Prussian numbers won an advantage. Thereafter other powers hurried to imitate Germany's model. World War I showed that the generals' lust for battle combined with the recently developed machine gun reduced war to mass slaughter. Though the result was to kill or maim much of Europe's youth, the idea that war is to destroy the enemy's main force in battle has continued to influence—and in many cases guide—our thinking to this day.

Yet the purpose of war is not battle at all. It is a more perfect *peace*. To attain peace, a belligerent must break the will of the enemy people to wage war. No nation goes to war to fight. It goes to war to attain its national purpose. It may be that a nation must destroy the enemy's army to achieve this purpose. But the destruction is not the end, it is only the incidental by-product or the means to the end.

If a commander looks at the peace he is seeking at the conclusion of war, he may find numerous ways of attaining it by avoiding the enemy's main force and striking at targets that may destroy the enemy's desire or ability to wage war. The great Roman leader in the Second Punic War, Scipio Africanus, weakened the Carthaginian hold on Spain by ignoring the enemy's armies and unexpectedly seizing the main enemy base, present-day Cartagena. In the final stages of the Napoleonic Wars in 1814, the Allies forced Napoleon's surrender by turning away from his army and capturing Paris, thereby causing the French people to lose heart and give up. Sherman's army fought very few military engagements in late 1864 and early 1865, but by marching through Georgia and the Carolinas, it destroyed the will of the Southern people to wage war and caused many Rebel soldiers to desert and go home to aid their families.

Clausewitz understood that the purpose of war is political and not military and actually expressed this in his writings. But his syntax and logic were so obscure and difficult that the soldiers who drew their inspiration from Clausewitz heeded less his qualifying limitations and more his sweeping phrases—the "bloody solution, destruction of enemy forces, is the firstborn son of war"; "Let us not hear of generals who conquer without bloodshed." Clausewitz's emphasis on battle likewise demonstrated a contradiction in his theory. For if war is a continuation of policy, the *goal* to be achieved in the war is the primary purpose. But in emphasizing *victory* in war, Clausewitz looked only to the end of the war, not the subsequent peace.

Although Clausewitz was actually saying that battle is the most usual way of achieving a nation's goal in war, generations of direct soldiers—unable to weigh his contradictions or decipher his obscurities—read that it is the only way.

We now can define the purpose of military strategy, or the broad conduct of war. It is to diminish the possibility of resistance. The great general eliminates or reduces resistance by means of movement and surprise. As Sun Tzu says, "Supreme excellence consists in breaking the enemy's resistance without fighting." To achieve this, Sun Tzu recommends that the successful general "march swiftly to places where he is not expected."[2] If the general appears at points the enemy must hasten to defend, the enemy is likely to be distracted and to weaken or abandon other points, thereby contributing to or ensuring his defeat. Speed and mobility are the basic features of strategy. Napoleon said, "Space we can recover, time never."

In the chapters ahead we will examine how great generals like Napoleon have carried out the principles of war. It may be

2. Ibid., 15, 25.

of help to summarize here briefly a few of the most salient principles so as to make the actions of great generals easier to follow.

B. H. Liddell Hart epitomizes much military wisdom in two axioms. The successful general, he says, chooses the line or course of least expectation and he exploits the line of least resistance.;[3]

Although these two admonitions may seem self-evident, generals rarely follow them or understand when these axioms are employed against them. The battles of Bloody and Heartbreak ridges were fought on the lines of maximum expectation and of maximum resistance. When the Germans invaded the Low Countries in May 1940, the British and French commanders could conceive of no response but to race into Belgium to counter frontally what they believed was the principal German assault, which they also thought was frontal. This permitted the Germans to follow the line of least expectation and drive through the "impassable" Ardennes and break out at Sedan. Now *behind* the Allies, they were able to rush to the English Channel along the line of least resistance. Likewise, American leaders in December 1941 were expecting an assault in the East Indies and perhaps the Philippines and were unprepared for the Japanese aerial attack on Pearl Harbor.

Genghis Khan and his great Mongol general Subedei Bahadur practiced another principle of war, shown to perfection in Subedei's invasion of eastern Europe in 1241. We don't know the name the Mongols used for it, but the early-eighteenth-century French army strategist Pierre de Bourcet conceived the same principle independently and called it a "plan with branches."[4]

Subedei sent four separate columns into Europe. One rushed into Poland and Germany north of the Carpathians and drew off all European forces in that direction. The three others entered Hungary at widely separated points, threatening various objectives and keeping armies from Austria and other states from combining with the Hungarians. The three Mongol col-

3. Liddell Hart, *Strategy,* 341, 348.
4. Ibid., 114.

umns then converged on the Danube River near Budapest to deal with the now-unsupported Hungarians.

Bourcet recommended that generals spread out their attacking forces into two or more advancing columns that could reunite quickly when necessary but take lines threatening multiple or alternative objectives which the enemy had to defend, thus forcing him to divide his strength and prevent his concentration. If the enemy blocked one line of approach, the general could instantly develop another to serve the same purpose. Union General Sherman used this method in his march through Georgia and the Carolinas in 1864–65. His widely separated columns threatened two or more objectives, forcing the Confederates to divide their forces to defend all—and therefore they were unable to defend any. This forced the Rebels in most cases to abandon their weakly held positions without battle.

Like Sherman and Subedei, the attacker using the "plan with branches" is often able to reunite his columns to seize one objective before the enemy can react and concentrate against him. A variation is for part of an army to converge on a known objective while the rest descends on its rear.

Stonewall Jackson in the Shenandoah Valley campaign of 1862 practiced a modification of the plan by using pure deception: he advanced directly on the main Federal force along the principal approach, then secretly shifted across a high mountain to descend unexpectedly on the Federal flank and rear.

Napoleon embellished Bourcet's plan with branches by spreading separate advancing columns wide, like a weighted fishing net. These columns could concentrate quickly and close around any isolated enemy unit that fell in the way.

Napoleon also owed much to another eighteenth-century French theorist, the Comte de Guibert, who preached mobility to concentrate superior strength against a point of enemy weakness and to maneuver against the flank or rear of the enemy. Using great mobility, Napoleon maneuvered his waving net, stretched wide over a large region. This greatly confused his foes, who were unable to fathom Napoleon's real purpose. They usually spread out their own forces, hoping to counter these mystifying movements. Napoleon then quickly coalesced his separate columns to destroy a single enemy force before it could be reinforced, or he descended with his army as a "grouped whole" on the enemy's rear.

The most deadly of Napoleon's strategic methods was this *manœuvre sur les derrières*. His method embodied the injunction of Sun Tzu: march unexpectedly away from the enemy's main strength and concentrate one's own strength against an enemy point that is weak, yet vital or important to the enemy. The art of war is to create this strength at the point of weakness.

Napoleon added another element by frequently seizing a terrain feature in the rear, like a mountain range, defile, or river, where he established a strategic barrage or barrier that prevented the enemy from retreating or getting supplies and reinforcements. Among others, he achieved victory with strategic barrages in the Marengo campaign in Italy in 1800 and in the Ulm campaign leading up to his victory at Austerlitz in 1805. By the time of the American Civil War it no longer was necessary to seize a terrain feature. Armies were relying on railroads for their supplies and new troops. A strategic barrage could be established merely by blocking a railway line in the enemy's rear. General Grant did this at Jackson, Mississippi, in 1863 and thereby isolated the Confederate forces at Vicksburg. This led to the surrender of the city, the opening of the Mississippi River to Union boats, and the loss of the trans-Mississippi states to the Confederacy.

Attacks on an enemy's rear are devastating for a number of reasons. If an enemy is forced to change front, he tends to be dislocated and unable to fight or to fight effectively. An army, like a man, is much more sensitive to menace to the back than to the front. For this reason a rear attack induces fear and distraction. In addition, a move on the rear often disturbs the distribution and organization of enemy forces, may separate them, threatens the retreat route, and endangers delivery of supplies and reinforcements. A modern army can exist for some time without additional food but it can't last more than a few days without ammunition and motor fuel.

An attack on the enemy's rear has grave psychological effects on enemy soldiers, but especially on the enemy commander. It often creates in the commander's mind the fear of being trapped and of being unable to counter his opponent's will. In extreme cases this can lead to paralysis of the commander's decision-making powers and the disintegration of an army.

A rear or flank attack must be a surprise to be wholly successful. This applies both to tactics, or actual battle, and to strategy. If an enemy anticipates a rear attack, he can often move to counter it and will usually be prepared to defend against it. In addition, a rear attack normally succeeds only when the enemy is "fixed" or held in place by other forces on his front and is unable to switch troops in time to meet the surprise blow.

Frederick the Great of Prussia did not fully understand this principle and suffered such severe battle losses that he nearly forfeited his state. Frederick always employed tactics of indirect approach, but his flank and rear assaults were made on a narrow circuit and did not fall unexpectedly. In 1757, for example, he found the Austrians strongly entrenched on the heights behind the river at Prague. Leaving a detachment designed to mask his design, he moved upstream, crossed the river, and advanced on the Austrian right. The Austrians saw the maneuver and had time to change front. The Prussian infantry fell in the thousands when they attempted a frontal attack across a fire-swept gradual slope. Only the unexpected arrival of the Prussian cavalry turned the scales.

The essential formula of actual battle is a convergent assault. A commander achieves this by dividing the attacking force into two or more segments. Ideally each segment attacks the same target simultaneously and in close coordination, but from a different direction or approach, thereby holding all enemy elements in the grip of battle and preventing any one from aiding others. Sometimes one part of a force fixes the enemy in place or distracts him while the other part maneuvers to gain surprise and break up the defense.

A true convergent assault is vastly different from a feint or "holding" attack by one force with the aim of diverting the enemy from the main blow. Unnumbered commanders over the centuries have wrecked their hopes with obvious feints that an astute enemy recognized, or they have tried to hit an objective so divided or spread out that the enemy was not distracted and could bring up forces to repel each blow.

A premier example of a convergent assault took place in 1632 during the Thirty Years War when Sweden's Gustavus Adolphus set up guns and burned straw to create a smoke screen while forcing one point on the Lech River in Bavaria. This held Marshal Tilly of Austria in place while another Swedish force crossed the Lech on a bridge of boats a mile upstream. Assailed from two directions simultaneously, Tilly was unable to defend either point. His troops fell back and Tilly was mortally wounded.

Napoleon's characteristic battle plan was "envelopment, breakthrough, and exploitation." He tried to rivet the enemy's attention with a strong frontal attack to draw all enemy reserves into action. Napoleon then moved a large force on the enemy's flank or rear next to his line of supply and retreat. When the enemy shifted forces from the front to shield against this flank attack, Napoleon broke a hole in a weakened section of the main front with suddenly massed artillery, sent cavalry and infantry through this hole to create a breakthrough, then used cavalry to shatter and pursue the disordered enemy.

In the Korean War, advancing Chinese Communist troops employed a somewhat similar formula. Since they could not counter United Nations air power and artillery, they shifted their main assaults to nighttime. Their general method was to get a force to the rear of enemy positions to cut off escape routes and supply roads. Then they sent in both frontal and flank attacks in the darkness to bring the enemy to grips. Chinese soldiers generally closed in on several sides of a small enemy troop position until they made a penetration, either by destroying it or by forcing the defenders to withdraw. The Chinese then crept forward against the open flank of the next small unit and repeated the process.

None of the axioms employed by great generals is difficult. Indeed, once they have been employed successfully they reveal their innate simplicity and appear to be the obvious and sometimes only logical solution. Yet all great ideas are simple. The trick is to see them before others. This book is about generals who possessed the vision to see the obvious when others did not.

1

The General Who Beat Hannibal

THE ROMAN REPUBLIC endured by far its gravest threat in the Second Punic War (219–202 B.C.) against the great commercial state of Carthage, founded by the Phoenicians and located near present-day Tunis in north Africa. The Carthaginians possessed, in Hannibal Barca, one of the great military geniuses of all time. Hannibal had vowed revenge on Rome for its defeat of Carthage in the First Punic War, which ended in 241 B.C. The fright he aroused so pervaded Roman thought that the cry *"Hannibal ad portas!"* ("Hannibal at the gates!") terrorized children for generations.

Hannibal decided to avoid a sea approach to Italy because of Roman command of the western Mediterranean. He chose to go around this water barrier by land with a great Carthaginian army he had formed in Spain, where Hannibal's father, Hamilcar Barca, had built a powerful base in the years after the First Punic War.

Beginning in March, 218 B.C., Hannibal's 50,000 infantry, 9,000 cavalry,[1] and eighty elephants crossed the Pyrenees and

---

1. At this time neither the stirrup nor the saddle with its raised pommel and cantle had been invented. A rider threw a cloth or hide over the back of the horse and held on by gripping with his legs. The absence of stirrup and saddle prevented a rider from delivering blows with the full power of the horse behind him. Carthaginian cavalry consisted of both heavy and light forms. The heavy was armed with the sword and a long pike or lance, the light with a spear but also missiles, like the javelin and the dart. The principal purpose of the heavy cavalry was decisive shock action, while the light cavalry's major aim was to harry

southern Gaul (France). Evading a Roman army, under the Roman consul Publius Cornelius Scipio the Elder, that belatedly tried to block him at Massilia (Marseilles), Hannibal turned north up the Rhône River. Scipio, instead of trying to chase after Hannibal, sent his army under the command of his brother Gnaeus to Spain to try to block the remaining Carthaginian forces there. He himself traveled to northern Italy to raise new forces and await Hannibal's arrival. This move was the fundamental strategic decision that gave Rome ultimate victory.

Hannibal moved east by way of the Drôme river valley into the Alps, already heavy with snow. There many thousands of men and animals perished from the cold and the fierce resistance of mountain tribes. Hannibal debouched from the Alps

----

enemy infantry bodies and pursue them if they became disordered. The heavy cavalry may have ridden larger and stronger horses than the light cavalry and possibly used some form of armor, either of leather or other material difficult for a sharp instrument to penetrate. The principal long-distance weapon of the Carthaginians was the sling, which delivered pebbles or leaden bullets with great accuracy and greater force than arrows could be shot by the bows used in the Mediterranean. The most famous slingers were from the Balearic Islands. There is no evidence the Carthaginians armed their cavalry with the compound bow and arrow. This bow, formed by combining wood, horn, and sinew, had immense power, though it was short, thereby making it easy for a man on horseback to handle. It had developed on the Eurasian steppes well over a millennium previously (see Chapter 2) but did not become a significant weapon in the Mediterranean. During his conquest of the Persian Empire, Alexander the Great (356–323 B.C.) encountered great difficulties with nomadic Sarmatian horsemen of the Saka tribe armed with this bow when he crossed the Jaxartes River (Syr Darna) into central Asia in 334 B.C. The Sakas rode around and around Alexander's army, firing arrows into his solid infantry phalanx but remaining virtually untouchable themselves. Alexander saved his army by throwing out his own cavalry on each wing of his phalanx and breaking up the menacing circling movement. Although Alexander created a force of mounted Asian archers, the concept of the horse archer was largely lost thereafter in the classical world. Alexander's cavalry was principally armed with the sword and spear or lance (*sarissa*). Although Xenophon (died 355 B.C.?) wrote of armor being used to protect horses, this practice was not common, and riders apparently used only small shields to defend themselves against enemy blows. See Legg, 64; Delbrück, vol. 1, 176–77.

HANNIBAL BARCA

Bettmann Archive

into northern Italy in October 218, with half of his infantry, two-thirds of his cavalry, and only a few elephants.

Consul Scipio rushed his cavalry to meet Hannibal at the Ticinus (Ticino) River, a northern tributary to the Po River, but Hannibal's much-superior African horsemen defeated them in November and drove them back. Scipio, reinforced by an army from Sicily under Tiberius Sempronius Longus, moved against Hannibal, located just west of the Trebia (Trebbia), near where this river joins the Po near Placentia (Piacenza).

Hannibal meanwhile had increased his army to over 30,000 by recruiting Gauls. Against the advice of Scipio, Sempronius allowed Hannibal to entice the Roman army of 40,000 to cross the Trebia in December and form up, wet and cold, on the western side. Now with the river at their back and unable to retreat in case of defeat, the Romans faced an attack by Hannibal, his infantry in the center advancing directly and his main cavalry force, elephants, and missile-throwing light troops on each wing driving away the weaker Roman horse and falling on the Roman flanks. While the Roman army was completely occupied with these assaults, a picked Carthaginian cavalry and infantry force of 2,000 under Hannibal's brother Mago—which had concealed itself in a ravine upstream—descended on the rear of the Roman army. The converging assaults to the front, sides, and rear shattered the Romans. Only 10,000 were able to escape, most cutting their way through the Carthaginian center. The remainder died. Hannibal probably lost only about 5,000 men.

Throughout the rest of the winter, Hannibal rested his men in the Po Valley and recruited Gauls. He also set up an elaborate spy network that examined the geography of the region and sounded out the dispositions of the Roman forces arrayed against him.

By spring 217 the Romans had assembled two armies blocking the main roads leading from the Po Valley toward central Italy and Rome. One army of 40,000 under Consul Gaius Flaminius Nepos was at Arretium (Arezzo) in the mountains of eastern Tuscany, and another of 20,000 was under Consul Cnaeus Servilius Geminus at Ariminum (Rimini) on the Adriatic Sea.

Hannibal, though all but one of his elephants had died in

the harsh Italian winter, had an army of about 40,000 men. His infantry was inferior in numbers to the Romans, but his pike- and sword-armed heavy cavalry and missile-throwing light cav- alry remained superior. He elected not to take either obvious, direct road south. If he followed this line of greatest expecta- tion, the two Roman armies would concentrate against him. He knew, as all great generals know, that the greatest uncertainty in war is not physical obstacles but human resistance. Although he had defeated the Romans twice, they remained a formidable opponent, and if Hannibal pursued the obvious course, they would be lined up and waiting for him, confident their leaders had picked the proper defensive location and sure their supe- rior numbers and fame as close-in fighters with javelins and short swords would give them victory.

Hannibal elected to confuse the Roman leaders. He turned away from the waiting Roman armies, climbed over the Apen- nines north of Genoa, reached the coast, and marched south along it. The Romans were surprised but not worried because they knew Hannibal had to cross the marshes of the Arnus (Arno) River in Tuscany, treacherous in any weather and reput- edly impassable in the spring floods. When Hannibal reached the marshes in April, therefore, the Romans had taken no pre- cautions to block him.

The Carthaginian, however, made a totally unexpected move that confounded the Romans and altered the strategic situation completely: he sent his army directly through the flooded swamps for four days and three nights of misery, the men now half drowned in the soft mud, now sinking deeply in the water. Many succumbed to exhaustion and died. Though he rode on the remaining elephant to keep above the water, Hannibal caught an eye infection and lost the sight of one eye.

Hannibal's army was in a stupendously favorable position, having emerged out of the swamps near Clusium (Chiusi), thirty miles south of Arretium, cut Flaminius's communications with Rome, and positioned itself closer to Rome than Flaminius. The Roman consul's officers urged him to wait until Servilius could join them in order to present the maximum force against the enemy. Flaminius refused, partly from arrogance and partly because he feared that Hannibal, with the road clear ahead of

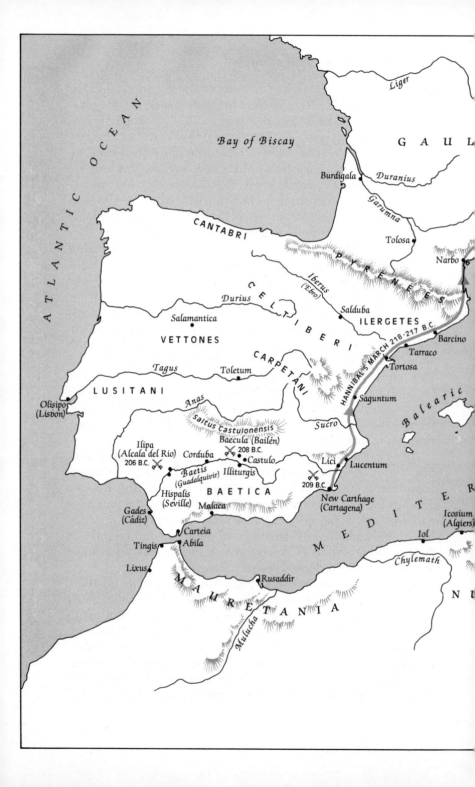

SECOND PUNIC WAR
219-202 B.C.

| 0 | 100 | 200 | 300 | 400 | 500 miles |

him, would strike directly for Rome. Hannibal gave this impression, but in fact moved only slowly, meanwhile devastating the countryside so as to incite Flaminius to pursue. Flaminius ordered his army to rush after the enemy to seek battle, sacrificing security for speed.

Hannibal planned a trap. He found a perfect place at Lake Trasimene (Trasimeno). There the road followed a course along the north shore of the lake. On the hills just above the road, Hannibal concealed the allied Gauls, his cavalry, and his pebble- or lead-bullet-throwing slingers from the Balearic Islands. In sight on rising ground to the east he encamped his African and Spanish infantry.

In early morning the Romans, in column formations, pressed over a pass just west of the lake and marched along the lakeshore road. They had made no reconnaissance, and heavy mists from the water made visibility poor. When the front of the column reached the massed Carthaginian heavy infantry, it halted and the rest of the column closed up behind. Hannibal ordered his cavalry to prevent retreat by blocking the pass on the west, then directed his light infantry to strike from the mountainside. The Romans were utterly surprised and panicked. With nowhere to go and in march, not battle, order, they were slaughtered like cattle, 30,000 of them, including Flaminius. About 10,000 fled in scattered groups through the mountains to notify Rome of the disaster. Hannibal lost 2,500 men. Lake Trasimene was the greatest ambush in history.

Hannibal did not march on Rome primarily because he did not possess a siege train and Rome's walls were formidable. Besides, Hannibal possessed no base in Italy and no regular supply line to Carthage and could not have conducted a long siege.[2] His strength lay in movement, his superior cavalry, and

2. A siege train consisted of catapults and ballistae (huge bows) to launch rocks and missiles, and towers, battering rams, and other devices to attack or scale walls. Since these items were heavy, it was impractical for Hannibal to carry them from Spain. See Dupuy, 38–39, 46, 82–84. Without control of the sea, Hannibal would have had difficulty getting siege engines from Carthage. He could have built them in Italy, of course. But Hans Delbrück points out (Delbrück, vol. 1, 338–39) that a siege of Rome would have required an army of 50,000

his supreme generalship. Accordingly he ignored Rome itself and concentrated on trying to break Rome's bonds with her Italian allies and to form a coalition of cities against her.

In the summer of 217, Hannibal rested his army in Picenum (Marche), opposite Rome on the Adriatic coast. During the autumn and into the winter he ravaged Apulia (Puglia) in the heel of Italy and Campania around Naples.

The Romans offered no serious resistance, because they recognized they could not cope with Hannibal on the battlefield. They appointed Quintus Fabius Maximus as dictator for six months. He adopted a course that has given to the world the generic concept of "Fabian strategy," a policy of evading decisive confrontation to gain time by using guerrillalike pinprick attacks and harassment to improve morale and preventing potential allies from joining the enemy.

The key to Fabius's strategy was that the Roman army should always keep to the hills to nullify Hannibal's decisive superiority in cavalry. The Romans hovered in the vicinity of the Carthaginians, cut off stragglers and foragers, and prevented them from founding a permanent base. The strategy avoided Roman defeat and dimmed Hannibal's glory. It successfully kept Rome's allies from declaring for Carthage, but it aroused great opposition among Romans themselves, for their state had thrived on a tradition of offensive warfare.

When Fabius's appointment ended, the Roman Senate was unwilling to extend his dictatorship and, passing a resolution that the army should give battle, named two consuls, the ignorant and impetuous Terentius Varro and the more cautious Aemilius Paulus. The Romans had assembled the largest army they had ever placed in the field, 80,000 infantry and 7,000

---

to 60,000 men. Since Roman ships prevented food deliveries from Carthage, Hannibal would have had to organize large supply lines functioning through a hostile countryside and passing by many cities and strongholds blocking his routes. In addition, the Romans could build a much larger army than Hannibal—keeping a strong garrison at Rome and still sending forces against Hannibal's supply lines. With insufficient strength to overcome the Romans completely, Hannibal devised a strategy aimed at wearing down and exhausting the Romans to the point where they would agree to a negotiated peace.

cavalry. It marched off toward Hannibal, Varro and Paulus alternating command each day.[3]

Paulus wanted to wait and maneuver for a favorable opportunity, but Varro took the first chance to offer battle, using his day of command to advance on Hannibal's 40,000 infantry and 10,000 cavalry at Cannae, on the Aufidus (Ofanto) River in Apulia.

Hannibal crossed to the west side of the Aufidus on August 2, 216, and lined up most of his army across the chord of an east-arching river bend, thereby securing his flanks against the stream banks. The river at this season was low, but it formed a barrier to retreat in case of defeat.

Both armies were arrayed in customary order, the infantry in the center and cavalry on both wings. But Hannibal pushed forward his less dependable Gauls and Spanish foot soldiers in the exact center, while holding back his strong African infantry on either side. This advance provided a natural magnet for the advancing Romans, who struck at the Gauls and Spaniards, forcing them back, just as Hannibal had intended.

The convex Carthaginian line, therefore, became concave, sagging ominously inward. The Roman legionaries, flushed with apparent success, crowded into this opening, believing they were breaking the enemy front.

At this moment Hannibal gave the signal and the African foot suddenly wheeled inward from both sides, striking the Romans in flank and enveloping them into a tightly packed mass. Meanwhile Hannibal's heavy cavalry on the left wing had broken through the weaker Roman cavalry on that side and had swept around the Roman rear to drive away the cavalry on the Roman left flank. Leaving the lighter Numidian (Algerian) cavalry on the right wing to pursue the Roman horsemen, Hannibal's heavy cavalry delivered the final stroke by bursting onto the rear of the Roman legions, already enveloped on three sides and so compressed they were unable to offer effective resistance.

3. Each year the Romans elected two consuls (essentially mayors), who also commanded the army. The consuls either divided the legions between them or, if they were together, alternated command each day. See Delbrück, vol. 1, 336.

BATTLE OF CANNAE
216 B.C.

positions held at onset of battle

positions held during battle

Retreat of Allied cavalry

Hasdrubal routs Allied cavalry, closes on Roman rear

Romans charge forward

Romans hemmed in by Carthaginians

Roman cavalry destroyed

Roman secondary camp

Aufidus River

CANNAE

Hannibal's camp

Roman camp

CHAZAUD

The battle now became a massacre. Only about 6,000 of the 76,000 Romans engaged were able to break out and get away. The rest died. Varro ironically was one of the survivors, while Paulus fell in battle. Hannibal's losses were around 6,000 men.

Cannae showed how elastically hinged wings of cavalry could exploit the disorganization created by a brilliant commander. Polybius, the principal chronicler of the war, wrote that Cannae was "a lesson to posterity that in actual war it is better to have half the number of infantry and superiority of cavalry, than to engage your enemy with an equality in both."

Cannae has gone down as the perfect battle of annihilation. Yet, such was their discipline and devotion to the state that the Roman people did not lose heart or even consider surrender. Although Rome had suffered unprecedented losses, she mobilized young boys and old men and marched two legions south immediately to encourage Rome's allies. A few went over to Carthage, but most remained loyal. Hannibal's lack of a siege train prevented him from assaulting well-defended cities. But he was relatively successful in building a base in southern Italy, although Carthage's lukewarm support and Roman naval superiority ensured that only a few reinforcements arrived. Hannibal had to maintain his army with halfhearted Italian recruits.

The war in Italy settled into a stalemate. Rome was unable to defeat Hannibal, but Hannibal was incapable of capturing the cities that would have forced Rome's allies to renounce Rome and join him, thereby giving him power and security.

Meanwhile an indirect attack on Hannibal was under way in Spain, where a Roman army was attempting to destroy his base there. While Hannibal was still approaching northern Italy in 218, Scipio the Elder's brother Gnaeus took advantage of Roman seapower, landed in northeastern Spain, and secured the region from the Ebro River to the Pyrenees. This cut Hannibal off from his main source of resupply and reinforcements. The next year, Scipio the Elder joined Gnaeus, and for several years they made significant advances in Spain, while effectively denying Hannibal substantial aid from the region. Most Roman leaders, however, were not greatly impressed by the Scipio brothers' victories, considering Spain a sideshow while

Hannibal was at the gates in Italy. Consequently they did not send substantial forces to Spain, and in 211 the Carthaginians defeated the Romans and killed the Scipio brothers in two separate battles on the upper Baetis (Guadalquivir) River in southern Spain. A major reason for the defeats was that the Scipios' native allies deserted them suddenly.

In 210 the situation of Rome was dismal. For eight years, Hannibal had ranged Italy, not conquering but himself unconquerable. Rome had achieved a few gains but had mostly followed Fabian strategy, which kept nearly all of its able-bodied men under arms yet reached no decision.

In Spain the situation was worse: the Roman survivors had been driven north of the Ebro River, and many of the Spanish tribes had forsaken them. Rome needed a proconsul there, and the Senate probably arranged that Scipio's well-regarded son be elected. He also was named Publius Cornelius Scipio, though known to history as Scipio Africanus. He was twenty-four years old and had fought at Cannae and somehow survived.

Scipio sailed with some reinforcements to Rome's last major base, Tarraco (Tarragona), in northeastern Spain. Unlike most Romans, Scipio saw Spain as a key to the whole struggle against Hannibal, because it remained his main base of operations and there he looked for most of his replacements.

It was not apparent at the time, but Scipio Africanus possessed a military genius equal to that of Hannibal. He commenced his campaign with a stunning surprise. The three major Carthaginian armies were widely separated, one near Gibraltar in southern Spain, another near the mouth of the Tagus around modern-day Lisbon, and the third close to modern Madrid. None was much closer than he was to the Carthaginian Spanish capital and principal port, New Carthage (Cartagena). Scipio resolved to seize this capital before the enemy armies could react.

New Carthage was the only Spanish port fit for a fleet, and it provided the direct sea crossing for Carthage from Africa. Moreover, the Carthaginians kept the bulk of their bullion, Spanish hostages, and war matériel there. It had not occurred to the enemy that an attack might come against New Carthage.

The city had strong walls and was situated on a peninsula jutting out into water, the harbor to the south and a lagoon to the north. It was connected to the mainland only by a 400-yard space at the base of the peninsula on the east. Fearing nothing, the Carthaginians had garrisoned New Carthage with only 1,000 trained soldiers.

Scipio recognized that his real objective was not the enemy armies but destruction of the will of the people to resist. Seizure of the capital would distract and demoralize the Carthaginians and cause the Spanish tribes to reconsider their loyalty. In most cases, war requires destruction of the enemy army to achieve such aims. But the Carthaginians had unconsciously uncovered New Carthage, and Scipio, following the line of least expectation, could seize it while the main enemy forces were far away. Nevertheless, Scipio had to break into the city quickly, before the enemy armies could march to its relief.

Before he left Tarraco, Scipio had developed just such a plan of rapid conquest. By telling no one except his naval commander, Gaius Laelius, Scipio reduced the likelihood that the enemy would hear of the move and march on New Carthage at the same time as he. Consequently, the Carthaginian armies were far away when Laelius brought the Roman fleet to blockade the port on the day Scipio's 27,500 men arrived overland at the city's walls in the spring of 209.

Scipio had found from fishermen at Tarraco that the lagoon on the north, though dangerous-looking, was shallow and easily fordable at low tide. This, Scipio saw, was the Achilles' heel of New Carthage. But to distract the attention of the defenders, he launched a furious frontal assault against the gate and wall facing the base of the peninsula on the east. This attack failed, with many Roman casualties. The Carthaginians were ecstatic and concentrated their troops and attention on this east wall, expecting the Romans to assault again.

Meanwhile, Scipio assembled 500 men with ladders on the shore opposite the lagoon. Scipio now followed the cardinal axiom of a tactical assault: just as the water reached its ebb and the men raced through the shallow lagoon and flung their ladders against the undefended wall above it, he launched a convergent attack at two other points to "fix" all enemy forces in

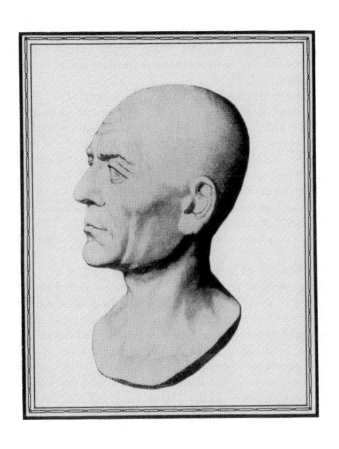

SCIPIO AFRICANUS
Warder Collection

place and prevent their moving to the lagoon walls. Men from the fleet attempted a landing attack on the harbor side, and a strong force tried once more to break the gate and scale the wall on the eastern side.

The 500 men quickly ascended the lagoon wall, cleared it for a substantial distance in both directions, then assailed the rear of the Carthaginians defending the eastern wall, taking them by surprise and opening the way for the main body. To break the resistance of the people, Scipio allowed civilians to be massacred while the citadel held out. But once it surrendered, he stopped the killings. Thereafter he freed all citizens of New Carthage and sent all Spanish hostages home as a gesture to build goodwill among the native tribes. Most of the other male prisoners he sent as galley slaves on captured vessels.

In a stroke the Carthaginians had lost their main base, key to their control of Spain, and the strategic initiative. If they attempted to recapture New Carthage, impregnable if it was properly garrisoned and the Romans held command of the sea, Scipio could threaten their flanks. If they moved directly against Scipio, he could choose his ground and, since he could move troops to New Carthage by sea, could threaten their rear. Faced with these realities, the Carthaginians could do nothing and had to accept the loss of their main base and best line of communications with Carthage.

Equally damaging, a number of the Iberian tribes came over to the Roman side. This tipped the power balance ominously toward Rome, and one of the Carthaginian commanders, Hannibal's brother Hasdrubal, decided in 208 to take the offensive before other tribes joined Scipio.

This failure to unite with the other Carthaginian forces was a boon to Scipio, who moved with about 35,000 men toward Hasdrubal near the town of Baecula (Bailén) on the upper reaches of the Baetis (Guadalquivir) in present-day Andalusia. Hasdrubal held a position on a small two-step plateau wide enough to deploy his 25,000 troops. On the lower plateau, Hasdrubal posted a screen of missile-throwing light troops, Numidian horsemen, and Balearic slingers. On the higher plateau he entrenched his camp.

In making his plans for battle, Scipio broke completely with Roman tradition, which relied mainly on the force of massed troops advancing directly on the enemy. It was this heavy forward thrust that Hannibal had exploited at Cannae, enticing the unwieldy legions to drive into his sagging center and then turning his heavy infantry against the legions' exposed flanks. Scipio, learning from Hannibal, divided his army into three parts: light troops *(velites)* in the center and heavy troops on each wing.

Scipio sent his *velites,* armed with javelins and darts, directly forward to scale the first plateau. Despite the rocky ascent and a shower of darts and stones, they drove the enemy troops back, inducing Hasdrubal to order forward his main body to what he thought would be the principal battle. This focused the Carthaginians' attention on the front, permitting Scipio to lead half his heavy troops around the left flank while his lieutenant, Gaius Laelius, led the other half around the right flank.

But the light troops were too weak to hold the Carthaginian heavy infantry in a firm battle embrace and prevent them from disengaging when the Romans struck their flanks. Though Scipio and Laelius caught the enemy main force while still on the move and drove it back in disorder, they did not shatter its cohesion, as Hannibal's heavy infantry had done to the Roman army at Cannae. And Scipio—with no cavalry capable of closing off the enemy's rear as Hannibal's horsemen had done at Cannae—got only two infantry cohorts (about 1,000 men) on the Carthaginian line of retreat, not enough to hold the army, though sufficient to cause many casualties.

Scipio thus failed to produce a Cannae, and Hasdrubal got away with about two-thirds of his army.

Scipio wisely did not pursue Hasdrubal into the mountainous interior for fear that the other enemy armies would converge and cut off his rear. Nevertheless, the battle of Baecula had vast consequences. Hasdrubal planned to march overland to Italy to reinforce his brother with his seasoned Spanish and African army. Baecula weakened this army and forced Hasdrubal to spend a winter in Gaul recruiting among the tribes.

When Hasdrubal arrived in Italy in 207, more than half his 50,000-man force consisted of unreliable Gauls. When a Roman army blocked him on the Metaurus (Metauro) River, Consul Caius Claudius Nero, confident the Gauls would not advance, withdrew a picked force facing them on the Carthaginian left flank, marched it entirely around and behind the Roman army, and struck the right rear of Hasdrubal's line, throwing the Carthaginian army into a panic. Hasdrubal saw all was lost and rode deliberately into a Roman cohort to die fighting. The Carthaginians suffered 10,000 men killed, and the rest scattered. Legend holds that Hannibal first learned of the disaster on the Metaurus only when the Romans catapulted Hasdrubal's head into his camp.

Hannibal gave up all hope of victory and withdrew his army to Bruttium (Calabria) on the toe of Italy, where he continued to hold the Romans at bay, despite his small (less than 30,000 men) and now poor-quality force.

In Spain, Scipio's victory at Baecula had alarmed the Carthaginian authorities, and they conceived a plan to descend on Scipio from two directions. A new general, Hanno, arrived with reinforcements from Carthage and joined another of Hannibal's brothers, Mago, who had been recruiting in the Balearic Islands, and together they began arming new levies in central and eastern Spain. Meanwhile another new Carthaginian general, Hasdrubal Gisgo, advanced toward Scipio with a large army from his base at Gades (Cádiz) in southern Spain.

If Scipio moved into the interior against his main threat, Hasdrubal Gisgo, he was likely to find Hanno and Mago across his rear. His solution was to make a surprise blow with stunning speed. While he watched Hasdrubal Gisgo, Scipio detached 10,000 infantry and 500 cavalry under a lieutenant, Marcus Silanus, to make a secret forced march against Hanno and Mago before they were aware of the danger. Silanus marched so fast no rumors of his approach reached the enemy, and he fell on the unsuspecting Spanish camp and routed the Spaniards before the Carthaginians could come up. Mago and the cavalry fled the scene, but Hanno and the new troops from Carthage were killed or taken prisoner. The Spanish levies scattered and could not be reformed.

Scipio had now secured his rear and moved with confidence against Hasdrubal Gisgo, who, alarmed, dispersed his troops into small garrisons in the various walled towns of southern Spain. Scipio wisely decided not to drain his strength by repeated sieges against these towns.

The war in Spain might have continued indefinitely in such a stalemate, but Mago encouraged Hasdrubal Gisgo to raise new levies and take the field in hopes of destroying Scipio once and for all.

In the spring of 206, Scipio marched south from his base at Tarraco to confront this imposing new threat. As he approached the Baetis River, Scipio began to appreciate the nature of his problem. He learned from spies that the Carthaginian army totaled 70,000 foot, 4,000 horse, and thirty-two elephants, far in excess of his own strength. In addition, perhaps half of Scipio's 40,000 men consisted of native levies. He was reluctant to rely on these natives, in part because his own father and uncle had been defeated and died in 211 when they had done so.

His solution embodied a use of deception and surprise that remains a model for tactical operations to this day. His problem was severe. The enemy army was superior overall and, moreover, possessed a solid core of seasoned African veterans who were a match man to man for the best Roman legionaries. Moreover, his Spanish levies might disintegrate if struck hard by these Africans.

The two armies came face to face at Ilipa (Alcalá del Río) on the Baetis, a few miles north of present-day Seville. The two camps faced each other across a valley between two low ridges. Hasdrubal Gisgo led his army out to offer battle. Scipio waited until the Carthaginians were moving before he followed suit. Hasdrubal Gisgo could find no advantage to induce him to attack and did not do so. Neither did Scipio. Near twilight the weary armies withdrew to their camps, the Carthaginians first.

This pattern repeated itself for several days: the Carthaginians marched out fairly late, the Romans followed, both sides stood under arms all day without action and finally returned exhausted to their billets. On each occasion, Scipio, following existing tactical doctrine, placed his solid Roman legions in the center directly opposite his enemy's Carthaginian and African regulars. He and Hasdrubal Gisgo placed their Spanish levies on the wings, again following doctrine, while the Carthaginian located his elephants in front of his Spaniards.

The belief took hold in both armies that this was the order that would be followed when the two sides finally came to battle. Scipio encouraged both the order and the sequence, always advancing his own troops to the field after the Carthaginians.

Scipio now acted. He ordered his troops to be fed late in the evening and armed before daylight and the cavalry horses readied. At dawn he sent his cavalry and light troops to attack the enemy's outposts. This unexpected move caught the Carthaginian cavalry and missile-throwing light forces napping and unready. The threat caused Hasdrubal Gisgo to order his whole army hurriedly under arms and into position. There was no time for a meal. At least as important, the Carthaginian was forced, because of the urgency, to repeat his normal troop dispositions, even if he'd wanted to alter them.

Scipio now hit Hasdrubal Gisgo with his second surprise. He reversed his usual order of battle, placing the Spanish in the center opposite the best Carthaginian forces, while locating his Roman legions on the two wings. Scipio now waited, allowing the effects of hunger to weaken the enemy army. He had no worry that Hasdrubal Gisgo would move his Africans opposite the Romans. Such a major troop shift in the face of the enemy would have left the army vulnerable to assault while the changes were in progress.

About 1:00 P.M., Scipio ordered the advance. But he directed the Spaniards in the center to move only at a slow pace, while the Romans on each wing moved faster. When the Spaniards were still several hundred yards from the Africans, the left and right wings of Romans, ahead, wheeled obliquely half left and half right and advanced rapidly on the Carthaginian flanks, guarded by the enemy's own Spanish irregulars, equally unreliable.

Scipio's Spanish center remained out of reach of the African infantry, yet these least dependable troops constituted a threat and, as Hannibal had done to the Roman legions at Cannae, fixed the most dependable enemy troops in place. Scipio thus overcame the weakness of his tactics at Baecula and, with great economy of force, rendered the Africans inactive and useless in the unfolding battle.

Scipio's Romans struck the weak Carthaginian flanks. At the same time, Scipio's light troops and cavalry wheeled outward and swept around even farther on the enemy's flanks. There the light troops were able to throw their missiles from enfilade (from the side) against the length of the enemy columns, while the cavalry drove the frightened elephants in on the Carthaginian center, spreading more confusion.

Scipio had achieved a convergent blow on each wing similar to what he had gained at Baecula, but in a surprising and unexpected manner. This forced the defenders to face attack in two directions at once and was more decisive because it fell not on the African veterans but on the Spanish irregulars—while Scipio's Spaniards were not engaged except as a threat.

The Romans methodically destroyed the enemy's wings, leaving the hungry and tired Carthaginian center with no choice but to fall back. The retreat at first took place in good order. But retreating under attack is one of the most difficult military tasks, and the Romans exerted relentless pressure.

The Carthaginians fled to their entrenched camp, but it was clearly incapable of holding off the Romans, and, under cover of night, Hasdrubal Gisgo ordered evacuation. Scipio, however, had placed a Roman force along his best route of retreat, to Gades, and the Carthaginians were forced to flee down the west bank of the river toward the Atlantic. In the retirement nearly all of the Carthaginians' Spanish allies deserted.

Realizing the enemy was broken and distracted, Scipio 1pressed his men to keep up close pursuit, sending cavalry ahead and forcing the enemy infantry to stand and fight and thereby giving the Roman foot time to catch up. When this occurred it no longer was a fight but a butchery. Hasdrubal Gisgo, Mago, and a few others got to the sea and took ship to Gades. Carthage's mighty military presence in Spain was ended forever.

After reducing all remaining resistance in Spain, Scipio returned to Rome with a new and, to the Romans, startling proposal: he wanted to carry the war to Africa.

Fabius, who had won fame by delay and inaction, spitefully ridiculed Scipio's plan. The danger, Fabius said, was Hannibal, and he was in Italy. There should be no assault on Carthage's heartland in Africa. Instead, the small army of Hannibal in the toe of Italy should be brought to battle and defeated directly. Liddell Hart points out that Fabius thereby showed himself as one of a legion of leaders down the centuries who have held as unimpeachable doctrine that the enemy's main army is the primary objective.

Scipio saw beyond Hannibal's army. The main deterrent to peace was the will of the enemy to continue. This will did not reside in Hannibal but in Carthage. An expedition to Africa might break this will and achieve Roman victory. But if it merely threatened Carthage, it at least would attain indirectly—and with no further loss of blood—the lesser goal that had evaded Rome for a dozen years: Hannibal's abandonment of Italy. This would occur, Scipio was certain, because Hannibal would be forced to come after Scipio in Africa.

The Roman Senate ultimately gave lukewarm assent to Scipio's proposal. For the next year he prepared for the expedition in Sicily. The principal reason for the delay was that Scipio saw an urgent need to build a strong cavalry force to counter what he realized was Hannibal's decisive weapon. It had been Hannibal's cavalry that had swept around the Roman flanks and rear at Trebia, had sealed off Roman retreat at Lake Trasimene, and had delivered the final blow against the Roman rear at Cannae.

Scipio realized, almost alone among Roman leaders of his time, that the Roman legion's great power for fixing an enemy by close battle was only half the equation: the other half was the cavalry, which, while the infantry held the enemy in place by figuratively grasping his throat, had the mobility to slip around behind the enemy and drive a dagger into his back. In Sicily, Scipio carefully built up a strong Roman cavalry force, following Hannibal's model. While still in Spain he already had convinced the formidable cavalry leader Masinissa to defect to the Roman side. Masinissa was a prince from Numidia (present-day Algeria) in North Africa. Thus, Scipio not only gained for his army these Numidian horsemen but took them away from the Carthaginians.

Also while in Spain, Scipio had made another preliminary move for an African expedition. He undertook a dangerous sea voyage to Numidia and sealed an alliance with Syphax, a rival of Masinissa, king of a large part of Numidia, and an ally of Carthage. But passion triumphed over diplomacy. Syphax renewed his ties with Carthage after the entreaties of his beautiful Carthaginian bride, Sophonisba, daughter of Hasdrubal Gisgo.

The invasion of Africa, by 30,000 Romans, took place in the spring of 204. The army landed near Utica, twenty air miles northwest of Carthage where the Bagradas (Medjerda) River falls into the sea. He invested Utica, with the aim of gaining it as a supply base, but was forced to give up the siege and retire to a small isthmus nearby after Hasdrubal Gisgo assembled 30,000 Carthaginian infantry and 3,000 cavalry and Syphax arrived with 50,000 foot soldiers and 10,000 horsemen.

Although Scipio prevented his army from being overwhelmed by fortifying the base of the isthmus, his situation was dangerous, since the Carthaginians and the Numidians set up strong camps a mile apart and about seven miles away from the Romans. Scipio decided to get around this danger by feigning fear and entering into negotiations to evacuate Africa in return for Hannibal's evacuation of Italy.

His purpose was not retreat but a sneak attack. To bring it off he needed to find out what was in the two camps, where the gates were located, and when and where the guards and vedettes, or mounted sentinels, were posted. The visits of his emissaries provided this information. Scipio determined that Syphax's camp was the more vulnerable, especially because some of the soldiers' huts were outside the entrenchments encircling the camp and many others inside were strewn about with little space between then and were built of inflammable material.

Scipio called off negotiations for an armistice. Even as he made final plans for a strike, however, he misled and confused the enemy by launching ships and mounting siege machines on board and sending 2,000 men to seize a hill near Utica, as if preparing a sea assault on the town. While the enemy had his eyes focused on Utica, Scipio waited until nightfall and marched his legions with as little noise as possible toward the two enemy camps, arriving around midnight.

Scipio divided his force, placing Masinissa and Gaius Laelius in charge of assaulting Syphax's camp while he directed the attack on the Carthaginian camp. Scipio said, however, that he would not move until Laelius and Masinissa had set fire to the Numidian camp.

Laelius and Masinissa divided their force as well, appointing special bodies to block all escape routes and assaulting the camp in a converging attack from two directions at once. The leading Romans set fire to every building they reached. Soon the whole camp was aflame. The Numidians assumed it was a natural fire and rushed out unarmed and fled in disorder. The Roman bands at the exits cut down the men as they emerged.

At the Carthaginian camp the soldiers, also assuming the flames were accidental, rushed to assist, only to be attacked by Scipio's men as they hurried over. Scipio's men launched attacks on the now-unguarded gates and quickly set fire to the nearest huts. Soon the whole Carthaginian camp was aflame, and as the men attempted to flee, Romans at the gates cut them down.

The result was a massacre. Perhaps 40,000 Carthaginians and Numidians were killed or died in the flames, and 5,000 were captured. Hasdrubal got away with about 2,500 men, taking refuge in a small town nearby and later fleeing to Carthage. Syphax got more of his men away and retired to a fortified position some distance away.

The abrupt change of fortune and the virtual disappearance of the two huge armies depressed the Carthaginians deeply and tempted Syphax to abandon the war. Syphax's wife, Sophonisba, pleaded with him, and when 4,000 Celtiberians arrived from Spain to bolster the cause, Syphax decided to stay loyal to Carthage. He and Hasdrubal recruited energetically and soon gathered a new, but still inadequately trained, army of 35,000 in the Great Plains, about eighty miles southwest of Utica.

Although Scipio had renewed his siege of Utica, he left only a small force there and immediately struck for the new enemy army before it became organized. The army faced Scipio with the Celtiberians, the best-trained troops, in the center, the Numidians on the left, and the Carthaginians on the right. Scipio's cavalry descended on the enemy wings and broke them quickly, proof that his decision had been right to strike before Hasdrubal and Syphax had trained their raw levies. Meanwhile, Scipio advanced part of his heavy infantry directly on the Carthaginian center. At Baecula, Scipio's light infantry in the center had been too weak to hold the main enemy force, but in this battle Scipio's heavy legionaries grasped the Celtiberians in a firm embrace, enabling other Roman heavy infantry to descend on each flank and surround them. The Celtiberians fought bravely, knowing they'd receive no quarter, since coming from Spain now constituted treason to Rome. They fought to the end and permitted many others to escape, including Hasdrubal to Carthage and Syphax to his capital, Cirta (Constantine, Algeria).

With no enemy army now to oppose him, Scipio sent Masinissa and Laelius in pursuit of Syphax and himself prepared to besiege Carthage, occupying Tunis, fifteen miles away, with little opposition and beating off an attempt by the Carthaginian navy to destroy the Roman fleet at Utica.

Masinissa and Laelius arrived in Syphax's Numidian kingdom of Massylia after fifteen days' march to the west. Syphax raised a raw, undisciplined force, but in the battle that followed, Roman training and discipline prevailed; the Numidians broke and fled, and Syphax was captured. Cirta opened its gates to the invaders, and Masinissa, promised the kingship, galloped off to the palace. There he was met by Sophonisba. She appealed to Masinissa's pride and passion, and he agreed not to hand her over to the Romans and married her that very day. Laelius was deeply annoyed and only restrained himself at the last moment from dragging her from the marital bed.

When Masinissa returned to Scipio's camp, the Roman decided on an indirect approach, reminding him of his duty and how wise it was to control passions. Masinissa got the message and sent Sophonisba a poisoned cup, telling her that though the Romans had prevented him from acting as her husband, he still would perform his second promise, "that she should not come alive into the power of the Romans." Sophonisba calmly drained the cup.

The frightened Carthaginian Senate frantically called Hannibal back from Italy, just as Scipio had predicted would occur when Carthage was threatened. It also ordered the return of Hannibal's brother Mago, who had been operating in Liguria (around Genoa) and had recruited a number of Gauls.

Carthage also asked for terms of capitulation. Scipio, looking toward a happy peace at the end of a long and destructive war, offered favorable conditions: withdrawal of Carthage from Italy, Gaul, and all Mediterranean islands, abandonment of any claim to Spain, loss of all but twenty warships, and a considerable, but not heavy, indemnity in money and grain. Unlike many victors in many wars before and after, Scipio did not impose terms that could not be fulfilled and thereby create grounds for another war.

The Carthaginians, however, regained their confidence and broke off negotiations when Hannibal landed in 202 with 24,000 men on the Gulf of Hammamet, some one hundred air miles southeast of Carthage. Although Mago died en route to Carthage, his army of about 12,000 joined Hannibal, as did 2,000 cavalry from a still-loyal Numidian kingdom under Tychaeus, new levies from Africa, and (according to the Roman historian Livy) 4,000 Macedonians sent by King Philip.

Scipio was placed in a dangerous position. He had fewer men in total, and all of Masinissa's cavalry and about 5,000 Roman legionaries were many days' march away in Numidia consolidating Masinissa's new kingdom. Most frightening, if Hannibal was able to reach Carthage and use this fortress as a base of operations, his situation would be superior to Scipio's.

Scipio now did an astonishing thing. Unlike an ordinary general, he did not interpose his army between Hannibal and Carthage or stand on the defensive until help arrived. Instead he marched off in a direction away both from Carthage and Hannibal: southwest up the Bagradas river valley!

It was one of the shrewdest indirect strategic moves in the history of warfare. The Bagradas Valley was Carthage's main source of food, supplies, and reinforcements from the interior. Scipio took every town by assault, appropriated all the grain and other food, and sold the people as slaves. Scipio struck not at Hannibal's army but at the ability of Carthage to resist, confident that the people would require Hannibal to go immediately after him and not wait to establish a secure base at Carthage. Besides, every step Scipio took southwest brought him closer to Masinissa and the detached Romans, who were moving to join him by forced marches.

Just as Scipio expected, Carthage sent urgent appeals to Hannibal to bring Scipio to battle and end the depredations in the Bagradas Valley. Hannibal, hoping to descend on Scipio before Masinissa and the remaining Romans arrived, complied and arrived at Zama, some seventy air miles west of the Gulf of Hammamet. There Hannibal lacked the reinforcements, maneuverability, and shelter in case of defeat that he would have had at Carthage.

Scipio now had the ground of his own choosing for the battle, on an open plain suitable for his cavalry and with water within a few yards. He also foiled Hannibal's purpose: Masinissa arrived with 6,000 foot and 4,000 horse, giving him about 36,000 men against Hannibal's 50,000.

Scipio placed his heavy Roman legions in the center, his Italian cavalry under Laelius on the left, and Masinissa's Numidian horsemen on the right. Behind as a reserve were Masinissa's light infantry. Scipio's heavy infantry was in the normal legion formation of three lines facing the enemy, each line being formed by a series of maniples (companies) of about 120 men, each separated from those on either side by an interval about the width of the maniple.

In a departure from ordinary Roman custom, however, Scipio did not stagger the second line of maniples to form a checkerboard pattern to cover the interval between the maniples of the first line. Instead, he formed all three lines so that the maniples were directly in a row, leaving unobstructed open spaces between each set of maniples. The purpose was to allow the light skirmishers (*velites*) in the front to move quickly to the rear once they had thrown their javelins and darts and also to provide a path along which Scipio hoped to direct the eighty elephants that Hannibal held in his front rank.

Behind the elephants and a screen of lightly armed troops, Hannibal deployed his front line of 11,000 heavy infantry mer-

cenaries: Ligurians, Gauls, and Moors. On the second line he
placed his 11,000 Carthaginian and African levies and the Macedonians. On the last line he held his own veterans, 200 yards
behind the others, as his solid, intact reserve, of about 24,000
men. On his wings, he placed his 4,000 cavalry, his Numidian
allies on his left and the Carthaginian horse on his right.

Hannibal was superior to Scipio in every respect except
cavalry. Scipio's efforts both in building a Roman force and in
attracting Numidian horsemen had come to fruition.

The battle opened as Hannibal ordered his elephants to
charge the Roman line. Scipio immediately directed a blare
from his trumpets and cornets, terrifying the elephants and
causing some to turn tail and rush on Hannibal's troops. This
unexpected movement threw the Numidian cavalry, Hannibal's best horsemen, into disorder just as they were preparing
to charge. Masinissa, seeing his opportunity, launched a counterstroke and threw the Numidians into flight, exposing Hannibal's left wing. Masinissa left the field in pursuit.

The remainder of the elephants charged on the Roman *velites* and trampled many, but the lanes between the maniples
provided a way for the survivors to withdraw. The elephants
also took the line of least resistance; some rushed down the
open lanes, but others, driven out of the lanes by darts, fled
toward the Carthaginian right wing and disturbed Hannibal's
cavalry there. At the moment of maximum confusion, Laelius
launched a charge against the Carthaginian horse and forced
them into headlong flight, thereby exposing Hannibal's right
wing. The Roman cavalry, too, left the field in pursuit.

Hannibal's flanks had been stripped bare. But Scipio realized an outflanking move was impossible in the face of Hannibal's reserves and advanced his whole line directly on the
Carthaginian front.

At first the Gauls, Ligurians, and Moors held an advantage,
because they were skilled in skirmishing. But they could not
break the Roman line, and the weight of the massed legionaries
pressed them back. Feeling they had been left in the lurch, the
frontline soldiers turned to flee but were repulsed by the com-
pact, tightly massed second Carthaginian line, now coming up,
which did not want to disarray its order by letting the broken
first line through. Members of the first line either died or fled

around the flanks of the second line.

The second Carthaginian line now pushed the Romans back, inflicting great bloodshed. Although the Romans began to waver, their line was longer than the Carthaginian line and overlapped it, and they gradually cut the Carthaginians to pieces. The third line of veterans would not allow the second line to penetrate, and survivors had to flee around the third line.

The Romans had now reached the hard core of the Carthaginian army, Hannibal's veterans, still fresh and under his personal direction. Seeing the danger he faced, Scipio ordered an immediate recall, and the discipline of the Roman legionary was such that all obeyed. Scipio realized he had fewer infantry than the third line (probably around 18,000) yet needed to make his line as solid as possible to confront the massed enemy. Intervals between maniples were now a disadvantage. He also saw that his blow should be as concentrated, yet as wide, as he could make it. He therefore ordered the second line to come up into the intervals between the first line and for the third line to move quickly outward to both flanks, thereby creating a long, solid, shallow line of six ranks, which now overlapped the Carthaginian front.

The Romans now advanced on the veterans. In such a stupendous contest between two supreme masters of war, both of whom had made superb use of the resources they had at hand, the resolution came down to which side would be worn away first. Hannibal relied on his veterans. Scipio had ordered his cavalry to break off pursuit of the enemy horse as soon as possible, return, and assault the rear of Hannibal's line. He bet his army on this countervailing chance. If Scipio's cavalry did not return in time, the relatively thin Roman line would ultimately be broken by the much deeper Carthaginian line.

Polybius, the principal historian of the war, writes that "the contest was for long doubtful, the men falling where they stood out of determination, until Masinissa and Laelius arrived providentially at the proper moment."

The cavalry charged the Carthaginian rear, and this sealed the fate of Hannibal's army. Hannibal lost 20,000 men killed and almost as many prisoners. Hannibal himself and some other survivors slipped away. Scipio lost 2,000, this smaller figure a reflection of the fact that most losses in ancient battles occurred when an army's formation was broken and the men were fleeing. In such cases battle became almost a massacre of disorganized and often unresisting men.

Zama was one of the decisive battles of history. Carthage disappeared as a power, and Rome gained complete command of the western Mediterranean. Rome's march toward world empire was assured. Yet the battle itself had pitted two of the greatest generals of all time, and both had made virtually foolproof dispositions. Hannibal prepared the way with elephants to break Roman ranks and throw the enemy in confusion. He forced the Romans to tire themselves and dull their swords on two lines of troops before the final and decisive engagement. Only two factors turned the scales in favor of the Romans: Scipio's brilliant decision to startle the elephants with trumpets and, more significant, the superiority of the Roman cavalry. It's ironic that the man who had shown the ancient world the combination of mobility and shock force that cavalry could provide would himself be defeated by this weapon.

Scipio granted Carthage generous terms. It retained its own laws and customs and all its traditional territory in Africa. It lost most of its navy and paid a significant indemnity, but payments were spread over fifty years. Unlike the more normal example of avaricious victors who impose impossible or destructive terms, Scipio achieved a more perfect peace. Carthage did not sully the settlement for fifty years and grew as rich and populous as ever in its history. Only the envy and deliberate provocation of selfish lesser men who followed Scipio brought Carthage down. Told to destroy their own city, the Carthaginians refused and suffered eradication at Roman hands. It was a sad end to a great state.

Hannibal also suffered a sad end. Angry that Carthage regained its prosperity so quickly, the Romans accused Hannibal of planning to break the peace, forcing him to flee in 196. In 183, pursued by vengeful Romans in Asia Minor, he committed suicide.

Yet Hannibal, the loser, has appealed ever since to the human emotion and has achieved enduring fame. Scipio, the winner who ensured the continued success of Rome and was one of the greatest statesmen of all time, has been largely forgotten.

2

Mongol Secrets

VELOCITY AND DECEPTION

FOR THOUSANDS OF YEARS, Eurasia was divided into two distinct and conflicting modes of life. On the oceanic peripheries rose a succession of great, wealthy, heavily populated empires or cultures based on agriculture, industry, and trade—Babylon, Egypt, Assyria, Greece, Persia, Carthage, Rome to the west, the Indus River civilization to the south, and China to the east. Deep in the vast interior, where man had to cope with temperature extremes and undependable rainfall, much harder societies grew—tribes of nomads deriving their sustenance from herds of cattle, sheep, goats, horses, or camels which they followed from one grazing ground to another.

An essential characteristic of the littoral empires was permanant settlement: people cultivating the same ground year after year, dwelling in villages and cities. In the heartland of Eurasia, society was a polar opposite: seasonal movements of entire peoples with their flocks, living in felt yurts or other temporary structures that could be broken down in an hour and carried with them.

Nowhere in the Eurasian interior were conditions easy. But the richest part was a great band of natural steppe grassland that stretched, roughly on both sides of the 50th parallel, over 4,000 miles from the relatively lush plains of the Ukraine in the west to the harsh rolling hills of Mongolia in the east. To the south of this great girdle of grass was a belt of semiarid land,

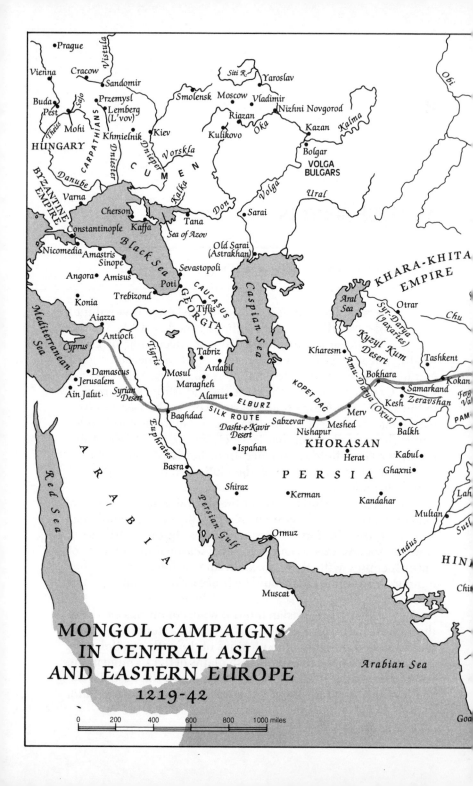

MONGOL CAMPAIGNS
IN CENTRAL ASIA
AND EASTERN EUROPE
1219-42

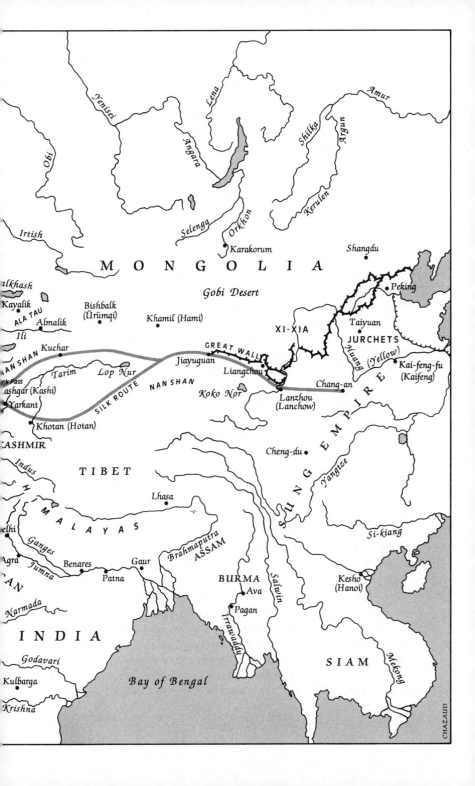

which trailed off in places into some of the bleakest, most forbidding deserts on earth: the Ust Urt between the Caspian and Aral seas, the Kara Kum north of the Kopet Dag mountain range of northeastern Iran, the Kyzyl Kum in Transoxiana between the Oxus (Amu Darya) and the Jaxartes (Syr Darya) rivers, the Takla Makan in the mountain-rimmed Tarim river basin, and the Gobi, the only natural barrier between China and Mongolia, a wild and empty region of gravel, salt plains, black basalt outcrops, and pink-yellow mountains of sand.

Since many grazing grounds were inherently less productive than others and since droughts or especially harsh winters affected growth of the grass, the tribes of inner Asia always were subject to fierce conflicts among themselves to gain or protect the pastures that meant the difference between life and death for their herds and themselves.

The innate insecurity of nomad existence and the battles to win or defend pastures created fierce and bellicose tribes of disciplined peoples with a capacity to overcome hardship.

The tribes, able to possess only what they could carry with them, were always drawn to the wealth, comfort, and luxuries of the littoral. Their lust for these riches was older than history and created a constant tension between the steppe and the sown, between the outer barbarians and the comparatively refined inhabitants of settled villages and cities.

If their discipline could be mobilized, the steppe tribes' avarice would constitute a formidable danger to the littoral. But for many centuries the nomads remained unable, because of distances and lack of mobility, to strike out of their enormous heartland. Instead they fought among themselves for grazing lands and endured their poverty.

However, early in the eighth century B.C., probably in the western grasslands north of the Black Sea, some tribesmen learned how to ride horses. This development revolutionized the life of the steppes and changed the world.

The revolution occurred despite the fact that the nomads rode without stirrups or saddle. Although their invention of the bit and bridle a millennium before had made possible the wheeled war chariot, it took centuries for the nomads to create the leather saddle with pommel and cantle to check excessive forward and backward movement and nearly another millennium for the stirrup, invented in India, to spread across the steppes.

Nevertheless, the subjugation of the horse was the final achievement of the steppe people, which made them potential world conquerors. Thereafter the nomadic tribesmen lived much of their lives on horses, treating their animals as virtual extensions of themselves. In the process they became natural cavalrymen. The horse gave them mobility on a continental scale, especially as the great river of grass running across Eurasia could serve as a source of food and a military highway to attack whatever region was weak and unprepared.

At least ten centuries previously, the steppe people had developed the other instrument that, combined with the horse, was to make them the most terrible warriors who had appeared on earth. This instrument was the compound bow, usually consisting of a layer of sinew on the back and a layer of horn on the inner surface or belly with a frame of wood in the middle. The bow could exert a pull of well over a hundred pounds, although it was short enough to be wielded easily by a man on horseback. Arrows shot from such a bow could kill at 300 yards and, equipped with sharp metal bodkin points, could penetrate the thickest armor.

The horse archers created battle tactics unlike anything seen before. Their essence was speed and surprise. Horse archers bewildered foot soldiers by the rapidity with which they could materialize before a phalanx, unleash a storm of arrows, attack to the front, sides, and rear, and disappear, without ever coming into collision with infantry swords or spears. A favorite technique was the feint. Combining the speed of the horse with a refined system of control and timing, horsemen rushed forward in a furious charge, then, pretending the onslaught had failed, withdrew, seemingly in panic and sometimes over the horizon. Only the most astute and controlled enemy forces could withstand the urge to rush after the supposedly fleeing horsemen and, in the process, go beyond their supports, lose their tight defensive order, and allow units or individuals to become separated. When this occurred, the horse archers suddenly regrouped, turned on the advancing enemy, and destroyed the disorganized forces one unit or soldier at a time. This device succeeded time after time and century after century against enemies unfamiliar with it.

Steppe horse archers burst out of the heartland upon the civilizations of the littoral. Sometimes the explosions came from tribes living along the frontiers who were bent on plunder. Other times impacts of tribe against tribe extending across much of Eurasia created movements of entire peoples that forced border tribes to flee into regions of settled civilization.

It was these or a combination of these forces in the centuries prior to Alexander the Great (356–323 B.C.) that brought on the great movements of Scythians, a people of Iranian stock, upon Europe, the Persian Empire, and Greece. After them came the Sarmatians, another Iranian people even more bellicose. Known to the Greeks as the Massagetae, they sent their young women as well as their men to war. This may have given rise to the myths of the Amazons.

The Sarmatians also developed a new weapon, heavy cavalry armed with a primitive lance, to counter the speed and the missile power of the horse archer and to permit cavalry to come to grips with massed enemy forces. The Sarmatians bred a horse larger and more powerful than the ponies the steppe bowmen rode. Combining this horse and long lance with a rider protected by leather or armor, the Sarmatians created a shock weapon that sometimes could survive arrow storms and offered a decisive advantage in close combat over enemies armed with shorter swords or spears.

Other nomads adopted the Sarmatian combination of heavy cavalry and traditional horse archer. Their campaigns to devastate and plunder littoral empires and weaker tribes within reach slowly taught their defeated enemies to copy the techniques that had given them victory.

However, the Romans, despite the example that Scipio Africanus had given of the effectiveness of cavalry, reverted after the Second Punic War to primary reliance on infantry. As a consequence, the compound bow never made enough impact on the Mediterranean world to become a major weapon. Rome, as a result, was unable to expand to the east. The Parthians, a steppe people who took over Iran and Mesopotamia, stopped the Roman legions with their mounted bowmen and heavy lance-wielding cavalry armored with plate and chain mail. One of Rome's greatest humiliations was the famous "Parthian shot," delivered by bowmen to the rear as they rode away. The Romans could not come to grips with these elusive horsemen and had no defense against their arrows.

Ultimately the Eastern Roman or Byzantine Empire adopted mounted warriors, including horse archers, as its major defense, and similar horsemen appeared across the Middle East. These developments reduced, but did not end, the disparity between the war capability of the steppes and the settled lands of the littoral.

In Europe, the tradition of the Sarmatian leather-girded lance-wielding warrior on a heavy animal descended directly to the knight clad in expensive armor and riding a great warhorse. He became the principal warrior in the Middle Ages. But the West did not adopt the other great contribution of the steppes to mounted warfare—the lightly armored or unarmored archer wielding the short compound bow from the back of a small, fast horse.

This failure led to profound social consequences in the West. Armor, swords, lances, and warhorses were very expensive, and kings assigned land and serfs to warriors to produce the means to buy them. This transformed warriors into a privileged, wealthy aristocracy and the rest of society into a servitor class, except for a small clergy allied to the aristocracy. Europe's reliance upon a single form of mounted warrior—heavy cavalry—and the consequent devaluing of inexpensive light cavalry (as well as infantry) was to have equally profound consequences when its chivalry came into contact with the greatest army that ever arose on the steppes.

This army was that of the Mongols, a small nomad people tending their herds in the spare grasslands of what is now southeastern Mongolia.

The Mongols rose to power in the waning years of the twelfth century under their khan, Genghis. With his principal *orlok*, or marshal, Subedei Bahadur of the Reindeer People, Genghis Khan infused the Mongols and their allies with an efficiency and discipline never attained before, carried the speed and the

GENGHIS KHAN
Warder Collection

deception of steppe warfare to its extreme limits, and gained victories on a scale no people or empire ever reached before or since.

Genghis Khan and Subedei are two of the greatest captains who have ever lived. Genghis, in addition, possessed high political skills, which permitted him to unite all the Mongols, defeat the Mongols' principal enemies, the Tatars, and force the Tatar survivors to join the Mongols, and bring other tribes in the region between the Altai Mountains on the west and Manchuria on the east into a single confederation.

In 1206, Genghis took stock. He wanted to keep enriching himself and his people, but his mind was divided between trade and conquest. He finally settled on conquest, but once he had bent central Asia to his will, he hoped to rebuild trade, and especially to reopen the great Silk Road that, beginning around the time of Christ, carried the refined products of the Orient to Rome, mostly in exchange for Western gold and silver.

The Silk Road was a great caravan route more than 4,000 miles long. It was a road in name only, and along many stretches it threatened great danger from unsettled peoples, great heat or great cold, and some of the highest mountains and bleakest deserts on earth. It started from China's former capital of Changan near present-day Xi'an and threaded through the oasis cities of the Tarim river basin to ancient Kashgar at the foot of the Mountains of Heaven (Tian Shan) and the Pamirs, its fields fed by mountain streams and noted for its grapes, apricots, peaches, cherries, rugs, and fine handicrafts.

Then the road went over the 13,000-foot Terek Pass in the Pamirs, down the great cleft of the Fergana Valley, where the Jaxartes River rises, to the caravanserai city of Kokand. From here the camels and horses crossed the Hungry Steppe to fabled Samarkand along the Zeravshan River, captured by Alexander the Great, enclosing within its five-mile-long walls great mosques and Islamic schools and famous for melons packed in snow, beautiful women who had beards and mustaches, and workshops for silk, paper, satins, and copperware.

The road then traversed the eastern edge of the Kyzyl Kum, a frightening desert region the size of New Mexico, covered with sand dunes and so arid many said it was impassable by man or beast, to Bokhara, where the Zeravshan River disappears into an interior delta and oasis. Bokhara was a city of flat-roofed houses of sun-dried bricks already eleven centuries old and famous for brocades, filigreed silver, falcons, and honey. At this point the Silk Road turned south across the Oxus River, the traditional frontier between the littoral and the steppe, ascended the Kopet Dag into the Khorasan region of northeastern Iran, turned west between the Dasht-e-Kavir desert and the Elburz Mountains to Baghdad and Mesopotamia, then across the Syrian Desert to Antioch and the Mediterranean.

After the Arabian conquests beginning in the seventh century and immense clashes that followed between Muslims and barbarians in and around Transoxiana, the Silk Road had become increasingly unsafe and untraveled.

In 1206, Genghis Khan decided to expand westward and to destroy the strong state of Kara-Khitai, a nomad nation of Turkish horse warriors, almost as formidable as the Mongols themselves, who dominated the region between the Jaxartes and Lake Balkhash. Kara-Khitai blocked Genghis's access to the Muslim empire of Khwarezm (Khorezm), which controlled from its capital at Samarkand a critical portion of the Silk Road. After he had disposed of the Kara-Khitans, Genghis hoped to enter into peaceful commercial relations with the Khwarezmian shah, Ala ed-Din Mohammed, and convince him that reopening the road would benefit him by increasing trade through his dominions.

Genghis Khan dared not turn his back, however, on two potent powers arching around the Chinese Sung Empire, which ruled the Yangtze river basin and southern China. These semibarbarian powers were alarmed by the expansion of the Mongols and were certain to strike into Mongolia the moment Genghis's armies moved west. They were the Jurchets, a former nomad people from Manchuria, who controlled northern China down to the Yellow River (Hwang Ho), and the Xi Xia, a Tibetan Tangut people occupying the vicinity of the Ordos Loop of the Yellow River in present-day Inner Mongolia and Ningxia province of China.

After long and difficult campaigns extending over twelve years, Genghis finally humbled both powers and opened the

Silk Road from Changan through the Tarim basin to Kashgar, while becoming enmeshed in trying to conquer the teeming millions of Sung Dynasty China.

Genghis himself, however, his rear now secure, turned abruptly away from China, leaving a small Mongol force to continue the war, and focused his attention on what he still considered to be his greatest danger, the Kara-Khitans.

Genghis saw a great opportunity to seize Kara-Khitai almost without bloodshed. The Kara-Khitan shah, Kuchluk, a Buddhist, had caused much discontent by persecuting the Muslim Turks who formed a great majority of his people. In 1218 one of Genghis Khan's marshals, Jebe Noyan, "the Arrow," at the head of two 10,000-man tumans, or divisions, rushed from the Korean border 2,500 miles to central Asia. Arriving, he declared he had come to restore religious freedom. The Muslim Kara-Khitans welcomed him, and within weeks Genghis had extended his power over virtually all the country.

Genghis was now face to face with Mohammed, the shah of Khwarezm. Mohammed's empire was also largely new. While Genghis was conquering central Asia, Mohammed was extending his rule over a great block of Muslim territory to the southwest. He had inherited Iran but had added Afghanistan almost to the Indus River and driven the Kara-Khitans beyond the Jaxartes, capturing all of Transoxiana. The shah could mobilize 200,000 men, considerably more than Genghis, and most of them were hardy Turkish horse warriors. Though not as tightly organized as the Mongols, the shah's army was also adept at the dizzying speed of steppe tactics, the compound bow, and the lance.

Genghis sincerely sought a peaceful relationship with Mohammed, at least for a period, and reopening the Silk Road was a high priority. Consequently Genghis sent an embassy to Samarkand, which presented the shah with the finest gifts he could offer, promised peace, but made the unforgivable error of saying he regarded the shah as his son, which to Mohammed's supersensitive ears suggested Genghis was calling him a vassal.

Unaware of the offense he'd given, Genghis prepared another caravan of a hundred camels, filled with articles of rare value, including many looted from China. The caravan crossed into Khwarezmian territory at Otrar on the lower Jaxartes. There the governor, Inalchik, seized the caravan and executed its leaders. Believing Inalchik might have acted without authority, Genghis sent a mission of one Khwarezmian and two Mongols to Mohammed, merely asking that the governor be punished. The shah chopped off the Khwarezmian's head and sent the Mongols back with their heads shaved, an insult beyond redemption.

Mongol tradition required revenge, and Genghis, sending out orders for his army to assemble, resolved to do more. He set about to conquer the lands of the vain and arrogant Mohammed. Genghis dispatched only one message to the shah: "You have chosen war. That will happen which will happen and what it is to be we know not; only God knows."

Mohammed decided to defend his northern frontier, the Jaxartes. But instead of concentrating his 200,000 men against the Mongols' 150,000, he divided most of his army into packets at various walled cities along 500 miles of the river. His competent son, Jalal ad-Din, pointed out that none of these points could be defended against a major assault without reinforcements from Samarkand. But Mohammed was convinced the Mongols could not conduct a siege or storm a fortified position and, trusting to his larger numbers, resolved to remain on the defensive.

In making this decision, Mohammed played into the hands of Genghis Khan, who possessed the most effective war machine in the world. It was built on four major foundations: extreme mobility, a superior weapon, an almost foolproof tactical system, and strategic genius, exemplified by Genghis himself and by his two chief *orloks,* Jebe and especially Subedei, both of whom rose to high command before they were twenty-five years of age.

The Mongols' entire army consisted of cavalry. In the vast open belt of deserts, steppes, and prairies that stretches from the Yellow Sea to the Danube River, horsemen held a decisive advantage over infantry because of their speed and mobility. And, since some time before the sixth century the stirrup had spread throughout Eurasia, a man on horseback possessed a platform from which he could shoot an arrow or wield a sword as easily as a man on the ground, and a horseman could deliver a lance blow with much of the force of the horse behind it. Each soldier, moreover, led with him a string of horses so that he could ride all day at full speed by changing horses as each got tired.

Although the Mongols had catapults and other siege artillery and used lances, swords, and javelins, their most important weapon remained the compound bow.

Considerable attention had been given to the bow in the Arab world, Byzantium, and China but it was more effective in Mongol hands, largely because the Mongols relied on it and devoted much of their time to perfecting their use of it. The Mongol bow, protected from the weather by waterproof lacquer, possessed a pull of 100 to 160 pounds, compared with about 75 pounds for the English longbow, which was made of a single material, yew wood. While the longbow—which did not achieve fame until over a century later at Crécy in France—had a range of 250 yards, the Mongol bow could shoot 350 yards and with greater velocity.

The Mongols had arrows that could penetrate any armor. They could shoot equally well from the saddle while advancing or retreating. They had long-range arrows, whistling arrows for signaling, and incendiary arrows that could set fire to wooden buildings and roofs.

Mongolian tactics were rigid in conception but flexible in execution and built on a framework of moves that resembled a battle drill. The repetition of tried techniques—directed by clear signals from the leaders—made for extreme efficiency and quick application and contributed greatly to Mongol success, since individual soldiers and officers were not expected to improvise on the spot. Mongol tactics were so quick and fast that they were usually irresistible.

The Mongol battle formation was in five ranks. Heavy cavalry made up the first two ranks and was intended for the major blow. The horses were armored. The men wore iron helmets and cuirasses of oxhide or leather-covered iron scales and carried twelve-foot lances, bows, and scimitars, battle-axes, or maces. Light cavalry, wearing light armor or none at all, and carrying small swords, javelins, and bows, composed the last three ranks.

Light troops spread out as skirmishers well ahead of the main body in three detachments—vanguard and both flanks. If the enemy attacked a flank, the light cavalry that met him would automatically become the vanguard and the other skirmisher units would swing either to the left or right, while the main body wheeled to face the threat.

Once the vanguard was engaged, the light cavalry in the three rear ranks of the main body would advance through the heavy cavalry to join the skirmishers. If the Mongols were advancing, the light troops showered the enemy front with arrows and javelins. If the enemy was advancing, the light troops retreated ahead of him, shooting arrows over their shoulders. The purpose in either case was to open the ranks of the enemy, whether cavalry or infantry. When this happened, the light horsemen broke away to either flank, leaving a path clear for the heavy cavalry to gallop in for the final blow.

If the light cavalry failed to create the necessary gaps in the enemy lines, the commander would order the light horse on one flank to assault the enemy's flank at right angles. At the same time the heavy cavalry would gallop around behind the same flank in a "standard sweep" and make their decisive charge in the rear of that flank.

The favorite Mongol tactic, however, was to use the *mangudai*, a specially selected unit that would charge the enemy alone. After a fearsome assault, the *mangudai* would break ranks and flee in hopes of provoking the enemy to give chase. Since all light cavalry learned this technique, occasionally half the light horse would practice it. It was usually so convincing that the enemy cavalry sprang after the fleeing Mongols, believing they were on the verge of victory. Unseen to the rear, Mongol archers waited. By the time they were upon the archers, the enemy horsemen were spread out and many would fall to well-aimed bow shots. Now disordered and suffering heavy casualties, the enemy would be vulnerable to the heavy cavalry, which now made its charge.

Mongol strategy was an exercise in masterful surprise and deception that confused the enemy and placed Mongol armies at decisive points where they were least expected. Genghis Khan and his *orloks* were about to demonstrate this strategy to Mohammed.

Genghis concentrated his main force on the Irtish River east of Lake Balkhash. Genghis chose Subedei to plan the invasion.

Subedei wanted to protect the assembling Mongol forces against a sudden offensive by Mohammed. He also wanted to cover his preparations and ensure secrecy. At Subedei's recommendation, Genghis sent his eldest son, Jochi, with a strong Mongol force toward the lower (northern) reaches of the Jaxartes in the spring and summer of 1219. Jochi laid waste the whole trough of country west of Lake Balkhash to the vicinity of Otrar. By the time Jalal ad-Din arrived with a strong Khwarezmian force to meet the supposed invasion, Jochi had accomplished his mission, sent back all the horses and forage available, and burned towns and fields, leaving a desolate landscape incapable of supporting an invading army. After a rearguard battle against Jalal ad-Din, the Mongols set fire to the dry grass on the plain and disappeared behind the barrier of smoke and flame.

Several months elapsed with no move by the Mongols. Then, early in 1220, Jebe Noyan moved west with two 10,000-man divisions (tumans) from Kashgar. He crossed the Pamirs through the Terek Pass, 13,000 feet high and deep in snow. Though the Mongols lost most of their supplies and suffered greatly, they arrived in the Fergana Valley and advanced on Kokand, which protected the southern end of the Jaxartes line. Jebe thereby directly threatened Mohammed's right flank and the two centers of Mohammed's power: Samarkand, 220 air miles southwest, and Bokhara, 100 air miles farther west.

Jochi's scorched-earth campaign the previous summer on the approaches to the northern Jaxartes convinced Mohammed that the Mongols would not strike again there, while Jebe's appearance in the Fergana Valley focused the shah's attention to the southern reaches of the Jaxartes. He reinforced the river line in that region and concentrated 40,000 men at Bokhara and additional men at Samarkand.

Meanwhile Genghis Khan was planning his major blows

elsewhere. He had divided his main striking force into three armies. One of these, of three tumans, he placed under Jochi, and another, also of three tumans, under two other sons, Ogedei and Chagatai. The third army of three tumans and the elite imperial guard tuman remained under Genghis, with Subedei as his chief of staff.

These three armies of over 100,000 men now advanced, carrying all their provisions with them, along the route they were *least* expected: directly over the land turned into a desert by Jochi. In February 1220, they unexpectedly debouched at Otrar on the left flank of the Jaxartes line. After seizing this city, they captured the governor, Inalchik, who had killed the Mongol envoy, and executed him by pouring molten silver into his eyes and ears until he died.

In the great rush of Mongol troops into Otrar, Genghis Khan's force of four tumans was not distinguished from the other two armies under Genghis's sons. The two armies under Genghis's sons turned south and began clearing the Jaxartes line, assaulting the fortresses and moving toward Jebe, who meanwhile captured Kokand and marched north toward a junction with them. The operations fixed Mohammed's attention on the Jaxartes line, and he sent all his reserves toward it.

But Genghis's army had not followed those of the princes. Instead it had disappeared north unnoticed and captured a Turkoman city, Zarnuk, for the sole purpose of acquiring a man who, informants had told Genghis, knew a way along a chain of oases through the Kyzyl Kum.

Genghis and his four tumans, with the Zarnuk guide, marched safely through the Kyzyl Kum and, at the beginning of April 1220, emerged at Bokhara and in the rear of Mohammed's armies, having traversed over 300 miles of supposedly impassable desert. In a single, stunning blow, Genghis had turned the shah's entire line and severed his connection with his provinces to the west, where many more potential troops remained uncalled. It was one of the greatest strategic maneuvers on the rear in the history of warfare and perhaps the foremost example of strategic surprise ever attained.

Genghis and Subedei left one gate of Bokhara unguarded. They hoped thereby to entice the main garrison outside the walls to fight in the open. This force consisted of mercenary Kanglis, a tribe of Kipchaks from beyond the Aral sea. The major portion of the Kanglis, 20,000 soldiers, rushed out the gate, pretending they were going to attack the Mongols but actually fleeing south. Next day the Oxus River blocked their path and the Mongols came up behind and cut them to pieces.

The remainder of the Bokhara garrison fled to the citadel while the Persian inhabitants surrendered the city. The Mongols soon captured the citadel after driving thousands of civilians ahead of their assault. In the battle most of the city burned, and Genghis ordered the walls pulled down.

Genghis and the other three Mongol armies now converged on Samarkand, from which Mohammed hurriedly fled. Fifty thousand Kanglis marched out on foot to meet them. The Mongols withdrew until they were able to wheel and fall on the Kanglis' flanks and thereby cut the Samarkand garrison in half. The remaining Kanglis offered to abandon Khwarezm, saying they were nomads like the Mongols and were willing to join the Mongol army.

Deserted by their defenders—since the 20,000-man remainder of the garrison withdrew into the citadel—the people of Samarkand surrendered. About 1,000 men slipped away by night from the citadel, but the Mongols soon assaulted it and killed the rest. They also surrounded the Kanglis outside the city and slaughtered them. Said Genghis: "A man who is once faithless can never be trusted."

A special Mongol force under Subedei now raced after Mohammed. The people in his remaining provinces had lost confidence in him, and, suspecting everyone, he become a fugitive. Mohammed died of pleurisy in January 1221, on an island in the Caspian Sea. Genghis, to protect his southern flank, methodically ravaged Afghanistan, and his son, Tului, killed most of the people of Khorasan.

In only a few months, Genghis Khan had virtually destroyed a great kingdom, almost entirely by strategic moves that had left the defenders unable to respond. By first striking in the south, he had focused the shah's attention away from the point of his first major blow, nearly 500 miles away at Otrar. Then, by fixing the enemy's forces in place by heavy but indecisive at-

tacks along the Jaxartes, he was able to march on the rear of
these forces, cut them off from reinforcements, seize a major
city, and uncover the capital. At every decisive point, Otrar,
Bokhara, and Samarkand, his surprise permitted him to assemble superior forces, though his overall strength was less than
Mohammed's.

In February 1221, Subedei and Jebe with 20,000 men began
a two-year reconnaissance into the western steppes to open a
path for further Mongol conquests. This campaign has remained the greatest cavalry raid in history. Though the expedition's strength was laughably small, Subedei and Jebe
destroyed Georgian, Cumen, Russian, middle-Volga Bulgar,
and Kangli armies, most of which were vastly larger. They also
recruited with gold large numbers of spies to inform them of
the situation in Europe and formed a secret alliance with the
Venetians, who had trading stations on the Sea of Azov. In
exchange for information about European geography and politics, Subedei and Jebe agreed to grant the Venetians a trading
monopoly wherever the Mongols rode.

Nevertheless, Genghis Khan's death in 1227 caused plans
to be suspended to subjugate the remainder of Iran, advance
into Mesopotamia, and reopen the Silk Road, along with plans
to conquer Europe. Genghis's second surviving son, Ogedei,
succeeded him, but Ogedei was preoccupied with subduing
the remaining Jurchets in northern China and, after 1235, with
a major attack on the Sung Empire of southern China.

But expansion in East Asia was limited by the sea. And the
western steppes of Russia offered the greatest opportunity for
conquest. These steppes had not been subdued in the 1221–23
expedition, yet had been allotted to Genghis's grandson Batu.
Subedei argued that they should be conquered to protect the
Mongol western flank and serve as a springboard to seize the
great grassed plain of Hungary. With this natural prairie as a
base and grazing ground for their horses, the Mongols then
could destroy the nations of Europe one by one.

Subedei's vision aroused great enthusiasm, and Ogedei provided 50,000 experienced troops for Subedei, under Batu's

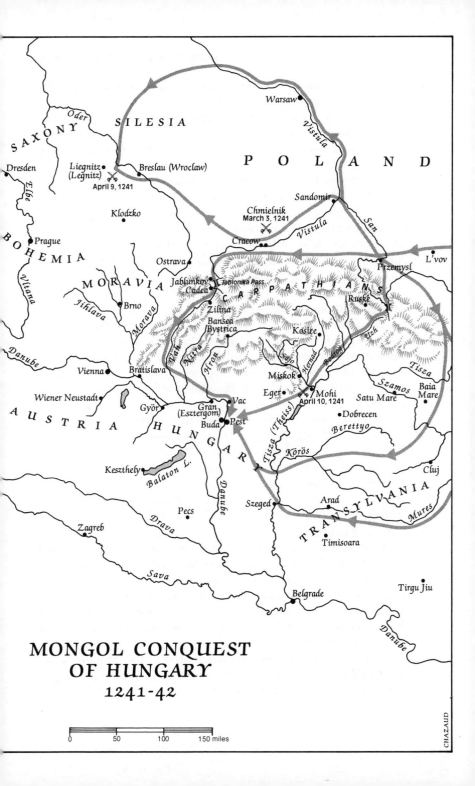

MONGOL CONQUEST
OF HUNGARY
1241-42

0   50   100   150 miles

nominal command, to conquer the western steppes with the aid of conscripts recruited in the region.

In 1236, Subedei secured his army's flanks by subduing the northern Bulgars on the upper Volga and the Kipchaks on the lower Volga, and in the winter of 1237, the Mongol army of 120,000 men crossed the frozen Volga into Russia.

For the next three years the Mongols systematically destroyed most of the Russian states, using the frozen rivers in winter as highways to penetrate deep into the country and avoid the thick forests. The campaign culminated in the seizure and destruction of Kiev in December 1240. Russian resistance now collapsed, and the Mongols quickly reached the Carpathian Mountains dividing Russia from Hungary.

The Mongols were now poised for the invasion of eastern Europe. Although European rulers had been aware of the Mongol intentions for at least two years, they were curiously unmoved. Pope Gregory IX was not sad to see the Eastern Orthodox Christians of Russia destroyed, but he was concerned about an invasion of Catholic Hungary. However, both he and the Holy Roman emperor, Frederick II, who ruled much of Germany and Italy, were distracted. They were on the verge of a violent conflict over power and could spare little attention to the pleas of King Bela IV of Hungary. It was left primarily to Hungary, Poland, and the German Teutonic Knights—now colonizing the Baltic coast of Prussia, Lithuania, and Latvia—to defend against the Mongols. But Poland was fragmented into nine principalities, and even in the face of imminent danger, the Hungarian nobility argued with King Bela for concessions before agreeing to fight.

Though European rulers knew practically nothing about the Mongols, Subedei and Prince Batu had been regularly informed about the political situation in Europe by their spies and informers. They were not concerned, therefore, that—with the need to garrison Russia and secure communications with the east—they could field only about 100,000 men to seize their first target, Hungary.

In January 1241, Subedei concentrated the Mongol army north of the Carpathians around Lemberg (Lvov) and Przemysl, near the present-day Polish-Ukrainian borders. Subedei's intention was to force the Carpathian passes and march on the Hungarian capital, Gran (Esztergom), on the Danube twenty-five air miles northwest of Buda and Pest. But it was dangerous to advance directly into Hungary with the Poles and Germans capable of falling on his right flank. Subedei had to crush these threats and also protect against possible thrusts from the west by the duke of Austria and the king of Bohemia.

Subedei therefore divided his army into four parts. Three he assigned to the main mission, Hungary, the fourth to removing danger on the right flank.

This last army, under Princes Baidar and Kadan, consisted of two tumans, or 20,000 men. It moved first, at the beginning of March 1241, crossing the Vistula at Sandomir, which it took by storm. The Poles were utterly surprised and had not gathered their forces. But the task of Baidar and Kadan was to draw the Poles and Germans away from Hungary. Therefore they had to stir the enemy into mobilizing.

Splitting their forces, Kadan moved northwest to spread alarm over as wide an area of Poland as possible and to threaten German states west of the Oder river, while Baidar continued southwest, directly toward the Polish capital of Cracow, burning and pillaging and drawing attention to himself. Baidar's men paused just before Cracow and began retreating, as if they were a raiding party returning to base. Like numerous enemy forces encountering the men of the steppes in centuries past, the chivalry of Poland did not recognize this move as a feint. Certain they were on the verge of a great victory, they threw caution to the winds, abandoned the walls of Cracow, pursued the Mongols on their heavy warhorses, and attacked.

Baidar's men broke and fled, allowing their prisoners to escape. Sure the Mongols were now on the run, the Poles chased after them. At Chmielnik, eleven miles from Cracow, a Mongol ambush awaited them: massed bodies of archers unleashed clouds of bodkin-pointed arrows that easily penetrated the Poles' armor. Most of the Poles died. The inhabitants of Cracow deserted the town and the Mongols burned it.

Baidar and Kadan planned to meet at Breslau (Wroclaw), the Silesian capital, but Baidar arrived before Kadan and found the inhabitants had burned their city and taken refuge in the

citadel. There he learned that Henry of Silesia had gathered an
army of 25,000 at Liegnitz (Legnica), forty miles west. Many
were armored knights wielding lances, especially Henry's
Silesians, French Knights Templar and Hospitallers, Teutonic
knights, and some surviving Polish horsemen. But most were
Polish and Moravian feudal levies, unmounted infantry, armed
mostly with pikes, who were virtually useless for offensive battle.

Baidar learned that King Wenceslas of Bohemia was marching to join Henry. Sending messages to Subedei and Kadan,
Baidar set out at full speed to get to Liegnitz before Wenceslas.
Kadan joined him on the road, and together they arrived at
Liegnitz on April 8. The next day Henry marched out to meet
the Mongols, not knowing that Wenceslas with 50,000 men was
only a day's march away.

Henry drew his army up on a plain beyond the city, and
when the Mongol vanguard approached in close order, it appeared so small that Henry sent only a small detachment of
cavalry to meet it. When this body fell back under the onslaught
of Mongol arrows, he ordered all the remaining horsemen to
attack. The Mongol vanguard, which had been a *mangudai,*
broke and fled, once again drawing the European chivalry after
it at a gallop. The European charge turned quickly into a spread-
out, disorganized race. Behind a screen of smoke bombs the
Mongol archers were waiting with armor-piercing arrows. When
the knights came within range, the archers struck down many
of them and brought the charge to a halt. Then the Mongol
heavy cavalry assaulted the confused knights, killing most of
the remainder. The archers now rode through the smoke screen
and shot down the infantry, while horsemen ran down and
killed Henry of Silesia. The Mongols filled nine sacks of right
ears cut from the slain and sent them to Batu.

In less than a month the Mongol detachment had raced 400
miles and fought two decisive battles. Poland was stunned and
prostrate, and the Germans west of the Oder were recoiling to
defend their lands. A large part of the task assigned to the Mongol detachment had been achieved.

Only Wenceslas remained a threat. When he heard of the
Liegnitz disaster, he retreated and collected reinforcements

from Thuringia and Saxony. The Mongols found his army drawn up at Klodzko in the Glatz defiles, sixty miles southeast of Liegnitz. Wenceslas hoped to entrap the Mongols in the defiles, but reconnaissance had already warned Baidar and Kadan of the danger, and they would not be drawn in. They also had lost many men in the Liegnitz battle and could not be certain of defeating Wenceslas's large army in open battle.

However, Wenceslas had already been drawn 250 miles away from the Hungarians mobilizing on the west bank of the Danube. Therefore Wenceslas's army was strategically useless, because it could not affect the decision in Hungary.

To make certain of holding Wenceslas in the north longer, the Mongol princes made a feint to the west, as if planning to march into Germany. This drew Wenceslas after them. The Mongols then broke into small bodies, rode entirely around the Bohemian army, and spread out in a wide band through Moravia, burning villages and stores and creating a desert to guard the Mongol flank.

Once through Moravia, the princes reassembled their men and turned southeast to join Subedei, ready to fall on the Austrians if they moved to the aid of Hungary. In this brilliant, whirlwind campaign, a moderate-sized Mongol force had eliminated all possibility of intervention by Polish, German, Czech, and Austrian forces many times its size and still managed to ride back to the main body in time to be of service if needed.

Subedei had expected protection from the flank campaign, but he had not relied entirely on it. The principal task of the commander seeking to maneuver is to deceive the enemy about his purpose so as to prevent effective opposition from being thrown in his path. That was why Subedei divided the main force into three columns, each to enter Hungary by a different route. Threatened from three directions at once, the Hungarians would be unable to concentrate against any one Mongol threat for fear the other two would descend on their rear or seize important cities or terrain they could not afford to lose. Therefore, Subedei was confident the enemy would not effectively contest any of the columns and all could reach the main barrier of the Danube unmolested and there reunite.

In addition, Subedei relied on unbelievable speed to place

the Mongols on the river before the stunned Hungarians could react.

The right or northerly column moved west from Przemysl in early March, shielded on the north by the Vistula and the princes' flank detachment, which had moved a few days before. The column then turned south through the Jablonika and neighboring passes of the Carpathians and, in two bodies, swept around in a long curving advance to emerge on the Danube on March 17, seizing Vac, on the east side of the river between Buda and Gran, and slaughtering the population.

Meanwhile the left or southerly column made a great arching sweep to the southeast through Moldavia and Walachia and broke through passes into Transylvania, and while part prevented the Transylvania nobility and clergy from bringing forces to Buda, another part under Subedei raced up the lower Tisza (Theiss) river valley, arriving at Pest on April 3.

The last to move was the central column, containing Batu and the elite guard. This column forced the pass of Ruske on March 12 and advanced directly by way of the upper Tisza Valley. The advance guard arrived on the Danube on March 15 and the main body two days later. The movement by the advance guard was one of the fastest in history: 180 miles in three days through enemy country deep in snow.

By April 3, Subedei had assembled his three columns opposite Buda, on the west bank of the Danube, and Pest, on the east bank, where Bela had concentrated his army of 100,000. Although the Mongols now controlled Hungary east of the Danube and Subedei's strategy had prevented a much larger European army assembling to meet him, he still was uncertain of the situation. He remained outnumbered, having perhaps 70,000 men, since a tuman was still in Transylvania, while the flank detachment in Silesia had not fought the battle of Liegnitz. It would be dangerous to force a crossing of the Danube under the eyes of the assembled Hungarian army. Moreover, the longer he lingered on the banks of the river, the more likely it was that other European rulers would send forces to aid Bela.

Subedei therefore practiced on a strategic scale the familiar Mongol tactical ruse: he withdrew eastward. The Hungarians immediately concluded that the Mongols had been frightened by their numbers and power, and they clamored to pursue the supposedly fleeing Mongols. Their mood changed abruptly from anxiety about a Mongol attack to a desire to share in the spoils and glory. King Bela ordered his army to go after the Mongols.

The Hungarians did not realize Subedei was luring them away from the protection of the Danube and a chance for reinforcement. Subedei carried out the retirement at a slow pace, taking six days to reach the Sajo River, about a hundred miles northeast of Buda-Pest. On the heath of Mohi, just west of the Sajo, shortly before it debouches into the Tisza, Batu and Subedei had decided to turn on their pursuers.

On April 9 the Mongol army rode over the heath, crossed the only bridge, made of stone, and continued on for ten miles into thickets just west of the hills and vineyards of Tokay. There the Mongol army found ample hiding places. When a Hungarian detachment that evening crossed the stone bridge and rode into the thickets, it found nothing.

The Hungarians camped on the heath, drawing up their wagons in a circle girded by chains and ropes and placing their tents inside. On the Hungarian right were the marshes of the Tisza, in front of them across the heath was the Sajo, and to their left were hills and forests.

The battle opened just before dawn on April 10. Batu, with 40,000 men, launched an attack on the stone bridge. The Hungarians defended fiercely, and the Mongols could not break across until they brought up catapults and bombarded the Hungarians with fire bombs, forcing them back and allowing the Mongols to get on the western side.

The Mongols, even so, were sorely pressed, being outnumbered well over two to one by the enemy, which drove repeatedly against the Mongol horsemen. Only archery fire saved the Mongols from being overwhelmed by the massed charges. For two maddening hours, Batu and his men withstood the incredible assaults, losing many men in the process but completely absorbing the attention of the Hungarian army.

At last Subedei and 30,000 more Mongols appeared on the Hungarian rear. While Batu had fixed the entire enemy to the front, Subedei, without the Hungarians suspecting anything, had built a bridge downstream across the Sajo and had led his men over it to descend on the enemy.

Stunned but too experienced to panic, the Hungarians made an orderly retreat to their encampment. But the Mongols surrounded it, pounded it with catapults, set fire to the wagons and tents with incendiary arrows, and shattered Hungarian confidence.

The Mongols now assembled for a charge but left a large gap toward the wide gorge through which the armies had entered the heath the day before. Although the bravest knights formed up in a wedge to meet the charge, many more Hungarian horsemen dashed for the opening and fled, a large number of them throwing away their weapons and armor to increase their horses' speed. The Mongols destroyed the Hungarian wedge with arrow fire and a charge by the heavy cavalry.

But the great mass of the Hungarian army was fleeing westward through the gorge, believing they were getting free but actually falling into a trap. The Mongol light cavalry, whose horses were generally faster than the heavy European warhorses, pursued the Hungarians on either side, shooting them down like helpless fleeing game. For thirty miles back to Pest the road was littered with Hungarian dead. At least 70,000 men died on the battlefield or on the flight westward.

Observers of the battle were impressed by the speed, silence, and mechanical perfection of the Mongol movements, which the men carried out in response to signals with black and white flags. They were also impressed with the deadliness of Mongol archery. While the European chivalry relied almost wholly on shock tactics, the Mongols, according to John of Plano Carpini, a contemporary chronicler, "wounded and killed men and horses and only when the men and horses are worn down by the arrows do they come to close quarters."

After the Sajo River holocaust, most Hungarian resistance collapsed. The Mongols pushed up to the Danube and burned Pest but did not venture over the river. Batu and Subedei rested the army and consolidated their hold on eastern Hungary. The pope declared a halfhearted crusade against the Mongols, but little came of it.

During December 1241, the Danube froze hard, and the Mongols crossed over on Christmas Day and stormed Gran, the richest city in Hungary and seat of the archbishop, and carried away most of the valuables. They also sacked Buda and advanced on a reconnaissance into Austria, while another force turned south to Zagreb and beyond in a vain search for Bela, who had escaped the Sajo River battle.

Europe lay open to invasion. No army capable of defeating the Mongols existed. Subedei's original plan to destroy each of the European states in turn seemed about to get under way.

But it was not to be. On December 11, 1241, a messenger had arrived from the Mongol capital of Karakorum with the news that Ogedei had died and his wife was acting as regent until a new khan could be elected.

The Mongol princes were eager to get back to compete for the succession and decided to return to the east with the imperial forces. Batu knew he could not hold Hungary without the imperial tumans, but he believed he could retain most of the rest of his dominions with Turkoman conscripts. He decided to evacuate Hungary, and the Mongols withdrew systematically and without interference. The Mongols destroyed everything in their path on the withdrawal, buildings and people. Batu returned to his base camp, Sarai, near the Volga sixty miles north of Astrakhan, and there established the capital of a Mongol empire that became known as the Golden Horde.

There was never another opportunity for the Mongols to invade Europe. What had happened seemed a nightmare and temporary aberration to the Europeans, and they invented all sorts of myths about how they had defeated and turned back the "Tartars," as they called the Mongols. But only the untimely death of the khan had saved them, for the Mongol warriors proved superior to the finest European men-at-arms, although the Europeans had superiority in numbers and armor.

Trade along the Silk Road grew soon after Mohammed of Khwaresm died, and the Mongols finally gained almost complete control of it when Mangu, one of Genghis Khan's successors, seized Iran, virtually destroyed Baghdad and most of its people in 1258, and trampled the caliph, the supreme leader of Islam, to death under the hooves of Mongol horses. Thereafter the Silk Road flourished for centuries.

The Mongol Empire expanded into China, but internal divisions among the chiefs and slowly growing resistance from subjugated peoples finally destroyed it. At its peak, however, it was the largest empire in area the world has ever known.

Mongol tactics were devastating because the soldiers did not close with their adversaries until they were disorganized by archery fire. They rarely allowed themselves to be drawn into clashes with heavy European cavalry but withdrew quickly at a signal when such a clash threatened, rallied at a distance, and assailed the enemy once more with arrows. They repeated this process until the enemy was weakened and only then launched a decisive charge with heavy cavalry.

By limiting their army to only one major arm, cavalry, the Mongols achieved simplicity and effectiveness. They avoided having to coordinate a mobile arm with a relatively immobile arm, infantry, a problem that always bedeviled European armies.

But principally the Mongols were victorious because they possessed a few generals who knew how to employ the exceptional mobility of their armies with destructive surprise attacks on the enemy rear and on points where they were least expected.

3

Napoleon and Wars of Annihilation

FOR A THOUSAND YEARS the horseman dominated warfare in the West. This superiority continued after the Mongols disappeared over the eastern horizons in the thirteenth century, never to return. Remaining to rule nearly every battlefield was the armored knight on a heavy warhorse, wielding a lance.

The horseman's power began to be broken by the English longbow and the crossbow, both of which could bring down a horseman by penetrating his armor. But the process was slow, despite the advantage demonstrated by the longbow over French chivalry at Crécy in 1346 and Agincourt in 1415.

It was not the bow but projectiles propelled by gunpowder that finally dethroned the knight.[1] By the middle of the fifteenth century, effective firearms had appeared, and by the beginning of the next century, their projectiles could penetrate body armor. In the seventeenth century, for the first time since the late Roman Empire, infantry once more became the queen of battle. Now armed with a single-shot, muzzle-loaded musket and aided by more mobile artillery, infantry filled the battle-

1. Swiss mountaineers armed principally with halberds (combining spear and ax in a single weapon) formed tight phalanxlike masses and defeated armored knights in the battle of Morgarten in 1315 and in subsequent engagements. Although the Swiss thereby preserved the independence of their cantons and Swiss mercenaries achieved fame throughout Europe, their innovation was a tactical cul-de-sac, doomed, like the knight on horseback, by firearms. For a full analysis of the Swiss achievement, see Delbrück, vol. 3, 545–656.

field and could maneuver well enough to get the better of cavalry.

But roving bands of ill-disciplined foot soldiers, especially hastily enrolled mercenaries bent primarily on loot, threatened to cripple Western civilization. In the Thirty Years War (1618–48), great stretches of central Europe became a depopulated wasteland, with thousands of towns and villages burned and abandoned. Over 8 million people perished.

The absolute kings who gained control of major European states resolved to halt these depredations and created professional standing armies kept separate from the civil population. Because the soldiers were largely drawn from the dregs of society, they were subjected to ferocious discipline. Being forced to remain on a permanent war footing, these armies were extremely expensive and consequently were kept as small as possible.

The necessity to restrain soldiers by discipline forced generals to limit their tactical operations severely. Unless watched nearly every moment, many men would desert. This led to close-order operations, always under the eyes of officers. Men were seldom even permitted to bathe in the streams unattended. Because soldiers were considered to be too vicious to forage for food on their own, generals fed their armies from supplies maintained at magazines in rear fortresses. This severely limited the mobility of armies and led to a strategy of attrition, not annihilation of the enemy's army. The main aim was not to strike at the enemy army but to maneuver on his supply line.

A great change was coming in society, however, propelled by Jean-Jacques Rousseau's writings extolling democracy and freedom. His teachings and those of others who wished to destroy the autocratic existing society set the stage for the French Revolution. This vast movement began in 1789 and led to the rise of the semidivine nation-state and patriotism. Former subjects of kings became citizens and formed attachments of love and loyalty to their nations, emotional bonds similar to those developed in the paleolithic hunter-gatherer tribe. In the tribe, human beings learned much of their sense of group identity and loyalty. But they also learned hostility toward strangers.

Tribe members followed a code of amity among themselves, a code of enmity to outsiders. As Herbert Spencer says, the result was internal friendship and external antagonism.[2] This pattern, inbred by nature and instinctive, was transferred to the new nation-states and inculcated aggression, conquest, and revenge toward foreigners. One intoxicating expression of this attitude was Rouget de Lisle's "Marseillaise" war hymn. It was not by accident that Nicolas Chauvin, a bellicose French soldier during the wars of this period, became the source of the word "chauvinism"—meaning boastful, unreasoning, militant devotion to one's country.

"Gentlemanly" wars between opposing sovereigns seeking limited territorial or other gains were about to give way to passionate warfare between citizen bodies, who had absorbed the myth that the sovereign will of the people is always right and who supported wars of aggrandizement to advance their nation at the expense of others.

As Europe drifted toward this mighty confrontation, the weapons and theories of war were also advancing at a rapid rate. With these new tools and with the enormous armies made possible by mass conscription and the concept of a nation in arms, a military genius, Napoleon Bonaparte, sought to create a great French empire. His plan ultimately came to ruin, but the methods he used transformed the way wars were fought.

The major changes waiting for Napoleon and others to exploit were based on the innovative ideas of a number of French army officers in the mid- and late eighteenth century. These included Pierre-Joseph de Bourcet (1700–80); Jacques Antoine Hypolite, Comte de Guibert (1743–90); Jean Baptiste Vacquette de Gribeauval (1715–89), and Chevalier Jean du Teil (1733–1820).

Bourcet advanced the idea of a "plan with branches": dividing an army into several dispersed columns and marching them on a number of separate targets. Although Bourcet apparently came upon this idea independently, it was essentially like the strategy Genghis Khan had practiced against the Khwarezmian

---

2. Herbert Spencer, *The Principles of Ethics* (1892), vol. 1, 322; Fuller, *The Conduct of War, 1789–1961*, 38.

empire and that Subedei Bahadur had employed against the
Hungarians over half a millennium previously.

Bourcet taught that since it was impossible for an enemy to
be in strength everywhere, a commander who divided his forces
could mislead the enemy, making him believe the main effort
was coming at some point other than the actual objective. The
strategy would force the enemy to abandon his own plans and
either disperse his troops to meet the new threats or, in concentrating to defend his main point, weaken secondary targets.
Therefore, a commander could gain at least one and perhaps
more of his objectives, provided his columns remained close
enough so two or more could combine quickly to overwhelm
an objective weakened by the enemy's division of his own forces.

Guibert wanted to establish a more mobile form of warfare
by dividing an army into permanent divisions, each of which
could march in a separate column, along a separate route. Wide
dispersal would confuse the enemy and permit a commander
to strike where he found the best opportunity. It also would
help end the prevailing practice of private contractors delivering food from rear magazines to armies on the march. Guibert
wanted army officers to learn supply and urged that in enemy
country the army live at the enemy's expense. Guibert's ideas
regarding feeding armies required a new type of soldier, which
came with the revolution: volunteers and patriots who were
not as likely as professionals to desert and could be trusted to
forage for food.

In the Italian campaign of 1796–97, Bonaparte employed
the divisional system, and in later years he expanded the concept into the "battalion square" *(bataillon carré)* or a separate
army corps containing several divisions and all arms which was
capable of standing alone against any enemy force for a day or
two and thereby permitting the other columns of his army to
close in upon the enemy from several directions.

Guibert sought to increase the mobility of artillery in order
to achieve quick concentration of fire to destroy a part of the
enemy's front and make a gap for a decisive breakthrough. He
also recommended that every defensive position taken up by
an enemy should be turned or flanked immediately by his new-
model army of divisions. This would force an end to static de-

NAPOLEON BONAPARTE

Musée du Louvre

fensive operations and make war more fluid.

Gribeauval proposed a radical reduction in the weight of field artillery in order to increase its mobility. Du Teil built on this concept and Guibert's ideas by using light horse-drawn smoothbore cannon to keep up with the troops, thereby uniting the most troops with the most guns at a weak point where the enemy's position could be forced.

By the time of the French Revolution, both the lighter, more mobile artillery and permanent divisions had been established in the French army. The way was open for ideas of dispersed attacks and movements advocated by Guibert and Bourcet to be seized by a general who understood the opportunities they presented.

Napoleon Bonaparte (1769–1821), a penurious member of the minor nobility in Corsica, received a military education at the French king's expense and was commissioned as an artillery officer in 1785. A significant part of his intellectual development occurred in 1788–89 when, still only nineteen years old, he commanded a demonstration squad at the Artillery Training School at Auxonne, where du Teil's new artillery theories were being tried out. Here, in practice and in reading military treatises, Bonaparte formed the basis of his military ideas.

The French Revolution and the ouster of the king brought on the resignation of most of the nobles who had dominated the officers corps during the *ancien régime* and opened up vast opportunities for poor but ambitious officers like Bonaparte. The first flash of his military genius appeared at the siege of the Mediterranean port of Toulon, which the British had occupied in 1793. He moved artillery to block the exits of Toulon's harbor and thereby forced the British fleet and troops to evacuate the city immediately.

Promoted to brigadier general, Bonaparte was in Paris when the royalists, hoping to restore the monarchy, instigated a revolt. Paul de Barras, given dictatorial powers by the National Convention, ordered Bonaparte to help stop the rebels. Bonaparte, with a "whiff of grapeshot" from the cannon he lined up, killed or wounded many rebels and stopped the march against the National Convention on October 5, 1795. Bonaparte's decisive action impressed the new government, the Directory, and he used his influence to gain command of the Army of Italy in March 1796.

Bonaparte had already developed a plan based on an earlier project of Bourcet's to defeat Sardinia-Piedmont and Austria, France's enemies in Italy. In this campaign, leading an ill-fed, partly mutinous army of only about 37,000 men at the outset, Bonaparte introduced a new form of warfare that sought total victory by mobility, surprise, and strategic movements the enemy could not counter. In a moment Bonaparte transformed the old system, which seldom sought more than to maneuver the enemy out of position and gain a partial success, into a war designed to annihilate enemy armies.

In this single Italian campaign, beginning in April 1796 and ending in April 1797, Bonaparte practiced virtually all the methods and strategies he was to employ with spectacular success in the vast wars that engulfed Europe until 1815.

The Directory's plan for 1796 was to make the major effort against Austria and its allies, several of the small states into which Germany was then divided. At the time Austria was a large empire covering much of central Europe. The Italian campaign was to be secondary and was intended primarily to divert Austrian attention from the German front by driving the enemy out of Piedmont and Lombardy in northern Italy. Bonaparte then was to march through the Tyrol and join the supposedly victorious French army moving through Germany. There was little hope such an ambitious joint campaign could succeed. The offensives were too far apart to support one another, the Alps separated the French armies, and if either campaign slowed the Austrians could transfer troops to the other flank. Bonaparte, however, saw that a decisive victory could be achieved in Italy alone and made plans accordingly.

In March 1796 the French Army of Italy was stretched along the Maritime Alps and the narrow coastal strip of the Italian riviera. Opposing them were 25,000 Piedmontese troops and a small Austrian detachment under an Austrian general, Baron Michael von Colli, spread in a thin line for about thirty miles from Cuneo on the west to Ceva on the east. East of the Pied-

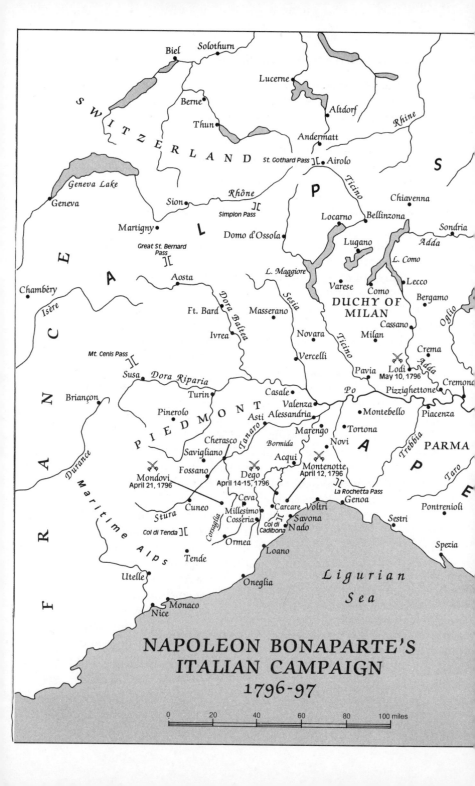

NAPOLEON BONAPARTE'S
ITALIAN CAMPAIGN
1796-97

0   20   40   60   80   100 miles

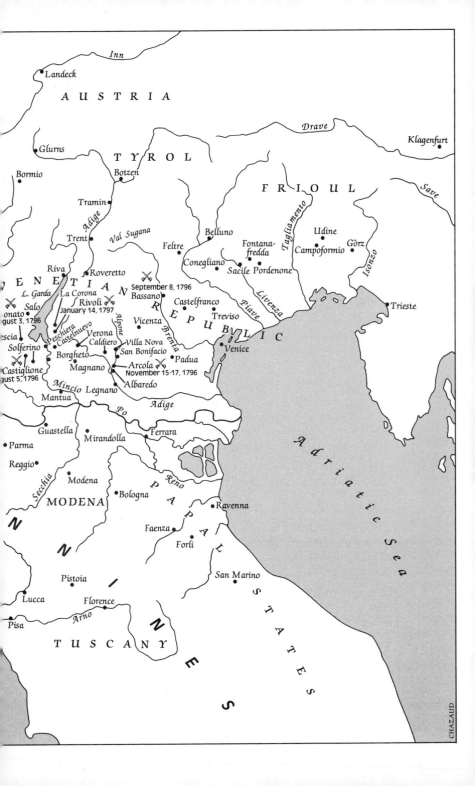

montese about 11,500 Austrians under General Count Eugen Argenteau occupied a thin outpost cordon for about forty-five miles along the hills from Carcare to the heights above Genoa. Behind in winter quarters in Alessandria and other Piedmontese towns were 19,500 more Austrians. The overall commander was General Baron Johann Peter Beaulieu, seventy-two years old, a competent officer but with virtually no initiative.

Bonaparte assembled 24,000 troops near Savona on the coast and planned to drive northwest from there over the Col di Cadibona in the Apennines to attack Carcare on April 15, 1796. This would place him with superior forces in what Bonaparte called the "central position" between the Piedmontese on the west and the Austrians on the east. He planned to turn first on the Piedmontese, already war-weary, and drive them out of the war, then move east to deal with the Austrians.

This first step by Bonaparte demonstrated a principle he enunciated somewhat later but always tried to follow: "The nature of strategy consists of always having, even with a weaker army, more forces at the point of attack or at the point where one is being attacked than the enemy."[3]

To deceive his opponents and keep their forces dispersed, Bonaparte used Bourcet's plan of advancing several columns at wide points along the front. As part of this plan, Jean-Baptiste Cervoni's brigade advanced on Voltri, just west of Genoa.

Beaulieu, believing he saw a chance to isolate and destroy Cervoni's force, launched an attack four days before Bonaparte's offensive was to start. Two columns advanced from the Apennines on Voltri, while General Argenteau was to swoop down through the Col di Cadibona on Savona and cut off French troops assembling in the vicinity.

However, Cervoni retreated safely toward Savona, and Argenteau got orders so late that Amédée E. F. La Harpe's French division was able to concentrate and check his advance. Bonaparte decided to go ahead with his plan to drive between the two enemy armies and on April 12 sent 9,000 troops against Argenteau's 6,000 at Montenotte, twelve miles north of Savona.

3. Delbrück, vol. 4, 428.

La Harpe's division made a frontal attack, which held Argenteau's force in a firm battle embrace, while a brigade under André Masséna worked around its flank. Argenteau saw the danger too late, and Masséna charged and routed the whole force. By dawn Argenteau had only 700 men under arms.

Bonaparte drove at once to the vital crossroads of Carcare, immediately to the south, placing him between the Piedmontese and the Austrians. On April 13, Bonaparte ordered Masséna with half a division to march to Dego, nine miles north of Montenotte, to block any Austrian advance and turned the rest of his force under Charles-Pierre-François Augereau on the Piedmontese fortress of Ceva on the Tanaro River, twelve miles west, toward which another of his divisions, under Jean-Mathieu-Philabert Sérurier, was advancing north down the Tanaro. This would concentrate 25,000 men at Ceva, where the Piedmontese under the Austrian General Colli were assembling 13,000 troops.

Unfortunately Augereau halted on the way and made several assaults, all of which failed, against 900 defiant Piedmontese grenadiers holed up in the ruins of Cosseria Castle on a steep hill. The attacks cost Augereau 900 casualties and the opportunity of storming Ceva quickly.

Bonaparte, exasperated, told Augereau to keep only a small force to guard the castle and march the rest of his men through the night on Ceva. Meantime Masséna found Dego occupied by a sizable Austrian force. Bonaparte ordered him to delay attacking until Augereau had gained the castle. The next day Cosseria Castle surrendered and Masséna struck the Austrians at Dego, capturing 5,000 prisoners. His men scattered in search of food and plunder and were surprised when five Austrian battalions attacked on the early hours of April 15, routed the French, and prepared the village for defense.

The danger of an Austrian descent on Bonaparte's right flank was now too great to ignore. He canceled the advance on Ceva, brought a strong force back to Dego, and successfully stormed the village. Once more Bonaparte held Dego, but it had cost him a day and 1,000 more casualties. Moreover, he was afraid the Austrian general Beaulieu might still drive on Carcare and cut his supply line to Savona. But Beaulieu had had enough and held his forces in the vicinity of Acqui, twenty miles north down the Bormida River, where he was protecting Alessandria and his line of communications back to Austria.

On the evening of April 16, Bonaparte, reassured that there was no danger on the east, turned back on Ceva and, with the 24,000 men he had massed, prepared to assault on the morning of April 18. During the night, however, Colli skillfully extricated his 13,000 Piedmontese and fell back a few miles to a strong defensive angle formed by the confluence of the Tanaro and Corsaglia rivers. Bonaparte, furious, ordered Sérurier to assault the new position frontally while Augereau advanced down the east bank of the Tanaro to outflank it. The French failed. Augereau couldn't find a river crossing, and Colli repulsed Sérurier's attack. The next day was an equal disaster. Sérurier's men scattered to loot and no attack could be organized.

Bonaparte called a halt for two days for his artillery to move up and prepared a three-divisional assault. He also changed his supply line from Savona to a new route through the Tanaro Valley to Ormea, allowing him to weaken the forces on his right flank. Dego was now unimportant, and Bonaparte moved Masséna's force westward to support the attack on Colli, set for the morning of April 21.

Again Colli slipped the noose. During the night he decamped and fell back on Mondovi, nine miles west. Bonaparte immediately ordered a cavalry pursuit, which denied Colli time to organize Mondovi for defense, while Sérurier made a frontal attack on the town and drove the Piedmontese into retreat.

This was the turning point of the campaign. At Mondovi, Bonaparte had reached the plains of Piedmont and had access to plenty of food and several routes of advance. Bonaparte ordered a march on the Piedmontese capital of Turin, his troops in three columns, each within a day's march of the others. This was another adaptation of Bourcet's "plan with branches": a series of independent columns moving forward, like an octopus with waving tentacles that could grip any opponent in its path while the others would automatically close up on it.[4]

4. Liddell Hart, *The Ghost of Napoleon,* 66.

The threat to their capital was too much for the Piedmontese, and on April 23, Colli asked for an armistice. Bonaparte drove his men forward even faster, separating the Piedmontese completely from the Austrians, and on April 28 worked out a temporary agreement with Piedmont: a cease-fire and permission to cross the wide Po River over the bridge at Valenza, eight miles northeast of Alessandria.

With Piedmont out of the war, the Austrians were far inferior in troops, 25,000 to Bonaparte's nearly 40,000 with new additions. Beaulieu ordered a retreat to the north bank of the Po. Valenza was on his route and also on the direct path to Bonaparte's next objective: Milan and the Austrian-owned duchy surrounding it. By receiving permission to cross there, Bonaparte focused Austrian attention on Valenza and deceived Beaulieu into concentrating at the point.

Bonaparte now undertook for the first time a *manœuvre sur les derrières,* which he used thirty times by 1815. Bonaparte customarily employed this rear maneuver on a wide front of many miles. The idea was to commit a strong force to hold the enemy army in place on his main line by a fierce attack or threat and to send a powerful column around the enemy's flank onto his rear and there establish a strategic barrage or barrier across his line of supply and retreat. This would force the enemy to withdraw from his main line and, if the barrage could be set in place in time to block the enemy, could result in his defeat or destruction. The maneuver became the most deadly of Bonaparte's strategic devices. Throughout his military career he never made a frontal attack when he could do otherwise and he always attempted to block the retreat of the enemy. He counted on the menace of a move on the rear, even if it failed, to shake enemy morale and to cause him to make mistakes that might give Bonaparte a chance to strike. The *manœuvre sur les derrières* led to victories in the Marengo campaign in Italy of 1800 and the opening stages of the Austerlitz campaign of 1805. In 1796 in Italy, Bonaparte demonstrated he had already worked out all of its essentials.[5]

5. Colin, 279–84. Karl von Clausewitz, who incorporated much of the essence of Napoleon's warfare into his treatise *On War,* which subse-

Ordering Masséna and Sérurier to mount diversionary operations threatening a major crossing at Valenza and thereby holding Beaulieu's forces in position, Bonaparte sent the rest of his army *east* along the undefended south bank of the Po to Piacenza, about forty air miles southeast of Milan. When he reached Piacenza on May 6, he had turned all the Austrians' possible lines of resistance. By crossing the Po on the ferries and boats assembled there, since the city was in the neutral duchy of Parma, Bonaparte threatened to get athwart the Austrians' line of retreat and destroy their army. Beaulieu, seeing his danger, abandoned Milan and the duchy without a fight and ordered a full retreat toward Lodi on the Adda River, twenty-two miles north of Piacenza. His swift withdrawal prevented Bonaparte from setting up a strategic barrage.

Practically the whole of the Austrian army had crossed the bridge at Lodi and was retreating eastward when the French arrived early on May 10 and launched a fierce attack against the Austrian rear guard there. Bonaparte could have crossed on fords elsewhere, but, hoping to fall quickly on Beaulieu's rear, he attacked directly over the bridge. The battle was extremely fierce and bloody, with several senior officers fighting at the head of the column and Bonaparte exposing himself to enemy fire.

The assault succeeded but took so long that the main Austrian army slipped out of Bonaparte's reach and moved back to the Mincio River, flowing south out of Lake Garda. Bonaparte broke across the Mincio at Borghetto on May 30, 1796, and his army scattered in several directions: Augereau advanced north on Peschiera, on the banks of Lake Garda; Masséna seized Verona, sixteen miles east; and Sérurier drove toward the fortress of Mantua, on the lower Mincio. The bulk of Beaulieu's army retreated northward up the eastern shore of Lake Garda to Trent in the Tyrol. But a detachment of 4,500 men, cut off from the main body, fled into Mantua, joining the fortress's garrison of 8,000 troops.

---

quently became the bible of the Prussian and later German General Staffs, completely misunderstood the significance of the *manœuvre sur les derrières*. See Chandler, 134.

The Austrians were shocked to discover that a large body of their forces had been locked up in Mantua. Although the fortress was virtually surrounded by the Mincio and extremely difficult to assault, it could be starved into submission. The Austrians set plans on foot to relieve it.

Thus Mantua, more by accident than by Bonaparte's design, became a bait to draw successive Austrian relief forces. Bonaparte, seeing the opportunity, sought to draw the enemy columns far from their bases and into his jaws. He did not, as would have been the practice of most generals at the time, entrench himself in a covering position and wait. Instead, he kept his forces mobile and in a wide and loose grouping that could be concentrated in any direction within a short time.

Meantime the Directory, suffering from a great need of resources, ordered Bonaparte to move southward into Tuscany and the Papal States to plunder their resources. Since Bonaparte knew the Austrians would need time to mount a relief expedition and also wanted to prevent any threat to his rear, he left Sérurier with a depleted force to guard Mantua and took most of his remaining army on a giant raid into central Italy. This operation gained much loot for France but left the region despoiled and prostrate for generations.

By mid-July 1796, Bonaparte, getting reports that the Austrians were about to advance, had brought his army, now totaling 46,000 men, back to defend Mantua, and Sérurier commenced a cannonade on July 17.

The Austrians had assembled 50,000 men under General Dagobert Würmser with the mission of relieving Mantua and driving the French out of northern Italy. Würmser divided his army into three columns, one going down each side of Lake Garda and the third a small diversionary force of 5,000 men moving down the Brenta River, which runs southeastward from the vicinity of Trent.

On July 29, Würmser's central column of 25,000 men, advancing down the Adige river valley east of Lake Garda, compelled Masséna to retreat south beyond the Mincio, abandoning Verona. General Peter Quasdanovitch with 18,000 men moved more slowly down the west side of Lake Garda and was checked by Augereau at Brescia on August 1. The danger now was that

Quasdanovitch and Würmser would unite south of Lake Garda, giving the Austrians great numerical superiority. Würmser, however, insisted on relieving Mantua, granting Bonaparte, in the central position between the two columns, just enough time to send Masséna against Quasdanovitch at Lonato while Augereau slowed Würmser's advance guard at Castiglione, only a few miles to the east.

Realizing he no longer could maintain the siege, Bonaparte instructed Sérurier on July 31 to move fourteen miles west to Marcaria on the Oglio River. There he could reinforce other French forces girding for the attack.

While Würmser wasted three days making certain the siege of Mantua had been raised, Bonaparte used the time to move up Augereau's division to cover Masséna's rear, while Masséna sent Quasdanovitch into retreat with heavy losses, then moved back to join Augereau and prepare for Würmser on August 4, 1796.

Despite his overall weakness, Bonaparte had assembled a superior force, 31,000 men against Würmser's 25,000. Würmser occupied a strong position on the heights of Castiglione and Solferino. To defeat him, Bonaparte unveiled a tactical plan that was to become his favorite and that he used numerous times to gain victory.

In this plan Bonaparte combined a series of deceptive maneuvers and du Teil's concept of massing artillery at a single point of attack. The first step was to send a strong force directly against the enemy main line in a fierce and determined attack designed to convince the enemy Bonaparte intended to break through, forcing the enemy to draw all of his reserves to contain it. Next Bonaparte directed a strong flanking column onto the enemy's rear to threaten his communications and line of retreat. This forced the enemy commander, who presumably had committed all his reserves, to detach some troops from his main line to counter the flank movement.

Because of the need for haste, these men had to be drawn from the point closest to the French flanking movement. Therefore Bonaparte could calculate in advance the point where the enemy main line would be denuded. In preparation he hid opposite this point and behind his main line a strong *masse de*

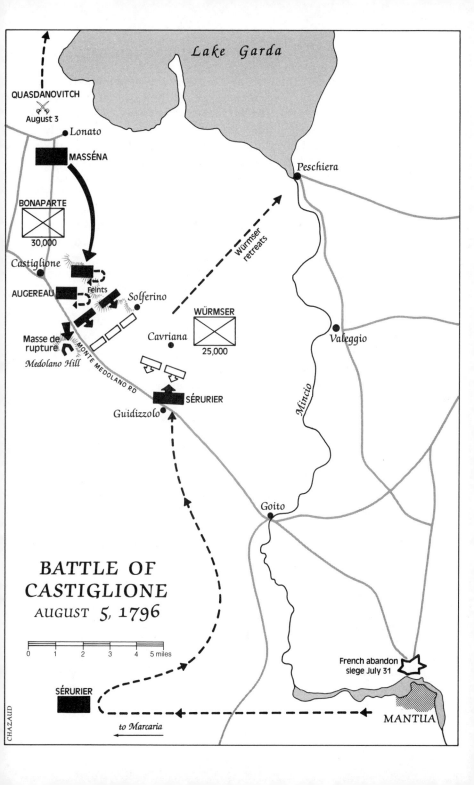

Lake Garda

QUASDANOVITCH
August 3

Lonato

MASSÉNA

BONAPARTE

30,000

Castiglione

AUGEREAU

Feints

Solferino

Masse de
rupture

Medolano Hill

MONTE MEDOLANO RD

Guidizzolo

SÉRURIER

Peschiera

Würmser retreats

WÜRMSER

25,000

Cavriana

Valeggio

Mincio

Goito

BATTLE OF
CASTIGLIONE
AUGUST 5, 1796

0   1   2   3   4   5 miles

SÉRURIER

to Marcaria

CHAZAUD

French abandon
siege July 31

MANTUA

rupture of cavalry, infantry, and artillery under command of a trusted lieutenant. When he detected a thinning of the enemy's line to meet the flank attack, Bonaparte ordered the special force's cannons to rush forward to blow a hole in the already thinned point with canister, which riddles infantry with deadly metal pellets and fragments. While the other infantry continued its heavy attacks all across the front, the *masse de rupture* infantry then rushed into the broken enemy ranks to shatter them and open a wide gap through which the French cavalry rushed. This breakthrough destroyed the enemy's equilibrium and sometimes led to the disintegration of his army and French pursuit of the disordered fragments.

Bonaparte's first venture at Castiglione on August 5, 1796, in this "strategic battle," as he called it, was not a complete success.

He ordered the divisions of Masséna and Augereau to make a frontal attack against Würmser's main line to draw him into a battle embrace and to force him to commit all his reserves. To start the action, however, Bonaparte resorted to an ancient strategem: he directed both French divisions, after taking up position, to feign withdrawal, seemingly fearful when they saw Würmser's strong positions on the Castiglione and Solferino heights.

The false retreat produced precisely the effect Bonaparte desired. Würmser, believing the French were about to run, swung his right or northern flank forward to crush Masséna on the French left and open the road to Quasdanovitch. This made Bonaparte's flank movement all the more effective. The previous day, he had ordered Sérurier's division to move from Marcaria, fourteen miles south, onto Würmser's left rear at Guidizzolo on his main line of retreat to Mantua. Thus Würmser's move on the French left pressed him even deeper into Bonaparte's trap.

As Würmser forced the attack on Masséna and the whole front erupted into battle, Sérurier's division arrived at Guidizzolo completely unknown to Würmser and opened the flank attack at 6:00 A.M. It came a trifle early, before Würmser had committed all his reserves and in time for him to turn part of his army to face the new threat. Also Masséna and Augereau did not press their fight hard enough to pin down all the Austrians facing them. Würmser fell back to his position on the heights, leaving his first line to stem Masséna and Augereau and sending his second line to form a new front against Sérurier's division.

These errors robbed Bonaparte of any chance to destroy Würmser's army, but the situation was still ripe to launch the *masse de rupture*. Bonaparte had drawn up this special force of three battalions of infantry, plus eighteen cannon and a cavalry force behind the French right wing. He ordered the artillery to gallop forward and open a point-blank cannonade against an Austrian battery on Medolano Hill, which had become the hinge linking the two Austrian fronts. After a fierce artillery clash, Bonaparte's infantry went in with the bayonet and crashed onto and over Medolano Hill, with the cavalry following. This effort did not make a complete breakthrough. However, Würmser's whole left wing soon reeled back, drawing the entire Austrian army with it. Würmser lost 3,000 men but was able to extricate his army and retreat to Peschiera, about ten miles northeast.

There were several reasons for Bonaparte's incomplete success. Sérurier's division was too small to dominate the roads east of Würmser, and thus the turning movement did not place a true tactical barrage across the Austrian line of retreat. Masséna and Augereau did not carry out the pinning attack along the front with the utmost vigor. The flank movement did not require Würmser to deplete his forces at the Medolano hinge. Also, the *masse de rupture* was too small to force a real penetration, and capture of Medolano exhausted its impetus, giving Würmser a chance to get away without great haste.

In later years Bonaparte polished and improved this "strategic battle" technique, especially in timing its successive stages, and with it he won the battles of Austerlitz, Friedland, and Bautzen. But the elements of all these successes were already present in the battle of Castiglione.

Würmser made only a brief stand at Peschiera, time enough to send two fresh brigades into Mantua, evacuate part of the sick, and resupply the fortress with food. This done, Würmser retreated northward toward Trent. He avoided any attempt to get the Mantuan garrison away. Bonaparte, after his victory at

Castiglione, occupied the central position between Würmser's main force and Mantua. If the Austrians had marched out of their fortress, Bonaparte could have destroyed them long before Würmser could have reached them. The Austrians' first attempt to relieve Mantua had cost the French 10,000 casualties but the Austrians almost 17,000.

The long-delayed French offensive in Germany had at last opened in July 1796. After Bonaparte's victory it appeared to the Directory that the next stage of its master plan could be launched, and it ordered Bonaparte to advance through the Tyrol and across the Alps and cooperate with the main Rhine army under General Jean Victor Moreau pushing into Bavaria. Bonaparte saw little possibility of success, since he had no means of communication with Moreau and it was now autumn and operations in the Tyrol would become increasingly difficult with the onset of winter.

However, he obeyed orders. He left 10,000 men to guard Mantua and small detachments to shield Verona and the lower Adige and marched the rest of his army, 33,000 men, north up the Adige River on Trent.

The Austrians saw an opportunity to profit by Bonaparte's direct advance. They formed an imaginative plan to slip about 26,000 men under Würmser through the Valsugana just southeast of Trent, drive down the Brenta River into the Venetian plain, then turn west to relieve Mantua. General Paul von Davidovitch, meanwhile, with about 20,000 men, would defend the Tyrol. The Austrians calculated Bonaparte would never ignore the threat posed by Würmser's advance onto his rear and, to prevent being caught between the two Austrian armies, would retreat the way he had come, to defend Mantua.

Bonaparte pushed back a blocking force of Davidovitch on September 4, 1796, and occupied Trent the next day. Only there did he get positive word that Würmser had already crossed the Valsugana and was marching down the Brenta river valley on his rear.

Bonaparte responded in a wholly unexpected manner. Instead of falling back down the Adige, he countered Würmser's indirect approach with an even more indirect approach of his own. Leaving 10,000 men to block the Tyrolean gorges north of Trent, Bonaparte turned the remainder of his army in hot chase of Würmser's army down the Brenta Valley! Here was a dramatic variation on the *manœuvre sur les derrières*. In a single movement he separated Würmser from Davidovitch, cut off his line of supply, and presented him only three options: to give battle on the Brenta, to turn tail and run for the Austrian base of Trieste on the Adriatic, or to fall back into Mantua and add to the Austrian forces in cold storage there.

Würmser, stunned by Bonaparte's move, ordered two divisions to block the French at Bassano on the Brenta, about forty air miles southeast of Trent. There, on September 8, in a fierce direct attack, Bonaparte defeated the Austrians, seized 4,000 prisoners, and split the enemy into two parts. One remnant fled northeast into the Frioul region of the Alps and completely out of the fight. The other, with Würmser, unexpectedly continued southwestward toward the Adige and Mantua, uniting with the remainder of his force and raising it to 16,000 men.

Würmser's dogged preoccupation with Mantua gave Bonaparte another opportunity, which he seized. Now east of Würmser, he blocked any possibility of Würmser's turning back and gaining safety at Trieste, thereby forcing him to fall back into Mantua. By September 12, Würmser was caged in the fortress, raising the garrison there to 28,000 troops, but imperiling its existence because food immediately began to run out. Soon the garrison was living off horse flesh, and by the new year 150 men a day would be dying of malnutrition.

Bonaparte had been unable to join Moreau in Bavaria, but this would have been virtually impossible anyway. Moreau retreated on September 19 and by late October crossed to the west bank of the Rhine. Bonaparte, however, had locked up a substantial portion of Austria's military capital in Mantua.

The Austrians decided they had to save their Mantuan garrison and conceived a new concentric advance. The senior commander, Baron Joseph d'Alvintzi, a veteran general with much service on the Rhine, in early November 1796 marched with 28,000 men to Bassano on the Brenta River and continued west, while Davidovitch with 18,000 drove south out of the

Alps to seize Trent and march down the Adige Valley. The two-pronged drive divided Bonaparte's forces and made it more likely that d'Alvintzi might unite his forces at Verona, Bonaparte's pivot for guarding Mantua.

Bonaparte left 9,000 men to guard Mantua, 4,000 as a reserve at Verona and 8,000 in the Adige Valley under General Charles-Henri Vaubois with orders to hold against Davidovitch. Bonaparte set out with his remaining 18,000 men in hopes of driving d'Alvintzi out of the Brenta Valley before falling on Davidovitch's rear. He had to change his plans, however, when Vaubois was routed on November 4 and fell back to Rivoli, only about twenty miles north of Verona.

Bonaparte immediately reinforced Vaubois and ordered his troops facing d'Alvintzi to retreat to the line of the Adige and the central position between Davidovitch and d'Alvintzi. His aim now was to prevent the junction of the two Austrian wings.

D'Alvintzi resolved to march to Davidovitch's aid before moving on Mantua and crossed the Alpone River at Villa Nova, fourteen miles east of Verona, with 17,000 men. The French drove back a preliminary probe toward Verona on November 11, persuading d'Alvintzi to close up his main body on the village of Caldiero, seven miles east of Verona, and, to guard his southern flank, to post 4,000 men at Arcola, about ten miles southeast on the Alpone near its junction with the Adige.

On November 12, Masséna assaulted d'Alvintzi at Caldiero but was defeated, losing 2,000 men, and was forced to seek shelter on the west bank of the Adige. Bonaparte was now in a precarious position. Two strong enemy forces threatened to converge on Verona. Bonaparte had only 18,000 men to oppose d'Alvintzi's 23,000. To achieve superior force he could raise the siege of Mantua, but this would place 17,000 more Austrians (the remaining active size of the garrison) on his rear.

Bonaparte resolved on another *manœuvre sur les derrières*, sending all available troops at Verona around d'Alvintzi's southern flank by way of Arcola onto his rear at Villa Nova, there to block his retreat and seize his supply park. This would compel d'Alvintzi to retreat. It also would force the Austrians to fight on ground of Bonaparte's choosing in the marshes and rice paddies between the Alpone and Adige, where the Austrians could deploy only on the area's few embankments and bridges and would lose the advantage of numerical superiority.

Bonaparte's plan was a great gamble. If Verona fell in the interim, all would be lost. Yet his confidence was so great that he did not flinch from committing virtually all his force for the rear maneuver, drawing only 3,000 men from Vaubois to defend Verona.

Bonaparte moved on the night of November 14, marching eighteen miles down the south bank of the Adige, then, at dawn, recrossing on a pontoon bridge into the marshes between the Alpone and Adige. While Masséna with 6,000 men moved northwest to defend against an Austrian advance on his rear, Augereau with 6,000 pressed on Arcola. However, Austrian cannon and Croatian infantry emplaced along a dike halted them. In desperation, Bonaparte sent 3,000 men over the Adige just south of its junction with the Alpone and ordered them up the east bank to seize Arcola. The movement took time, and d'Alvintzi, seeing what Bonaparte was attempting, retreated toward Villa Nova. Although the French seized Arcola at 7:00 P.M., at least half the Austrian army was already safely in place at Villa Nova.

At this time Bonaparte got news that Vaubois had been driven back closer to Verona. For safety, Bonaparte abandoned Arcola and withdrew to the south side of the Adige in case he had to march north to aid Vaubois.

By the next morning, November 16, Bonaparte had heard nothing more of an advance by Davidovitch, and he resolved to renew his attack on Arcola. His men had to fight for everything again in a bitter day among the dikes, assaulting toward Arcola and also defending against the Austrian force on the west that was trying to drive the French against the Alpone and destroy them. Both efforts, those of the French and the Austrians, failed, but d'Alvintzi's nerve was severely shaken.

On the morning of November 17, Bonaparte prepared for his third attack against Arcola. By now the situation had turned to his advantage, since a third of d'Alvintzi's army was fighting in the marshes on the west, where it was isolated. While Masséna attacked Arcola frontally from the west, Bonaparte ordered Augereau to cross the Adige below the junction with the Alpone and move up to seize Arcola. Augereau had great difficulties pressing up the east bank against strong opposition.

Bonaparte resorted to a tactical ruse, a rarity for him, sending four trumpeters to the Austrian rear to sound the charge. The Austrians, already shaky, feared a heavy attack and retreated rapidly northward. The French pressed on their heels to Villa Nova. There d'Alvintzi, believing he was facing a major attack, ordered his army to retreat overnight to Vicenza, twenty miles northeast.

On November 17, Davidovitch at last had launched his long-awaited attack from the north, beating the French back to Castelnuovo, near the southern end of Lake Garda. On the 18th, Bonaparte shifted his infantry back to assist Vaubois, with Augereau marching up the eastern bank of the Adige in an attempt to envelop Davidovitch north of Castelnuovo. The Austrian general recognized his peril in time, however, and retreated rapidly toward Trent.

It was a brilliant victory for Bonaparte. With inferior forces, he had used his central position to prevent junction of the two Austrian wings, inflicted 7,000 casualties against 4,000 French, defeated both Austrian armies, and thwarted the third attempt to relieve Mantua.

By the end of November 1796 the French government urgently wished to end the war. Despite great expense, its major offensives through Germany had failed. The Directory opened negotiations, but the efforts crashed against the Austrian determination to save Mantua. Vienna demanded the right to reprovision it while peace talks went on. This would have nullified many of the gains Napoleon Bonaparte had made and was out of the question to the French.

Relief of Mantua now became a matter of great urgency to the Austrians. The garrison was beginning to starve. Meanwhile the Directory raised Bonaparte's force to 45,000, of which he detailed 8,000 to besiege Mantua and kept 37,000 mobile to meet the Austrians' fourth effort to relieve the fortress.

Bonaparte placed forces to block d'Alvintzi's three routes of attack: down the Adige Valley; on the French rear by way of the west side of Lake Garda; and through the Brenta Valley, thence westward by two routes, one on Verona, the other, by way of Legnano on the lower Adige thirty miles southeast of Verona, directly on Mantua.

By January 13, 1797, Bonaparte had figured out d'Alvintzi's attack plan. By the Brenta, d'Alvintzi had sent Baron Adam von Bajalich with 6,000 men on Verona, and Johann Provera with 9,000 on Legnano, with the hope of breaking through to Mantua, relieving the garrison, and attacking the French rear. Meanwhile d'Alvintzi moved the bulk of his army, 28,000 men, directly south to crush Barthélemy C. Jourbet's 10,000-man division guarding the Adige Valley. On this day, d'Alvintzi pushed Jourbet out of La Corona, twenty miles northwest of Verona.

Leaving 3,000 of Masséna's men to guard Verona and Augereau with 9,000 to block Provera, Bonaparte ordered Masséna with his remaining 6,000 men and Antoine Rey with 4,000 from west of Lake Garda and Claude P. Victor with 2,000 at Castelnuovo to march at all speed for the plateau of Rivoli, a good defensive position between Lake Garda and the Adige, about three miles south of La Corona.

Before these reinforcements arrived, d'Alvintzi attacked at Rivoli on the morning of January 14, following a highly complex plan involving six columns. While three attacked frontally on the Rivoli plateau, one moved around each of the French flanks, while the sixth advanced down the east bank of the Adige, with the aim of crossing over behind Bonaparte's main body.

D'Alvintzi's move east of the Adige failed, but the frontal assaults pushed back Jourbet and Masséna and his eastern flanking column reached the plateau and threatened the French right flank, while the western flanking force, 4,000 men, took a long time marching but at last appeared along the ridge south of Rivoli, threatening to block the French line of retreat.

Bonaparte ordered a brigade to attack this force on his rear and sent every other man he could find into a successful artillery and infantry attack against the right flank attack. This threw back the Austrian penetration. Bonaparte now concentrated on a direct attack into the Austrian center, splitting the enemy army into two parts. Meanwhile, Rey's and Victor's troops, approaching from the south, destroyed the 4,000-man Austrian force on the French rear. These actions virtually ended the battle, and D'Alvintzi pulled back out of contact, having lost 8,000 men.

However, Bonaparte's position was still precarious, for Augereau had been unable to prevent Provera's 9,000-man Austrian force from crossing the lower Adige, and it was marching on Mantua. Leaving Jourbet with less than half the French force to guard d'Alvintzi, Bonaparte hurried the remainder south to stop Provera.

The next day Jourbet held off a second attack by d'Alvintzi at Rivoli, then drove the discouraged Austrians north in disorder, taking close to 5,000 prisoners. Meanwhile, Augereau, with part of the Mantua besieging force, halted Provera's advance within sight of Mantua on January 15. When Bonaparte came up on Provera's rear in the afternoon with the force from Rivoli, Provera had no choice but to surrender.

In five days of superb marching and fighting, Bonaparte had kept the Mantua garrison bottled up and reduced d'Alvintzi's 48,000-man army to 13,000 fugitives. Masséna's division, for instance, fought three engagements and marched fifty-four miles in 120 hours.

The destruction of d'Alvintzi's campaign meant the fall of Mantua. Würmser surrendered on February 2, 1797. Of the garrison only 16,000 were fit enough to march into captivity. This completed the French conquest of northern Italy. The Austrians, with most of their field forces gone, fell back helplessly to the Alps. In late February, Bonaparte advanced toward Austria, crossing the Alps and seizing Klagenfurt, 150 miles southwest of Vienna, on March 29.

With this effort Bonaparte exhausted his strength. He turned to diplomacy, pressing the Austrians to agree to peace, using as threats his position at Klagenfurt and Moreau's preparations, at long last, to cross the Rhine and join him in a converging move on Vienna. The Austrians signed a preliminary agreement at Leoben on April 18, 1797. In this armistice, modified somewhat in the Peace of Campo Formio on October 17, Bonaparte demonstrated he also possessed great diplomatic talents. Although he forced the Austrians to give up Belgium to France and to cede the duchy of Milan to a new French-dominated Cisalpine Republic in northern Italy, he offered the Austrians a great gain as well: annexation of the proud Venetian Republic and several territories around the northern end of the Adriatic.

Napoleon Bonaparte created a new, far more mobile and

devastating method of waging war. Yet he did not practice total war by inflicting so much destruction on enemy people and property that they gave up all will to resist. Rather, his aim from first to last was destruction of the enemy's army. Although this gave him great victories, it did not result in permanent gains. He believed he could achieve his goals by defeating enemy field forces. Consequently, his enemies never completely lost heart and renewed the struggle after seemingly crushing defeats.

In attaining his goal of destroying enemy armies, Bonaparte exploited the new concepts of warfare pioneered by Bourcet, Gribeauval, du Teil, and Guibert, and he continued the practice of the new revolutionary armies of living off the country, either by forced exactions from the enemy or allowing his troops to forage.

Bonaparte conceived little new in warfare. But his implemention of what he had inherited produced stunning victories against enemies still operating with the mental baggage of eighteenth-century ideas of war. He subordinated every other consideration to achieve his principal objective, destruction of the enemy's main army. He constantly sought to place his army on the enemy's flank or rear to arouse fear and to cut the enemy off from his supplies, reinforcements, and route of retreat. At the same time he sought to keep his own lines of communications safe and open.

Bonaparte understood that wars are won much the same way as boxing matches are won. While hitting, the boxer must also guard himself. To strike effectively, the boxer must catch his opponent off guard. For the general, this means he must disperse his forces in order to force the enemy to disperse his own. Yet, as Bourcet had taught, he had to be able to reassemble his army at a selected point before the enemy could do so. This became Bonaparte's aim throughout his military career and was the secret of his success: hitting while preventing the enemy from hitting him. To achieve this, Bonaparte perfected three methods that his opponents never were able to copy effectively and that gave him victory after victory.

The first was the *manœuvre sur les derrières*, a great strategic descent with a large force or entire army on the enemy's line of communications.

The second was the "strategic battle," his favorite tactic: pinning the enemy down with a frontal attack, sending a force around the flank onto his line of communications, finally winning the battle with a breakthrough of a select artillery-infantry-cavalry force at the point in the enemy's line he had partially stripped to counter the flanking movement. His methods followed the principles that Hannibal, Scipio, and the Mongols had used before: holding the enemy in a tight battle embrace along the front, then hitting decisive blows on the enemy's flanks or rear.

Bonaparte's third recipe for victory was the strategy of the "central position," or movement between two or more enemy armies within supporting distance and defeating one army before turning on the other. By this means, Bonaparte, though his forces were smaller than the enemy's total, could concentrate superior numbers against each of the opposing armies.

Bonaparte combined these startling innovations with extreme mobility and audacity and used them to acquire supreme power in France and to create an empire for himself. As Emperor Napoleon, however, he possessed such enormous armies and so much confidence in his military ability that he no longer depended upon speed and surprise but relied upon sheer *mass* or offensive power to win his victories.

After his spectacular defeat of the Prussians at Jena in 1806, he was concerned exclusively with battle, because he was confident he could crush his enemy if only the enemy could be brought to battle. Napoleon demonstrated this in his new artillery tactics: massing great numbers of guns to blast a hole at a selected point in the enemy's lines.

From this point on, Napoleon purchased victories at the cost of great losses of manpower—on both sides. With virtually a blank check on the resources of his empire, Napoleon lost his resolve to win by guile and deception. In the end the losses became too great and his enemies were able to overpower his weakened armies. As Basil H. Liddell Hart says: "He paid the penalty for violating the law of economy of force, to which mobility and surprise are the means."[6]

6. Liddell Hart, *Ghost of Napoleon*, 102–3.

4

Stonewall Jackson

"MYSTIFY, MISLEAD, AND SURPRISE"

Few soldiers and fewer politicians recognized that the conditions of warfare changed fundamentally between the end of the Napoleonic Wars in 1815 and the outbreak of the American Civil War in 1861.

Nearly everyone saw the cause—the introduction of the long-range single-shot infantry rifle—but no one at first recognized that this change altered warfare so profoundly that a new method of combat had to be devised. The rifle increased the defensive power of infantry to such a degree that the attacks that had generally won battles in the Napoleonic wars and the Mexican War of 1846–48 rarely worked any longer. The new rifle had an effective range of 400 yards, four times that of the smoothbore musket with which troops had been armed previously.[1] This rifle doomed seven out of eight Civil War attacks to failure and abruptly ended the method Napoleon had used in his later wars to win victories: rolling up smoothbore cannon within 200 yards or so of an opposing line and blasting a hole in it with case or

---

1. Rifled firearms had been used for centuries. But gunpowder quickly fouled the rifling grooves, making sustained fire impossible. In 1849, Claude-Étienne Minié, a French army officer, invented a self-cleaning cylindrical bullet with a hollow base. When fired, the base expanded to fit against the rifling grooves and cleaned them as the bullet spun forward. The Minié-ball rifle was highly accurate at 200 yards and remained deadly, though less accurate, at 1,000 yards.

canister, which riddled the enemy with deadly metal balls and fragments.

No general in the Civil War found a solution to the defensive power of the rifle, because there was none. Although long-range rifled artillery appeared for the first time in quantity in the Civil War, it could not dominate the rifle, because shells exploded by gunpower were not strong enough to replace canister, which remained the principal weapon against infantry. The solution required artillery with chemical explosives more powerful than gunpowder, better fuses for artillery shells, and a method for cannon to be fired accurately while out of sight of the target and beyond enemy rifle range. These developments came only in the decades after the war ended.

Faced from the start with an insoluble problem, most generals on both sides ordered direct attacks on defensive positions, accepted the terrible losses, and hoped somehow to force the enemy to despair and give up.

One Confederate general, however, realized that the South, with only a third the white population of the North, could not long sustain great battle losses and would inevitably lose a war of attrition. He attempted to avoid frontal attacks wherever possible and to achieve victory by indirection and guile and by striking where he was least expected. This general was Thomas Jonathan Jackson, nicknamed Stonewall because the Southern army rallied around his resolutely standing brigade in the battle of First Manassas on July 21, 1861.

Stonewall Jackson proposed a strategy shortly after First Manassas to go around the Union Army and strike behind Washington at Union railways and cities, thereby damaging Northern property so heavily that the people would allow the South to have its independence. The Confederate president, Jefferson Davis, did not possess the imagination of Jackson and rejected his bold move.

Jackson persevered and unveiled a variation on the same strategy in the campaign he conducted in the Shenandoah Valley of Virginia in the spring of 1862. This campaign contained all the elements of the broader war-winning strategy Jackson proposed and demonstrated he had worked out an antidote to

THOMAS J. "STONEWALL" JACKSON
Bettmann Archive

the ruinous problem of direct attacks on infantry armed with the rifle.

Stonewall Jackson, from western Virginia, was thirty-seven years old when the war started. A West Point graduate, he had distinguished himself in the Mexican War but had resigned from the U.S. Army in 1851 to become professor of tactics and mechanics at Virginia Military Institute. He was tall, eccentric, and extremely religious, and found it difficult to express his views to most people. However, he was deeply interested in military problems and could concentrate his mind exclusively on the subject at hand.

In the spring of 1862 the chief of the Union Army, Major General George B. McClellan, presented Stonewall Jackson with the opportunity he was seeking. McClellan had built an army nearly three times the size of the force commanded by the senior Confederate commander, Joseph E. Johnston. But he had no real comprehension of strategy and did not know how to exploit his strength. He transferred most of his army by ship through Chesapeake Bay to Fort Monroe, an army post the North still held at the tip of the peninsula between the York and James rivers southeast of Richmond. From there he planned to drive directly up the peninsula and seize Richmond, the Confederate capital, railway hub of Virginia and the South's major munitions-manufacturing center.

McClellan did not take the precaution of sending part of his army directly against Johnston's army in the vicinity of Manassas in northern Virginia, thereby holding it in place and forcing the South to divide its already inadequate forces. As a consequence Johnston was able to withdrew most of his army to meet the sole threat of McClellan.

Since the Union president, Abraham Lincoln, was extremely sensitive about protecting the Federal capital, McClellan had been forced to leave behind a large garrison manning forts the Federals had built around Washington, plus three major field forces: a 40,000-man corps under Irvin McDowell south of Washington to protect against any direct move by the Rebel army on the capital, a 23,000-man army under Nathaniel P. Banks guarding Stonewall Jackson and his tiny army of 4,600 men in the lower (northern) Shenandoah Valley, and a 15,000-man army under John C. Frémont approaching the valley from the Allegheny Mountains to the west.

Although Johnston had only about 57,000 men to fend off McClellan's approximately 90,000, the Federal commander consistently exaggerated Confederate strength and pressed Lincoln to release McDowell's corps to him, saying he could not guarantee a successful attack on Richmond without it. Lincoln relented and said that as soon as there was no threat to Washington, McDowell's corps could join McClellan.

Stonewall Jackson was left with a threefold task. The first was to protect the Shenandoah Valley, the wide rich region between the Alleghenies and the Blue Ridge Mountains, whose farms were important for feeding the Rebel army and whose northern exit at the Potomac River afforded a protected point where Southern forces could invade the North. Jackson's second job was to prevent Banks from detaching a large number of troops to reinforce McClellan. Jackson himself, not General Johnston, conceived his third responsibility: to prevent Mc-Dowell's enormous corps from joining McClellan. Against such an increase in strength, Johnston would find it nearly impossible to protect the Confederate capital and would have to retreat, possibly leading to an early Southern surrender. Johnston, a solidly conventional officer, saw no way that Jackson's tiny force in the valley could influence McDowell's movements. But Jackson, knowing Lincoln's fears about protecting Washington, thought otherwise.

On March 11, 1862, Banks pushed Jackson out of Winchester, some thirty miles south of the Potomac. Jackson ordered a night attack on the Federals bivouacked about four miles north of town. But his officers marched the troops six miles south, making the return trip too far to ensure surprise. Jackson angrily abandoned the planned attack and, behind a screen of cavalry under Turner Ashby, retreated forty-two miles south up the macadamized valley pike to Mount Jackson.

Banks quickly figured out the size of Jackson's force and, wanting to participate in McClellan's campaign, left 9,000 men in the valley under James Shields and began moving his remaining troops eastward toward Manassas. Turner Ashby,

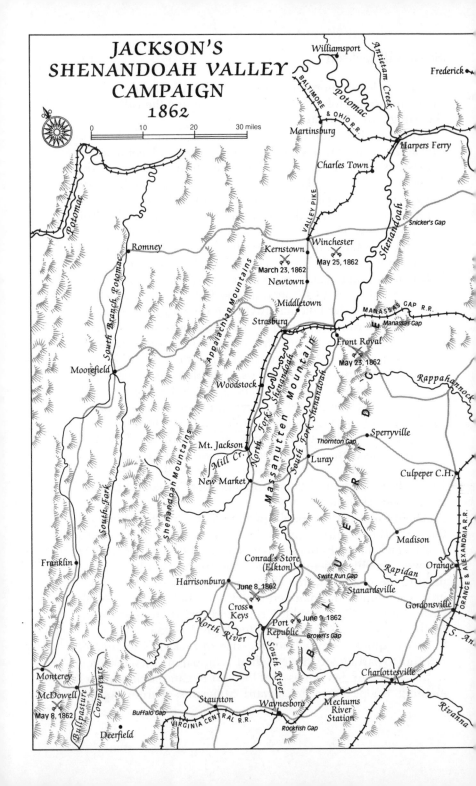

through spies, learned of the movement and got reports that most of Shields's force also was about to depart to the east.

Jackson reacted instantly, marching his men so fast down the valley pike that only 3,000 were still in ranks on March 23 when he found Ashby facing what he assured Jackson was only a Federal rear guard at Kernstown, four miles south of Winchester.

Leaving Ashby on the pike to demonstrate with his artillery, Jackson sent most of his men three miles to the west up a long ridge, hoping to get around the Union flank. Ashby's information was wrong: Shields's entire division was hiding north of Kernstown, and as soon as Jackson made his move, Colonel Nathan Kimball, in charge since Shields had been slightly wounded, dispatched a much-superior force to block Jackson.

Fighting raged bitterly, and Jackson, seeing he was facing a much larger force than his own, sent forward his last three reserve regiments. However, the commander of the Stonewall Brigade, Richard B. Garnett, fearing the Rebel line was about to crack, ordered a retreat. This sent Jackson's entire army into disorderly flight four miles south. Jackson lost 718 men, nearly a fourth of those engaged. He relieved Garnett of his command for retreating without orders.

It was a severe tactical setback for Jackson. Yet the strategic outcome of the battle of Kernstown was astonishing. Shields could not believe Jackson would have attacked without large reinforcements. Lincoln, fearing for the safety of the Shenandoah Valley, sent back most of Banks's army and transferred a 7,000-man division to Frémont west of the Alleghenies. Most significant, however, Lincoln ordered McDowell's corps to remain near Washington, reassuring McClellan, irate at the news, that McDowell could march overland to Richmond as soon as any threat to the capital disappeared.

Though Jackson had lost a battle, his decisive action had kept a major force from joining McClellan and had absorbed the attention of two Union armies, Banks's and Frémont's. In effect, nearly 80,000 Union soldiers had been immobilized by Jackson's 4,000-man army.

Meanwhile the Confederate military leadership—President Davis; Robert E. Lee, Davis's chief of staff; and George

W. Randolph, secretary of war—rejected a proposal of General Johnston to withdraw to the doorstep of Richmond and ordered him to defend a weak line of entrenchments running across the lower peninsula from Yorktown to the James River. McClellan was so cautious he refused to assault this line and began a siege, which lasted a month.

Jackson remained as the only Confederate commander capable of making a strategic move. He increased his army to about 6,000 men by recruiting, and Johnston gave him access to an 8,000-man division under Richard S. Ewell, resting on the eastern slopes of the Blue Ridge. In the Alleghenies west of Staunton blocking Frémont's entry into the valley was a 2,800-man force under Edward Johnson.

Banks, now with 19,000 men, and Frémont, with over 15,000, began to move on Jackson, who had retreated southward after Kernstown and on April 17 abandoned New Market, nearly fifty miles below Kernstown, and fell back to Harrisonburg, twenty-five miles north of Staunton. Jackson's primary aim was to keep Banks and Frémont apart. If they joined they would have twice the men Jackson could muster.

As Banks moved into Harrisonburg, Jackson marched his army fifteen miles due east to Conrad's Store (now Elkton). This town lay at the base of Massanutten Mountain, an enormous block in the midst of the Shenandoah Valley, running forty-five miles from Harrisonburg and Conrad's Store on the south to Strasburg and Front Royal on the north. Only a single highway crossed Massanutten's 3,000-foot ridgeline: about halfway between the northern and southern ends a road ran twelve miles from New Market on the west to Luray on the east. Down the narrow Luray Valley to the east runs the South Fork of the Shenandoah River; to the west the North Fork courses through the main Shenandoah Valley. The two join at Front Royal.

At Conrad's Store, Jackson was safe behind the South Fork and able to escape, if necessary, through Swift Run Gap in the Blue Ridge just to the east. However, Edward Johnson's tiny force, which had withdrawn to about seven miles west of Staunton, could not keep Banks and Frémont apart. And the situation had worsened greatly in eastern Virginia. McDowell's corps was about to march to Fredericksburg, halfway to Richmond, and continue on to join McClellan in front of the Confederate capital. If he was to be stopped, something decisive had to be done. Jackson now undertook a strategic move that ranks as one of the most deceptive in the annals of war.

He ordered Ewell to march to Conrad's Store. But as Ewell arrived, Jackson's own army was on the move. Jackson merely told Ewell to remain at Conrad's Store and attack Banks if he marched on Staunton. Jackson led his own army twelve miles south to Port Republic and then east over the Blue Ridge! He emerged at Mechums River Station on the Virginia Central Railroad about nine miles west of Charlottesville.

Few marches have had such consequences as this. By moving east, Jackson deliberately instilled the idea that he was going to Richmond to fight McClellan or toward Fredericksburg to block McDowell. This caused the Union secretary of war, Edwin M. Stanton, to tell McDowell his first job was to protect Washington and to halt at Fredericksburg until Jackson's intentions were better known. By moving east of the Blue Ridge, Jackson also avoided direct assistance to Edward Johnson's force, thereby deceiving Robert H. Milroy, leading Frémont's advance guard, and giving him no reason to rush up substantial reinforcements.

At Mechums River, Jackson loaded the army in railway cars he had assembled there. But instead of moving east as his men were expecting, the cars rolled west back into the valley! Arriving at Staunton on May 4, Jackson interposed his army between Frémont and Banks and was in position to defeat each Union force separately. His immediate objective was General Milroy, now isolated with a small force some thirty-five miles west of Staunton.

Jackson's roundabout march had the unexpected additional benefit of cutting Banks's army in half. Banks, wanting out of the valley into the larger arena to the east, assured Stanton that Jackson was "bound for Richmond" and suggested his whole force be sent to McDowell or McClellan. Stanton and Lincoln refused but ordered Banks to send Shields's division to McDowell, leaving him only 10,000 men to defend the valley.

Jackson arrived at Staunton the day after General Johnston

pulled out of the Yorktown line and withdrew to the outskirts of Richmond. The battle for the Confederate capital was beginning.

Jackson quickly joined forces with Edward Johnson and marched against Milroy's advance guard. At McDowell on May 8, twenty-seven miles west of Staunton, they ran against Milroy with 4,000 men. While Jackson maneuvered a force around his flank, the Union general attacked the main Confederate body posted on a high hill east of the village. Though he caused considerable Rebel casualties, his position was hopeless, and the Federals retreated during the night toward Franklin. Jackson pressed behind, seizing Franklin and driving Frémont's forces far into the Alleghenies, where they could play no military role for some time.

Jackson now turned back into the valley. Banks, all at once feeling his isolation, withdrew fifty miles north to Strasburg, fourteen miles south of Winchester, where the Manassas Gap Railroad brought him supplies from Washington. He ordered 7,500 of his men to entrench at Strasburg and placed 1,500 men at his rear base at Winchester and 1,000 at Front Royal, ten miles east, where the railroad crossed the Blue Ridge.

Jackson wired General Johnston that Banks was fortifying Strasburg and he was moving down the valley, with Ewell's division, to attack him. Johnston replied that an attack would be too hazardous and said Banks should be left "in his works" and Ewell should come eastward to help defeat McClellan while Jackson remained to observe Banks. Jackson had no intention of leaving Banks "in his works," nor of attacking them directly. But he needed Ewell's division and got Lee to intervene with President Davis to rescind Johnston's order.

Without expenditure of a single soldier, Jackson had halted McDowell's march on Richmond for the second time. He had assembled an overwhelming force to drive back Frémont's advance guard and throw Frémont's whole army out of the strategic picture for the present. Now Banks was isolated with 10,000 men in the lower valley, while Jackson was descending on him with nearly 17,000 troops.

Banks waited astride the valley pike at Strasburg, confident that his entrenchments, rifles, and cannon could defeat the direct assault he believed Jackson would have to make.

Jackson deliberately fostered the idea this was what he had in mind. He ordered Ewell to send Richard Taylor's Louisiana Brigade around the base of Massanutten Mountain from Conrad's Store to New Market on May 20, leading Federal spies and scouts to believe he was consolidating his entire force there preparatory to striking straight down the pike to Strasburg.

However, Jackson was about to demonstrate fully his ability to "mystify, mislead, and surprise."[2] While Turner Ashby's cavalry rushed northward the next morning all the way to Strasburg with orders to impose a cavalry screen between Jackson and the Federals, prevent any spies from getting through, and give the impression the main army was coming behind, Jackson, riding in the van, quietly turned the head of the column to the right—up the sloping road over Massanutten Mountain to Luray!

When his wondering soldiers filed into the Luray Valley some hours later, they realized what their commander had achieved—for there waiting was Ewell's division. In a single maneuver Jackson had concentrated his entire command on the flank of the Federal army. Now only the hopelessly outclassed 1,000-man garrison at Front Royal stood in the way of the Confederates' getting on the Federal rear.

On the morning of May 23, Jackson's entire command nearly wiped out the unsuspecting Union force at Front Royal, capturing 600 prisoners and causing over 300 casualties.

Thus, in one swift move Jackson severed Banks's direct rail link with Washington, cut his retreat route to the east, and placed himself as close to his rear base at Winchester as Banks himself.

2. Brigadier General John D. Imboden quotes Jackson as saying there are two things a commander should never to lose sight of: "Always mystify, mislead, and surprise the enemy, if possible; and when you strike and overcome him, never let up the pursuit so long as your men have strength to follow; for an army routed, if hotly pursued, becomes panic-stricken and can then be destroyed by half their number. The other rule is, never fight against heavy odds, if by any possible maneuvering you can hurl your own force on only a part, and that the weakest part, of your enemy and crush it. Such tactics will win every time and a small army may thus destroy a large one in detail and repeated victory will make it invincible." See Johnson and Buel, vol. 2, 297.

Banks reacted with stunned immobility to the astonishing news. All of May 23 he refused to evacuate his now-useless works at Strasburg, despite the urgings of his senior commanders. When Colonel George H. Gordon pleaded with him to save the army while he could, Banks burst out: "By God, sir, I will not retreat! We have more to fear, sir, from the opinions of our friends than the bayonets of our enemies!"

Jackson had worked on the mind of the Union commander, distracting him to such a degree that he was incapable for a while of making a rational judgment. It was not until the morning of May 24 that Banks at last recognized his peril and ordered precipitate retreat toward Winchester.

Jackson had hoped to cut off Banks's force between Strasburg and Winchester. But on this day his usually reliable cavalry failed him. The Shenandoah Valley horsemen who made up Jackson's cavalry were brave and determined. But Turner Ashby was no disciplinarian, and the men could not resist pillaging the Union supply wagons they found fleeing up the road toward Winchester, and especially they could not ignore the many Federal horses they found free for the taking. The Confederate cavalry had to supply their own mounts, and this to some extent explains why many of the Rebel horsemen led captured animals back to their homes, taking one or two days to make the trip and abandoning the army for the period. Because of failure of discipline, Ashby's cavalry was unable to cut off the Federal retreat and most of Banks's army rushed back to Winchester, although Jackson scattered Banks's rear guard at Middleton, a few miles north of Strasburg, and pushed his exhausted infantry until 1:00 A.M. on May 25 in pursuit.

Nevertheless, Banks's position at Winchester was desperate. He was greatly outnumbered and had been so distracted that he had failed to occupy a highly defensible ridge at the south edge of town above Abrams Creek. On the early morning of May 25, Jackson discovered Banks's force standing along a broken ridge some eight hundred yards to the north. About 400 yards closer on another ridge were eight Union rifled guns and sharpshooters. These caused severe damage to Confederate batteries and two brigades Jackson sent onto the ridge above Abrams Creek.

Jackson's main effort was a two-brigade attack around the Federal west flank, led by Taylor's Louisiana Brigade. The assault sent the already shaky Federals reeling back into retreat. Seeing the Federal line disintegrating, Jackson ordered the entire Confederate line forward, 10,000 men in a magnificent charge from the flank and the hill above Abrams Creek, all the men joining in the wild "Rebel yell" and sweeping into the streets of Winchester and out again to the north.

If Turner Ashby's horsemen had been in place, Jackson might have carried out a huge roundup of Banks's panic-stricken army. But they had largely disappeared, and Jackson had to be satisfied with 3,000 Federal losses, mostly prisoners, and capture of many rifles, guns, and supplies. Although the cavalry's indiscipline was the principal reason for the failure, Jackson's excessive fear of divulging his plans contributed. He had every reason to believe he might bag Banks's entire force between Winchester and the Potomac River. But he did not inform his cavalry commanders in advance. If he had they would have made extraordinary efforts to carry out his wishes.

Jackson's rout of Banks and his march to the Potomac River set off a panic in Washington. Secretary Stanton telegraphed the Northern governors to alert all their armed forces to defend the capital. Lincoln halted McDowell's march on Richmond for the third time and ordered him, in conjunction with Frémont, Banks, and Rufus Saxton at Harpers Ferry, to cut off Stonewall's retreat and destroy his army. He also wired McClellan that he thought Jackson was making a general move into the North and "the time is near when you must either attack Richmond or give up the job and come to the defense of Washington."

Jackson's strategy demonstrates how indirect action against an enemy's vulnerable point—in this case the Union capital—can immobilize an enemy with little loss of life. By threatening along the Potomac, Jackson prevented McClellan from receiving the corps he believed was mandatory to defeat the Confederates in front of Richmond. This stopped McClellan from attacking and gave Johnston and Lee more time to prepare defenses and bring up reinforcements to defeat him.

Without doing anything further, Jackson had achieved a great Southern victory. However, Jackson believed he was in a position to win the war. The vast bulk of the Federal army was locked in front of Richmond and would be unable to react for days and perhaps weeks if Jackson swept behind Washington, seized Baltimore and perhaps Philadelphia, severed the rail connections with the capital, and began systematically destroying Northern factories. He immediately renewed with President Davis and General Lee the proposal for such an invasion that he had made after the battle of Manassas in 1861. Now he asked for enough reinforcements to increase his army to 40,000 men. With them, he informed Davis and Lee, he would cross into Maryland, "raise the siege of Richmond and transfer this campaign from the banks of the Potomac to those of the Susquehanna."

It was a spectacular proposal. It would move Southern strength away from Federal strength—McClellan's army in front of Richmond—and strike at a point that was largely undefended: the cities and railways north of Washington. If the capital could be isolated and its food supply cut off, there would be intense pressure for Lincoln's government to evacuate the city for fear members would be captured. In such a case, the Northern people would lose much confidence in their government, and Britain and France, whose textile industries were hurting because the Union naval blockade of Southern ports was preventing export of cotton, might recognize the Confederacy and force an end to the war.

At the very least, a move by Jackson into the North would end the siege of Richmond without a single Confederate soldier losing his life. And it would throw the North onto the strategic defensive.

As Jackson's emissary, Colonel A. R. Boteler, a former U.S. congressman, rushed off to Richmond to present his plan to Davis and Lee, Jackson retreated southward up the valley to get behind Federal forces converging in hopes of cutting him off.

Jackson's withdrawal would not prevent his sweeping northward again if he received additional troops and authorization to invade the North. He had already worked out a plan to neutralize Union forces attempting to block him and to march into the North virtually unopposed. Jackson expected to cross over to the eastern slope of the Blue Ridge and move north. This would lock Union forces opposing him in place. Troops protecting Washington could not move for fear he might strike directly at the capital. Forces in the valley would remain immobile for fear he would seize it. By alternately threatening Washington and the valley, Jackson could prevent Union forces from joining, defeat any single force that dared attack, bypass the remainder, and cross the Potomac. Beyond the river, there were no strong Federal field forces.

Although Lincoln and Stanton hoped to cut off Jackson and destroy him, there was little hope the Union commanders could pull off such a maneuver. Frémont, in the Alleghenies eighty miles southwest of Jackson, was in the best position. But he was extremely sensitive to his supply lines, and when a small Rebel force blocked the main pass leading to the valley, he turned north down the South Branch of the Potomac, then turned east to converge on Strasburg, toward which James Shields with 10,000 men from McDowell's corps also was marching, followed by another 10,000 men under James B. Ricketts.

Because of Jackson's audacious advance, both Frémont and Shields exaggerated his actual strength and neither was willing to take him on alone. As a consequence, both held back and Jackson got his army unscathed through Strasburg on June 1, 1862, and headed south up the valley pike.

While this was happening, General Johnston was sending his army into an attack on McClellan just east of Richmond. This battle, known as Seven Pines in the South and Fair Oaks in the North, was mismanaged. A double envelopment planned by Johnston failed, and the battle degenerated into a series of frontal assaults that cost the South 6,000 casualties and the North 5,000. Johnston sustained a severe wound, and President Davis placed Robert E. Lee in command of the Confederate army.

Once Jackson was south of Strasburg, Frémont began making fierce attacks that the Confederate rear guard had difficulty stopping and that finally took the life of Turner Ashby in a bitter fight near Harrisonburg. Meanwhile Shields, at Front Royal, turned south up the Luray Valley in hopes of getting on Jackson's rear at New Market by marching from Luray over the only road crossing Massanutten. In case this failed, Shields ordered his cavalry to seize the bridge over the South Fork of the Shenandoah at Conrad's Store, so that his division could press around the southern base of Massanutten and block Jackson at Harrisonburg.

Jackson had anticipated these moves and sent some of his native cavalry, who knew every road and byway of the valley, to burn the two bridges over the South Fork at Luray and the single bridge at Conrad's Store. When Shields's division arrived at Luray, the links were gone, and the river was in spate, as a result of heavy rains that had been sweeping the valley. And when Shields's cavalry arrived at Conrad's Store, the bridge there, too, was destroyed. Shields, with no pontoon bridge, was isolated east of the South Fork.

There was still one bridge over the South Fork: at Port Republic, twelve miles southeast of Harrisonburg, where the North and South rivers come together to form the South Fork. This bridge spanned the North River, while fords gave passage over the South River. Jackson had taken a calculated risk and left this bridge intact, because it provided his bolt hole to Brown's Gap in the Blue Ridge just to the east. Jackson had to get his army to this gap, where it would be safe from attack and from where he could move to Richmond if Lee called or toward the Potomac if Lee and Davis authorized an attack behind Washington.

Both Jackson and Shields began a race for the Port Republic bridge. Jackson won by a single day, arriving on June 7. The next morning a detachment of Federal cavalry crossed a South River ford, captured part of Jackson's staff, nearly captured Jackson, and was driven into retreat only by a hastily organized attack by Rebel forces over the North River bridge and into the village.

Jackson now was in what Napoleon called the "central position" between the two enemy forces, able to turn on one before he had to deal with the other. Jackson's most immediate danger was from Shields. Although he had allowed his division to become widely spread out up the Luray Valley, Shields could still block Jackson's escape through Brown's Gap and seize his wagon train only a short distance below Port Republic, and he might drive on to Waynesboro and cut the Virginia Central Railroad.

Jackson, therefore, resolved to turn on Shields and send him flying northward. Then he intended to turn back and defeat Frémont.

Unfortunately, Frémont on June 8 unexpectedly came up on General Ewell's division at Cross Keys, five miles northwest of Port Republic, forcing Jackson to deal with him first. Although Frémont had twice the force of Ewell, he advanced only about a fifth of it against the Confederate right, where Isaac R. Trimble's brigade shattered the assault, then moved around the Union left flank, forcing the line to retreat a mile. Jackson, seeing that Frémont was going to do nothing more for at least a day, left two brigades to guard him and turned the remainder of his force to dispose of Shields's advance guard, only a short distance north. Jackson hoped to destroy this vanguard, then move back and shatter Frémont.

Shields's forward force of 3,000 men was commanded by an outstanding soldier, Colonel Erastus B. Tyler, who took up a formidable position along a sunken road and a small stream about two miles north of Port Republic in a mostly open valley about a mile wide between the river and the heavily forested slopes of the Blue Ridge. He had posted eight cannon on an open "coal hearth" where charcoal was prepared on a high terrace just below the Blue Ridge. These cannon dominated the position.

Jackson advanced with the Stonewall Brigade and the Louisiana Brigade behind, expecting the remainder of his force to cross an improvised bridge of boards laid over wagons pulled into a South River ford. The bridge proved to be rickety, and the soldiers refused to cross except one at a time. Officers in charge failed to correct the problem, and it took much of the day to get the army across. Meanwhile the Rebel soldiers on the firing line nearly buckled from artillery fire from the coal hearth and Union assaults. Only when the Louisiana Brigade and part of Ewell's division flanked the coal hearth by way of the Blue Ridge was Tyler's position turned and his brigades forced to retreat nine miles north, where Shields had formed a new defensive line.

Before the battle was over, Jackson had realized he had no hope of turning back and defeating Frémont, and he ordered the brigades guarding him to retreat to Port Republic, burn the bridge, and cross to the east bank. They accomplished this with speed.

As the day ended, Jackson had achieved a great deal: his army was safely on the east bank of the South Fork and within reach of the Blue Ridge, Shields had been pressed out of the fight to the north, and Frémont remained isolated on the west side of the river. Jackson called off the pursuit of Tyler and marched his army to safety onto the lower cove of Brown's Gap.

The next day, Shields withdrew toward Luray, although McDowell had authorized him to remain if he had a reasonable chance of defeating Jackson. Apparently Shields decided he did not, because he gave as his excuse that he was supposed to march with McDowell's corps on Richmond. But this march had been indefinitely suspended because of Jackson's presence in the valley. Frémont, seeing Shields had departed, withdrew as well. Pursued by Rebel cavalry, he retreated first to Harrisonburg and by June 24 all the way to Middletown, ten miles south of Winchester, where Banks, leading Federal forces advancing from the Potomac, had stopped.

In this anticlimactic way the valley campaign ended. Jackson brought his army down from the Blue Ridge on June 12, pitched camp near Port Republic, and gave his men a five-day rest.

Just prior to the battle of Cross Keys, Jackson had received a short message from Davis that he could not send additional troops for the proposed offensive north of Washington. Now, having disposed of Shields and Frémont and having kept McDowell immobilized for fear he would march again northward, Jackson hoped to get permission for the invasion.

He called in Colonel Boteler on June 13 and sent him to the capital to take another letter explaining his invasion plan and asking his army to be raised to 40,000 men. With such a force, he said, he would cross to the east side of the Blue Ridge and proceed northward until he found a gap through which he could descend on the rear of Banks's army and defeat it. Then he would invade Maryland and Pennsylvania.

But Jackson's hopes for a counteroffensive received little attention in Richmond. Davis and Lee had been distracted by the unsatisfactory outcome of the battle of Seven Pines and by Johnston's wounding. But the real reason was that Davis and Lee had a fixed belief that the defense of Richmond was the most important task facing the Confederacy. They could not see that Jackson's proposal offered not only a guarantee of ending the siege of Richmond but also a strong chance of winning the war.

Lee had written Davis on June 5 that "the character of the war" would be changed if Jackson could be reinforced as he requested. But Lee wanted no troops removed from Richmond and suggested only that the governors of the Carolinas and Georgia be persuaded to dispatch troops. Davis was unprepared to press these states, and the matter lapsed.

Lee sent Jackson 8,000 reinforcements, but his purpose was solely to deceive the Federal commanders into thinking Jackson was preparing another strike down the Shenandoah. For he ordered Jackson to make secret preparations to move his whole army to Ashland, just north of Richmond, to help in the counterstroke he was preparing against McClellan.

When Boteler arrived at Lee's office and presented Jackson's letter, Lee responded: "Colonel, don't you think General Jackson had better come down here first and help me drive these troublesome people away from before Richmond?"

And when Lee sent Jackson's letter to Davis, his endorsement said: "I think the sooner Jackson can move this way [toward Richmond] the better—The first object now is to defeat Mc-Clellan." Davis endorsed the letter, saying, "Views concurred in."

Neither Lee nor Davis understood the strategic opportunity that McClellan had presented when he placed his army east of Richmond where it could not block the North from invasion. They were obsessed with defeating the North's main army and were unwilling to look at Jackson's wholly different strategy: striking at the North's will to win.

Jackson wanted to move away from the Union armies and succeed indirectly. Lee sought to win by frontal attack into the teeth of McClellan's enormous military power. His battle plan, which finally came into operation in the battles of the Seven Days, June 26 to July 1, 1862, drove McClellan into a defensive position at Harrison's Landing, on the James River twenty air miles southeast of Richmond. But the cost in killed and wounded was incredible: over 20,000 men, one-fourth of the entire Southern army.

Lee never surmounted his urge to resort to direct solutions. Jackson tried once more, after the Seven Days, to convince Lee and Davis to undertake an indirect offensive into the North to avoid the Union field army and prey on the morale of the Northern people. Again he failed. Thereafter, Jackson sought to defeat the Union forces in battle and thereby make the North defenseless against attack. Four times Jackson tried to persuade Lee to conduct a campaign to sweep around the flanks of the Federal field army, surround it, and defeat it. Four times Lee refused or failed to carry it out. Finally, on his fifth attempt, Jackson got Lee's authority to attack the rear of the Union army of Joseph Hooker at Chancellorsville on May 2, 1863, to cut off its retreat and to destroy it. Unfortunately Jackson was fatally wounded at the moment he was bringing about this spectacular maneuver and it was never carried out.

In the battle of Gettysburg, fought two months later, Lee reverted to his direct method of battle, his policy culminating in ordering the disastrous charge of 15,000 Confederates under George Pickett on the third day. The resulting near-annihilation of this force destroyed the last offensive power of the Confederacy. Thereafter, Lee could only strike out like a wounded lion at the enormous Federal armies that gathered to beat him into the ground.

5

Sherman

THE GENERAL WHO WON THE CIVIL WAR

AT THE BEGINNING OF 1864 the Union armies facing Robert E. Lee's Confederates in Virginia were little farther along than they had been when the war started in 1861. Despite horrendous losses, Lee's Army of Northern Virginia still stood defiantly in the path of the Federal forces seeking to capture Richmond.

The situation was radically otherwise in the western theater, beyond the Allegheny and Appalachian mountains. By January 1864, Union forces—which had consistently faced Confederate commanders inferior to Lee and Stonewall Jackson in Virginia—had seized the entire valley of the Mississippi River, Kentucky, and Tennessee, and had driven Rebel forces beyond Chattanooga to Dalton in the mountains of northern Georgia.

With the states beyond the Mississippi isolated, the Confederacy in the west had been reduced to parts of Mississippi and to Alabama south of the Tennessee River. Nevertheless the Confederacy still retained a bastion of great strength: the four old eastern states where the Southern culture had originated, Georgia, North and South Carolina, and Virginia. The lower anchor of this heartland was Atlanta, pivot of the remaining rail links between east and west and site of vital foundries, machine shops, and munitions factories.

If the Confederate commander at Dalton, Joseph E. Johnston, could keep the Federals from Atlanta and Lee could protect Virginia, the South might hold out long enough for Northern voters, weary with the war and appalled at the losses, to elect a Democratic peace candidate in the November 1864 presidential elections, oust Abraham Lincoln and the radical Republicans, and bring about a negotiated peace between North and South.

Lincoln was well aware that a tide of pacifism was sweeping the North. He knew 1864 was the crucial year of his presidency. Unless he made dramatic advances before the election, he was certain to be defeated. Lincoln had learned from bitter experience that his primary lack in the east was a general who would advance, no matter the consequences. He had never had such a general. Time after time an eastern general had marched into the terrible jaws of the Confederate lion, had suffered devastating losses, and had withdrawn, anxious never to measure himself again against Lee or Jackson.

In the west, however, Lincoln had such a bulldog of a general, Ulysses S. Grant. Grant and his chief lieutenant, William Tecumseh Sherman, had fought brilliantly to seize Vicksburg and open the Mississippi in 1862–63 and in November 1863 had won the battle of Chattanooga and thrust the Rebels into the mountains of northern Georgia.

On March 4, 1864, Lincoln made a profound decision. He summoned Grant to Washington and conferred on him command of all the Federal armies. Like nearly all the Republican political leadership, Lincoln was still preoccupied with Lee's army and capture of the Confederate capital of Richmond and told Grant he should supervise personally the Union Army of the Potomac in its attacks against Lee.

Grant agreed, named General Sherman to command in the west, and worked out a grand strategy to defeat the Confederacy. Grant's main objectives were Lee's army behind the Rapidan River in Virginia and Johnston's army at Dalton. Grant would direct the campaign against Lee; Sherman would lead the campaign against Johnston. To distract the Confederates, he ordered separate moves against the strategic flanks of the two Rebel armies. Against Lee, a Union army under Benjamin F. (Beast) Butler was to advance westward along the south bank of the James River towards Richmond. Against Johnston, Union

General Nathaniel P. Banks was to seize the port of Mobile,
Alabama, and open an alternative gate into Georgia from the
extreme south. In the event, neither flanking movement succeeded. Small Confederate forces bottled Butler up against the
James east of Petersburg, and Banks was so slow that Sherman
had to advance directly on Atlanta without the possibility of
creating a threat to the Confederate rear.

Grant envisioned the campaigns to end the war as direct
attacks with little subtlety. By 1864, frontal assaults had become extremely dangerous and costly. The long-range killing
power of the rifle loaded with the Minié ball had been combined with trenches, earthen embankments, and log embra-
sures to make nearly any position taken by troops in the field
virtually impregnable. Grant ignored this reality because he
could think of no other course of action and because Lincoln
assured him of his full support and unrestricted access to the
manpower of the North. Consequently, Grant adopted a bru-
tally simple strategy: to make repeated hammer blows against
Confederate field fortifications, beating down the enemy by
main strength. The prospects were for casualties on a scale
even more enormous than had been suffered previously.

As was to be seen, however, General Sherman was acutely
aware of the perils of frontal assaults and developed an entirely
different approach, although he was forced to conduct a direct
campaign along a single corridor leading from Dalton to Atlanta, since he was locked, for his supplies, to the single-track
railway running from Chattanooga to Atlanta.

Sherman, an 1840 graduate of West Point, saw no active
service in the Mexican War but earned a growing reputation for
military excellence during the long operations in the west, especially in the Vicksburg and Chattanooga campaigns. Even
so, there had been little hint of the radically different approach
to warfare that he was about to unleash in the drive for Atlanta
and the marches through the heart of the South he made thereafter. These campaigns won the Civil War for the North when
the strategy of Ulysses S. Grant came to the verge of losing it.

Grant, in a letter to Sherman on April 14, 1864, said he
would stay with the Army of the Potomac and order its com-

WILLIAM TECUMSEH SHERMAN

Bettmann Archive

mander, George G. Meade, to keep Lee's army as his sole objective, "that wherever Lee went he would go also." Grant thus renounced from the outset any plan to get *around* Lee's army. To Sherman, in whom he had great confidence, his instructions were less specific. Sherman was to move against Johnston's army, break it up, and get into the Confederate interior and do as much damage as possible "against their war resources." He left Sherman free to execute the task in his own way.

Sherman had come to realize that destroying the Southern people's will to pursue the war was more important than destroying Johnston's army. Once the people wearied of war, their armies would melt away. So long as they remained adamant, they would continue to throw up armies or, failing that, guerrilla bands, which could lead to endless war. The only sure solution was to inflict so much damage on Southern property and way of life, and not merely "war resources," that the people would prefer surrender to continued destruction. Stonewall Jackson had recognized this principle early in the war and had wanted to apply it against the Northern people. But the Confederate leadership had refused. Now Sherman, on the other side, was about to embark on it.

Nevertheless, Sherman had to deal first with Joe Johnston's army standing at Dalton and blocking the way through the mountains to Atlanta, eighty air miles away. Johnston had about 60,000 men, with a corps under Leonidas Polk on the way from Mississippi. Sherman had assembled just shy of 100,000 men, with almost as many more guarding his railway supply line leading back from Chattanooga through Nashville to Louisville, Kentucky.

The 3:5 ratio of Confederate to Union strength was comfortable to hold such naturally defensible country as northern Georgia's mountains, especially as Johnston had covered the low valley north of Dalton through which the railway ran with strong entrenchments on either flank.

Johnston had already renounced a proposal of President Jefferson Davis to take the offensive northeast of Chattanooga, turn west into middle Tennessee, and hope to compel Sherman to fall back to save Nashville. Johnston told Davis he did not have enough horses and mules to undertake the campaign.

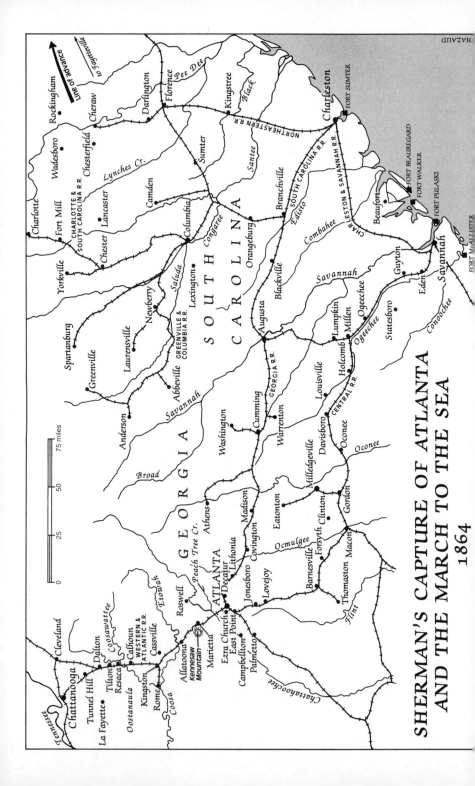

SHERMAN'S CAPTURE OF ATLANTA
AND THE MARCH TO THE SEA
1864

Johnston, convinced of the power of field fortifications, believed his best chance of defeating Sherman lay in remaining entirely on the defensive.

He was certain Sherman intended to attack him directly at Dalton, since the Federals were dependent on the railway and a move along the rail line would be the most obvious and simple course. For that reason he concentrated his two corps (under William J. Hardee and John Bell Hood) at Dalton with his 6,000 cavalry under Joseph Wheeler farther out, watching the approaches to Dalton.

This reliance on the defensive—and especially on defending a particular point along the railway—was Johnston's fatal mistake. Sherman knew a frontal assault against the entrenchments at Dalton would be deadly and did not consider making it. Instead, on May 4, 1864, start of the offensive in Virginia and Georgia, he ordered his main force—the 61,000-man Army of the Cumberland under George H. Thomas and the 13,000-man Army of the Ohio under John M. Schofield—to demonstrate directly against Dalton, holding Johnston's army in place. Meanwhile he sent the 24,000-man Army of the Tennessee under James B. McPherson through the mountains around Johnston's left or western flank to seize Resaca on the railroad, fifteen miles south of Dalton.

This was a stunning version of Napoleon's most deadly practice, the *manœuvre sur les derrières,* and was designed to interpose a strategic barrage or barrier directly on Johnston's route of retreat. If McPherson marched firmly and seized Resaca, the Confederate army would be unable to retreat except along impracticable mountain roads east of the valley and was likely to be destroyed.

Thomas's and Schofield's armies pressed the Rebels at Dalton but, on Sherman's orders, made no serious attack on the immensely strong Confederate entrenchments. However, the distraction of their advances cloaked McPherson's flank move. On May 8 his leading division, against no opposition, occupied Snake Creek Gap, about five miles west of Resaca.

Meanwhile James Cantey's brigade of Leonidas Polk's corps arrived at Resaca. Johnston still had no hint of McPherson's approach on his rear but, confused by Federal attacks edging around his position at Dalton, ordered Cantey, with his 2,000 men, to remain at Resaca until the situation clarified.

On the morning of May 9, McPherson's army of 24,000 debouched into the valley about four miles west of Resaca, drove back a small Rebel cavalry patrol, and came within sight of a small line of entrenchments that Cantey's men had hurriedly built. Although ordered by Sherman to attack boldly and seize the village, McPherson took up defensive positions with four divisions while sending his fifth division forward with orders to cut the railroad and then *fall back* to the mouth of Snake Creek gorge. The "attack" was so tepid that just eighteen men got to the railroad and succeeded only in breaking a small section of telegraph wire.

Johnston, alarmed, hurriedly sent three of his seven divisions at Dalton to Resaca. They arrived early on May 10. But this day McPherson rested his men and made no attack. Johnston, believing the maneuver was only a Union demonstration, recalled his troops, leaving two divisions at Tilton, eight miles north of Resaca, so they could move in either direction, and ordering Polk's corps, now arriving, to concentrate at Resaca. Sherman was bitterly disappointed at McPherson's failure but said only: "Well, Mac, you have missed the great opportunity of your life."

Sherman ordered Thomas to leave one of his three corps to keep up a feint attack at Dalton, while the rest of his army and Schofield's force moved around Johnston's left flank to join McPherson and attack Resaca. Sherman hoped Johnston would stay at Dalton until he could get his main force to McPherson, but this was unrealistic, because surprise was gone. Johnston's cavalry got enough signs of Sherman's movement on May 12 to persuade him to retreat, thus giving up his impregnable positions at Dalton without a battle. By the morning of May 13, Johnston's army was in force at Resaca.

McPherson advanced on the village, while Thomas and Schofield deployed to the north. In hours, the Rebels threw up field fortifications west and north of the village. On the 14th the Federals tested Rebel strength at various points but found no weak point.

Johnston was a solidly conventional soldier and had failed

to grasp the radical nature of Sherman's strategy. The ease with which Sherman had evicted the Rebels from Dalton indicated such a move was likely to be repeated. Building entrenchments was no antidote. Once Johnston had committed his army to fortifications, Sherman could simply go around them. For this reason, a Confederate policy solely of defense was a guarantee of ultimate defeat. Unless Johnston could make an offensive move that would force Sherman back, he would be driven from one entrenched position after another until he had fallen back to Atlanta.

Sherman's vulnerable point was his line of communications. The Union forces relied on the railway from Chattanooga. In the rough mountains of northern Georgia, the troops would have starved without food delivered by this railroad. If Johnston had sent strong forces around Sherman's flanks to block this railway, he might have brought the Federal offensive to a halt. He had enough troops to interpose strategic barriers requiring major efforts to break up. Such a policy would have distracted the Federals, and even if most Rebels had been forced to retreat, they might have escaped through the mountains and forests on either side of the railway. The wild nature of the country would have permitted large numbers of semiguerrilla Rebel bands to operate all along the railway, killing guards and repair crews, blowing up bridges, and interrupting rail traffic.

Johnston never attempted a major campaign against Sherman's rail line. Rather, he reverted at Resaca to an obvious tactical pattern: sending Hood to strike Sherman's left wing in flank, hoping to cut him off from his line of retreat. Such a narrow turning movement had little hope of success, given Union numerical strength, and the Federals parried the blow. Anyway, Sherman's pontoon bridge had already been thrown across the Oostanaula River southwest of Resaca preparatory to another move around Johnston's flank.

On May 16, hearing the Federals were across the Oostanaula and moving on his rear, Johnston abandoned Resaca and fell back twenty miles to Cassville. The last of Polk's divisions had arrived, and Johnston, with 75,000 men, hoped to fall on an isolated Union column and destroy it. Sherman, however, marching in the way Napoleon had advanced, spread out a wide waving net of columns that could swiftly concentrate against any enemy force. Rather than ambushing a Union column, Johnston was in danger of being enfolded by Sherman's even-wider-spreading columns. Reluctantly, he ordered withdrawal south of the Etowah River, causing deep gloom to his soldiers, sentenced to one more retreat.

Johnston entrenched positions covering the steep, narrow Allatoona Pass, through which the railroad ran fifteen miles northwest of Marietta. Sherman had no intention of following Johnston into such a trap and on May 23 outflanked Johnston's line again, pushing his whole army due south across the Etowah, with the intention of swinging again on Johnston's rear.

The Federals were now in a region of good farming country and foraged for their food—but also commenced Sherman's design to force the Southern people to end the war. The foragers ruthlessly set fire to houses, barns, and other property, marking the beginning of a pattern of wanton destruction that Sherman intended to cut all the way through Georgia. Sherman wrote his wife: "We have devoured the land and our animals eat up the wheat and corn. . . . All the people retire before us and desolation is behind."

Johnston detected Sherman's move south and got his army into blocking position near Dallas, fifteen miles southwest of Allatoona. The two armies clashed violently for several days, but on May 28 Sherman began sidestepping eastward toward the railway, forcing Johnston on June 4 to retire fifteen miles southeastward to new entrenchments on Kennesaw Mountain covering Marietta, only twenty-five miles from Atlanta.

The Federals were held up for weeks by wet weather, and on June 27, Sherman ordered the only direct attack of the campaign: two separate but simultaneous assaults a mile apart against the entrenchments of Kennesaw Mountain. Since he had avoided such attacks, he hoped the Confederates would not be expecting them. Both assaults failed utterly, the Federals losing 3,000 men in a few minutes to the Rebels' 630, the Confederate losses almost entirely due to artillery fire.

The attack on Kennesaw Mountain proved once more that there is never justification for a direct assault on an unshaken enemy in position. To his credit, Sherman tried it only once.

When it failed, he immediately planned a new move to his flank.

Sherman acted far more wisely than Grant in Virginia. After the Army of the Potomac had clashed headlong with Lee in the Wilderness on May 5–7, 1864, Grant ordered a left-flank march to Spotsylvania Courthouse. Lee beat him there and Grant assaulted his entrenchments directly, suffering severe losses but failing to break the Confederate line. Grant then slipped off southeastward, ending at Cold Harbor, only a few miles northeast of Richmond, where again he attacked frontally, with horrendous casualties. In a month's campaign Grant lost 55,000 men, nearly half his original strength, and nearly double Lee's losses. Grant had ruined the offensive power of his army. He crossed the James River on June 12 and began a siege of Petersburg, but the Army of the Potomac lay largely paralyzed in front of the Confederate entrenchments. The war in Virginia settled into a long stalemate.

The outcome of Grant's Virginia campaign—appalling losses and baffled hopes for victory—deeply depressed the Northern people and caused many, led by the Democratic Party, to doubt whether the war should be continued. Even within the Republican Party, leaders began to criticize Abraham Lincoln's policy, and his strongest supporters feared his chance for reelection was hopeless.

In the gloom that settled over the North in July and August 1864, only Sherman's continued advance offered any relief. If he captured Atlanta and demonstrated the weakness of the South, the North would take on new heart and see the war to a successful conclusion. If he failed and his campaign, like Grant's, degenerated into a stalemate, Lincoln would be defeated and the Union dissolved.

The final approach to Atlanta commenced only four days after Sherman's repulse at Kennesaw Mountain. McPherson slipped around Johnston's left or western flank and reached only three miles short of the Chattahoochee River in the Confederate rear. Johnston detected the danger and withdrew his army on July 2. Sherman discovered the retreat early on July 3 and sent his forces in hot pursuit, hoping to prevent the Confederates from getting across the Chattahoochee and using it to build a formidable new line.

Johnston, however, had decided to meet the Federals in front of the Chattahoochee, taking a dangerous chance because the army, if defeated, would have difficulty retreating with the river at its back. Johnston took the risk to surprise Sherman, fortifying a six-mile bridgehead where the railroad crossed the stream.

Sherman had no intention of crashing into these new Rebel entrenchments. While some of his cavalry probed downstream as if searching for a crossing below Johnston's bridgehead, other horsemen found two unguarded fords, Phillips Ferry, about ten miles upstream, and Roswell, about twenty. Sherman sent Schofield's army over Phillips Ferry on July 8, forming a strong bridgehead on the southern bank, while Union cavalry crossed at Roswell and established another bridgehead, quickly reinforced by an infantry corps.

Taking the only course open to him, Johnston retired to Atlanta before the Federals cut him off. Once more he had been outwitted by Sherman, obliged not only to forfeit his fortified position but also to give up the Chattahoochee as his forward line of defense. Sherman took quick advantage of the situation, using his bridgeheads over the Chattahoochee to swing Thomas's army onto the Confederates' first entrenchments along the east-west line of Peach Tree Creek, five miles north of Atlanta, while Schofield occupied Decatur, seven miles east of the city, and McPherson moved seven miles farther east to break Hood's main railroad connection with the Carolinas and Virginia, the Augusta Railroad.

Johnston's last retreat was too much for President Davis. On July 17 he relieved Johnston and gave his command to John Bell Hood. This was wonderful news to Sherman. Hood was notorious as a "fighting soldier," a man of little intellect who had never grasped the profound change in warfare brought on by the Minié ball and field fortifications.

Hood still believed the recipe for victory was an attack and, playing directly into Sherman's hands, hoped to strike the Federals as they were crossing Peach Tree Creek. On July 20, Hood's forces came out of their entrenchments behind the creek and attacked Joseph Hooker's corps of Thomas's army. A desperate frontal battle developed, lasting four hours and including much hand-to-hand fighting. Hood, even after initial assaults had failed and surprise was lost, repeatedly renewed the attacks, gaining nothing but adding to Confederate dead and wounded. Meanwhile, McPherson, moving west from Decatur, threatened the east side of Atlanta, and Hood had to call off the attack and divert troops to stop McPherson from entering the inner defenses of Atlanta. Hood fell back to the main lines protecting Atlanta after losing 4,800 men to the Federals' 1,700.

Holding these lines with two corps, Hood made a wide circuit with Hardee's corps on the night of July 22 to get on McPherson's left rear. But McPherson had anticipated the move and posted Grenville M. Dodge's corps to meet it. Dodge shielded McPherson's rear, repulsed Hardee's leading two divisions, and forced Hardee to strike the flank, not rear, of Frank P. Blair, Jr.'s, corps, protected by field entrenchments. Blair parried the first Rebel strikes, but Hood still ordered repeated hopeless assaults that gained nothing but cost horrible casualties. He lost 8,500 men to the Federals' 3,700, including McPherson, who was killed. Hood was forced to fall back into the Atlanta entrenchments.

Sherman did not have enough men to besiege Atlanta. His plan was to cut off the railway lines and, threatening starvation, to force the Confederates to evacuate the city. The railroad to Augusta was already broken, and Sherman now moved McPherson's army under its new commander, Oliver O. Howard, around Atlanta to cut Hood's last remaining rail connections, the line running southwest to Montgomery and the one southeast to Macon.

On July 28, Howard's army had just taken up positions near Ezra Church, a couple miles west of Atlanta, when Hood launched a frontal attack against it with a division. Howard's men had erected a rough breastwork of logs and were able to halt the blow. Hood brought up two more divisions and renewed the vain direct assaults, finally losing 4,600 men to Howard's 700. This third terrible defeat undermined the morale of the Rebel soldiers. Even in the first onslaught it was clear the men had lost their former élan. Hood, by his wrongheaded tactics, was well on the way to destroying his army.

Although Sherman attempted to seize East Point, seven miles south of Atlanta, junction of the Montgomery and Macon railways, delays gave Hood enough time to strengthen the East Point works and protect the railways. The situation began to look unpleasantly like a stalemate, since Hood had been upbraided by President Davis for his direct assaults and could no longer be induced into attacks.

Now almost the entire Rebel cavalry force, under Joseph Wheeler, began long-range raids to break Sherman's railroad connection to Chattanooga, cutting several points between Marietta and Dalton. Sherman discovered, however, that Wheeler did not intend to keep the line broken, which would have forced Sherman to send back a major relief expedition to open it. Instead, he rode into Tennessee, hoping to cut rail lines there and induce Sherman to retreat. This had no hope of success. Men on horseback presented a large and easy target for rifle-firing infantry. To fight infantry, cavalry had to dismount, thereby losing their mobility. Cavalry consequently had to adopt a hit-and-run policy, because enemy infantry guarding rail lines could soon surround and destroy any static cavalry force.

With Wheeler gone, Sherman was able to repair the line back to Chattanooga, where he had a large stock of food and other goods already assembled, thereby relieving him of anxiety about supplies.

With the Rebel cavalry force unavailable to discover Federal movements, Sherman also was able to swing most of his army below Atlanta on August 28, destroy several miles of the Montgomery railroad, and on August 31 approach Jonesboro, on the Macon railroad, twenty miles south of Atlanta, with the intention of breaking this line as well. On this day Hardee, in command of two corps, obligingly launched another hopeless Confederate attack, suffering heavy losses against Federals behind hastily erected field fortifications.

Hood decided irrationally that a direct attack on Atlanta was imminent and drew all his forces back to the city except Hardee's corps, which he ordered to protect Macon. Hardee retreated eight miles south to Lovejoy, while Sherman's men broke the railway. Atlanta was now isolated. Hood realized he no longer could hold the city and on September 1 ordered the retreat, moving most of his forces southeast, then west to join Hardee. On September 2, Sherman telegraphed Washington: "So Atlanta is ours and fairly won." The news electrified the Union, revived hope of victory, made Lincoln's reelection a certainty, and sealed the fate of the South.

General Sherman had resolved to convince the Southern people that "war and individual ruin are synonymous terms" and set about at once to demonstrate his intentions. He ordered the entire population of Atlanta to evacuate, forcing men, women, and children out of the city by way of a station, Rough and Ready, just south of Atlanta. Homeless, destitute civilians spread across Georgia, seeking shelter, food, and comfort. Many suffered great privation. Although Sherman did not want to commit the troops necessary to garrison a populated Atlanta, his real purpose was to punish every Southerner he could reach for seeking to leave the Union. "If they want peace," he wired Washington, "they and their relatives must stop war."

In allowing plunder, arson, and destruction of the farms of northern Georgia and in his vindictive act against the entire population of Atlanta, Sherman demonstrated his intent to destroy the wealth and if possible ruin the lives of all Southerners in his path. He was to expand this program in the months ahead into a vendetta of organized ruination that had no parallel in modern history. He thus struck at the South's most vulnerable element and ultimately broke the will of the people to pursue the war.

Sherman had already decided on his next move after capturing Atlanta: to march to the sea, living off the country and destroying everything in his path. His target would be either Savannah, 220 air miles away, or Charleston, 260 miles distant. At either point, Union ships could resupply his army. At Atlanta he was 450 miles from his real base of supplies, Louisville, and dependent on a single railroad that could be cut by Confederate raiders almost anywhere.

General Hood had no inkling of Sherman's radical idea, and in late September, supported by President Davis, he turned his back on Sherman's army and planned to march into Tennessee, seize Nashville, sever Federal rail connections with Louisville, and force Sherman to abandon Georgia by cutting off his supplies. First, however, Hood's soldiers raided up the railway to Chattanooga, broke the line between Allatoona and Marietta, and moved north to Dalton. But Hood did not intend to invade Tennessee through the northern Georgia mountains, where there was little food, but turned west to Gadsden, Alabama, preparatory to moving more directly on Nashville. Meantime the Confederate raider Nathan Bedford Forrest frightened the Union garrison at Athens, Alabama, into surrendering and rode into middle Tennessee.

Sherman pursued Hood with most of his army but realized that to continue doing so into Alabama would play into the Confederate game to draw him away from Georgia. Accordingly, he called off his pursuit, sent General Thomas back to Nashville to protect Tennessee, and transferred to his command Thomas's army, Schofield's force, and all the cavalry except a 5,000-man division under Judson Kilpatrick. In all, Thomas had about 71,000 men, with another corps en route from St. Louis. Sherman was left with four corps and Kilpatrick's horsemen, about 60,000 men in all.

On October 9, 1864, he wired Grant: "It will be a physical impossibility to protect the roads, now that Hood, Forrest, and Wheeler and the whole bunch of devils are turned loose without home or habitation. . . . I propose we break up the railroad from Chattanooga and strike out with wagons for Milledgeville, Millen, and Savannah. Until we can repopulate Georgia, it is useless to occupy it, but the utter destruction of its roads, houses, and people will cripple their military resources. By attempting to hold the railroads we will lose 1,000 men monthly and will gain no result. I can make the march and make Georgia howl."

Grant reluctantly agreed to Sherman's plan but had misgivings, especially after President Lincoln, who had almost no understanding of military strategy, complained that "a misstep by General Sherman might be fatal to his army."

Neither Grant nor Lincoln recognized, as did Sherman, that President Davis and Hood had committed an irretrievable error in expecting to pull the Federal army out of Georgia merely by marching on Sherman's communications. Instead, Hood's departure opened a virtually uncontested road to Savannah. Only a few state militia and cavalry stood between him and the sea. If Hood had relied on Forrest to break Sherman's railway and had barred an advance into Georgia with his army, he might not have stopped all of Sherman's columns but he very likely could have destroyed one or more, seriously threatening Sherman's campaign.

Hood, whose army now numbered about 31,000 men, moved far to the west in order to get closer to Forrest's cavalry force of about 7,500. On October 31 he gained a foothold across the Tennessee River at Florence, Alabama, 150 miles west of Chattanooga, but there his advance halted for three weeks because of lack of supplies. Hood's move clinched Sherman's resolve to march on Savannah, because the Confederate army now was so far west it had no possibility of countering him.

Grant wired Sherman on November 1, casting new doubt on Sherman's plan. "Do you not think it advisable now that Hood has gone so far north to entirely settle with him before starting on your proposed campaign?" Grant asked. Sherman responded with patience that pursuit of Hood would be like chasing a will-o'-the-wisp. He would withdraw southwestward, "drawing me as a decoy from Georgia, which is his chief object," Sherman wired. Grant now dubiously endorsed Sherman's project, consoling himself that Thomas, with over twice Hood's strength, had enough troops to destroy his army.

Sherman now moved with alacrity, repairing the breaks in the railroad Hood's men had made, sending back into Tennessee all his sick and wounded and bringing forward supplies for his march, then destroying the railroad as far back as Allatoona and the bridge over the Etowah River.

Sherman divided his army into two wings, each of two corps, the right under Oliver O. Howard, the left under Henry Warner Slocum, while Kilpatrick's cavalry were directly under Sherman. Each corps, its transportation pared to the bone, was to move on a separate road. The army carried 200 rounds of ammunition per man and per cannon and twenty days of rations. But the rations were only for emergencies, for Sherman authorized his troops to live off the country. From the beginning the distinction between foraging and pillaging was lost, for Sherman intended to destroy everything of value as his army passed.

General Hardee was in command of the few troops the Confederates had to throw in front of the march. The only immediate force was 7,000 men, composed mainly of Wheeler's cavalry, who had returned from Tennessee, and Georgia militia with little fighting potential. There were about 12,000 more men in various garrisons in Georgia, South Carolina, and Florida. The Georgia government, from the capital of Milledgeville, proclaimed a *levée en masse* of all able-bodied men to defend the soil, but this was a gesture of despair and little came of it. Hardee did not adopt his best policy, which would have been to disperse his slender forces into guerrilla bands to harass the Union forces. Sherman feared such a tactic, saying ambushes could kill nearly every Union officer.

Just prior to the start of the march, on November 15, 1864, the Federals burned the business part of Atlanta—machine shops, mills, warehouses, and stores—and then abandoned the city.

The march itself confused the Confederates greatly. With four columns moving on widely separated routes, sometimes fifty miles apart, they could not determine Sherman's actual target. The right wing appeared to be aiming at Macon but actually passed north of it, while the left wing created the impression it was moving on Augusta. According to Sherman, this placed the enemy "on the horns of a dilemma." As the eighteenth-century French strategist Pierre de Bourcet proposed in his "plan with branches," by threatening alternative targets Sherman forced the enemy to keep troops protecting both Macon and Augusta, leaving a clear avenue for Sherman to march directly between them and seize Milledgeville on November 22.

Rebel forces at Macon swung around to Savannah, while Wheeler's cavalry barely got ahead of the Union columns. Confederate General Braxton Bragg rushed to Augusta to take supreme charge of the campaign. He had about 10,000 men there.

On November 24, Sherman departed Milledgeville, sending Kilpatrick's horsemen to the left flank to convey the impression the spearhead was aiming at Augusta. This kept Bragg in place and unable to intervene when Kilpatrick swerved southeast to cut the Savannah-Augusta railway. Wheeler nearly foiled this effort, but Kilpatrick, gaining support of some Union infantry, drove Wheeler back sharply, forcing the Rebel cavalry to follow in the wake of the Union forces, doing little damage, for the rest of the march.

Kilpatrick's feint to the northeast gave almost free passage for the rest of the Union forces to Millen on December 9.

By now a path of desolation 200 miles long and as much as 60 miles wide had been cut through the center of Georgia. Houses, barns, and other buildings were burned, crops eaten or destroyed, cattle and horses seized, the people reduced to destitution. Behind the pillaging army ranged another army of freed slaves, excited and eager to follow the Federals wherever they went. The Federals were not happy with this clog of humanity and removed a pontoon bridge over a large stream to keep them from crossing. A great crowd of blacks, however, stampeded down the bank and into the stream, where many drowned.

At Savannah, General Hardee had gathered 15,000 Confederates, but his orders were to abandon the city rather than sacrifice the troops.

As Sherman's army approached the city on December 10, he moved first on Fort McAllister, south of the city. Its formidable defenses on the ocean side barred contact with the Union fleet offshore, but Sherman calculated correctly that its landward defenses were weak, and the Federals captured the fort in a quick assault.

Sherman opened communications with the Union navy and found an order awaiting him from Grant to fortify a base on the coast, leave his artillery and cavalry, and transport the bulk of his infantry to Virginia to help in the campaign against Lee! This astonishing order demonstrates Grant's lack of strategic insight. Sherman's army would be far more devastating if it advanced on Lee's rear through the Carolinas than if it were brought around to attack him frontally.

Sherman was disappointed at Grant's command but replied he would come directly as sea transport arrived. But, anxious to seize Savannah beforehand, he tried to bluff Hardee into surrendering. Hardee refused but retreated northward into South

Carolina on December 20, abandoning the city to the Federals.

Sherman's march to the sea sent a deep wave of gloom over the South, demonstrating that the Confederacy could not protect its territory or its people. The people's faith in their government and their cause suffered a near-mortal blow. Sherman had been right: the quickest way to end the war was to attack the people's will to wage it.

While Sherman was closing in on Savannah, Confederate general Hood advanced on Union general Thomas at Nashville. Hood was propelled by desperation. He had made the wrong decision in marching his army away, opening the door to Savannah and to destruction of central Georgia. Now the only chance he had of pulling Sherman out of Georgia was to seize Nashville or defeat Thomas badly. Yet he had little hope of either with an army half the size of Thomas's and morally shaken by its terrible losses.

Moreover, Hood—despite the disasters his army had suffered against Sherman—had still not learned that frontal attacks against entrenched positions were a recipe for destruction.

Accordingly, when he came up November 30 on Schofield's isolated force at Franklin, twenty miles south of Nashville, he threw his men in repeated frontal assaults against the Federal entrenchments. The attacks failed utterly and cost him 4,500 men, triple the losses of the Northern defenders. This was the final blow to Confederate morale, for the men realized Hood's tactics were destroying them.

Schofield withdrew to Nashville, where the entire Federal army had concentrated. It was folly for Hood to follow, but he did, lacking the understanding that his army had been crippled and that to bring it within the reach of the Federal army was almost certain to complete its ruin. He might have achieved real gains if, instead, he had slipped past Thomas and menaced Kentucky and the Ohio Valley.

Thomas struck on December 15, throwing the bulk of his army against the left flank of the entrenched Confederate line, forcing Hood to a shorter line two miles south. Despite the fact that Thomas, too, had launched a frontal attack, his losses were only 1,000 men, demonstrating that the Rebels no longer were fighting with their former resolve. Indeed, the roads to the south were filled with Southern stragglers.

The next day a sudden Federal infantry attack on a weakened part of the Confederate line was a signal for a general collapse of the entire army. About 4,500 Rebels fell prisoner, but the bulk got away to the south, finally halting at Tupelo, Mississippi, where the shattered forces were reorganized under new leadership.

Even before he had captured Savannah, Sherman set about to persuade Grant to rescind his order to move Sherman's infantry to Virginia. On December 17 he asked permission to march north through the Carolinas and especially to punish South Carolina—the first state to secede from the Union and a particular object of Sherman's enmity.

He had an ally in Henry W. Halleck, chief of staff of the Union Army, who wrote Sherman: "Should you capture Charleston, I hope that by *some accident* the place may be destroyed, and, if a little salt should be sown upon its site, it may prevent the growth of future crops of nullification and secession." Sherman responded to Halleck: "The whole army is burning with an insatiable desire to wreak vengeance upon South Carolina. I almost tremble at her fate."

Grant at last agreed to Sherman's plan, not because he understood the strategic advantage of cutting through the remaining heart of the Confederacy and onto the rear of Lee but because he had learned it would take transports two months to bring Sherman's army to Virginia.

Sherman adopted another "plan with branches" to reduce the Carolinas. He had left Augusta untouched on purpose to confuse the Rebels as to his objective—Augusta or Charleston. When the march northward of his 60,000-man army commenced on February 1, 1865, Sherman aimed one wing at Charleston, the other at Augusta. As had happened in the march through Georgia, this placed the Confederates "on the horns of a dilemma" because it induced them to divide their 33,000 men to protect alternate targets. Instead, Sherman marched *between* the two cities on Columbia, the South Carolina capital, capturing it on February 16.

Confederate looters caused some damage during the evacuation, but drunken Union soldiers and a desire for vengeance on the part of the Federal leadership led to much burning and arson. A gale wind that came up during the night of February 17 turned these separate fires into an inferno that burned half the city, leaving thousands homeless.

Sherman's march on Columbia separated the Confederate forces and prevented any chance of the two halves uniting. As a consequence, the Rebels were unable to assemble a strong enough force to challenge Sherman's army. In addition, the march on Columbia severed the main railroads to Charleston and compelled the Confederates to abandon the port city on February 15. The senior Rebel commander, Pierre G. T. Beauregard, ordered his scattered forces to assemble at Chester, forty-five miles north of Columbia, to protect Charlotte, North Carolina, and the railroads leading to Richmond.

But Sherman sent his army northeast in numerous wide-spreading columns through Cheraw, South Carolina, to Fayetteville, North Carolina, with the intention of moving on northeastward to Goldsboro, where a corps of 21,000 men under Schofield had been sent by way of New Bern, a North Carolina port that the Federals had held since 1861. At Goldsboro, Sherman expected to resupply his army.

The Confederates, once more finding themselves out of position, were unable to interpose any effective forces to block Sherman's progress, although the remains of Hood's army at Tupelo, Mississippi, had been rushed through Georgia by way of Augusta to reinforce the Confederates.

In the crisis, President Davis reinstated Joseph E. Johnston as supreme commander. Johnston realized the only way to stop Sherman was to exploit the central position between the two Union armies that the Confederate forces possessed. To do so, Lee had to bring down a substantial portion of his army from Virginia and unite with Johnston's 40,000 men. The now-superior Confederate army could defeat Sherman, then turn back on Grant. Sherman had feared this strategy from the start of the Carolinas campaign, questioning whether Lee "would permit us, almost unopposed, to pass through the states of South and North Carolina, cutting off and consuming the very supplies on which he depended to feed his army" and remarking that "if Lee is a soldier of genius, he will seek to transfer his army from Richmond to Raleigh or Columbia; if he is a man simply of detail, he will remain where he is, and his speedy defeat is sure."[1]

Johnston proposed such a strategy to Lee on March 1, 1865, but Lee replied he was unwilling to turn against Sherman until the Federals had reached the Roanoke River, only fifty-five miles south of Petersburg. This demonstrated Lee's lack of strategic vision and eliminated any possibility of defeating Sherman.

Yet Lee recognized that Sherman's march was rapidly destroying his own army. He had written the governor of North Carolina on February 24: "The state of despondency that now prevails among our people is producing a bad effect upon the troops. Desertions are becoming very frequent and there is good reason to believe that they are occasioned to a considerable extent by letters written to soldiers by their friends at home . . . that our cause is hopeless and that they had better provide for themselves."

Sherman crossed the Cape Fear River at Fayetteville on March 15, feinting temporarily north with his left wing in the direction of Raleigh to make Johnston and Hardee, the Rebel commander on the spot, believe that the North Carolina capital was his objective, while actually moving his entire army northeast on Goldsboro.

Lee, realizing his supply depots in eastern North Carolina were in danger of being overrun, wired Johnston on March 14 that unless Johnston could strike a blow against Sherman, Lee's army would be forced to evacuate Petersburg. This spurred Johnston to seek battle. To prevent being overwhelmed by superior numbers, Johnston had to catch one part of Sherman's army out of reach of the rest. Getting word from his cavalry on March 17 that Goldsboro was the Union objective and that Sherman's left wing had turned in that direction, Johnston set his army in motion for Bentonville, ten miles west of Golds-

1. Liddell Hart, *Sherman: Soldier, Realist, American,* 356; Sherman, 271.

boro, where he hoped to intercept its march. He believed Sherman's right wing was moving along routes well away to the east. In choosing Bentonville, Johnston unwittingly invited disaster, for this crossroads was the very point Sherman had selected for his two wings to converge!

Johnston, however, beat the Federals to Bentonville, because his roads were better and heavy rains delayed the Federal advance. The two lead divisions of the Union left wing were still eight miles short of Bentonville on the night of March 18, while the other two divisions were eight miles farther back. Meanwhile the right wing, marching on roads to the east, was behind the left wing.

Sherman, believing the Rebels were concentrating to protect Raleigh, ordered the right wing to move directly on Goldsboro instead of turning north to Bentonville. Consequently, the two lead divisions of his left wing under General Jeff. C. Davis were alone when they reached Bentonville at midday on March 19 and bumped into a long line of Confederate entrenchments. The Union troops tried to carry the enemy lines but found they were ominously strong and hurriedly dug in. Johnston's right arm under Hardee enfolded the Federal line, rolling back Davis's left flank, but Johnston's left had been stunned by Davis's initial attack and the commander there, Braxton Bragg, called for reinforcements. Johnston sent over a division that otherwise might have swept behind Davis's left and caused disaster. This gave time for part of the left wing's other two divisions, under A. S. Williams, to come up and form a solid line.

By nightfall the Confederate attack had clearly failed, and Johnston, realizing the remainder of Sherman's army would be arriving, drew his army into a convex semicircular defensive position, seeking only to remove his wounded before retreating northwest toward Smithfield.

Meanwhile Sherman had turned his right wing toward Bentonville, seeking to frighten Johnston back, not to attack, because his main objective was Goldsboro, junction with Schofield, and replenishment of supplies, which had run dangerously low. Although a division of the right wing made a deep penetration into the Confederate position, Sherman ordered it back, and Johnston was able to get his army away.

Sherman continued into Goldsboro and completed the

greatest march in history through enemy territory, 425 miles. Sherman's march had cut the heart out of the Confederacy, in both a physical and a moral sense. The denouement now came quickly, for Lee's army in Virginia was ready to collapse at the first heavy blow. The disintegration of this army was partly because of the strain of trench life at Petersburg and partly increasing hunger as Sherman's advance contracted Confederate supply sources. But the greatest reason was letters from home, which reflected the despair and helplessness of families and friends who had watched Sherman's unchecked progress and witnessed the destruction of their property. Soldiers in this situation turned to their fundamental loyalty, their families, and deserted in great numbers to get home to protect those dearest to them as best they might.

On March 29, Union general Philip H. Sheridan's cavalry threatened Lee's right south of Petersburg, and the next day Grant turned this threat into an infantry stroke, overthrowing a Confederate detachment. On April 2 a general Federal assault broke into the outer defenses of Petersburg, forcing Lee's withdrawal and his surrender at Appomattox on April 9. This led to Johnston's surrender at Greensboro, North Carolina, on April 26.

The Civil War ended, and Sherman's strategy of indirect attack had gained the victory. Unless he had seized Atlanta before the presidential election, Lincoln would not have been reelected. And the march through Georgia and the Carolinas destroyed the South's will to continue the war.

But Sherman's remorseless pattern of deliberate *personal* injury to the Southern people sowed seeds of hate that were to bear bitter fruit. If the purpose of war is to bring about a more perfect peace, Sherman failed dismally. The memory of the damage he and his men did was passed from parent to child throughout the South for a century after the Civil War. Sherman's march evoked an enduring folk memory of wanton havoc that embittered the Southern people against the North, the Republican Party, and the national government for generations. This was why the South remained "solid" in voting Democratic for many years and why an element of distrust exists to this day against a federal government that could have perpetrated such violence against part of its own people.

6

Palestine 1918

BREAKING THE DEADLOCK OF
TRENCH WARFARE

ONE CAMPAIGN WAS FOUGHT in World War I that demonstrated that the generals commanding the armies could have found means to win the war other than beating their heads against the impervious entrenchments of the western front in France and Flanders. This was the Palestine campaign of 1917–18, which ended in the destruction of three Turkish armies, the capture of Arabia, Palestine, Syria, and Mesopotamia, and the abrupt withdrawal of Turkey from the war.

The Palestine campaign was one of the most decisive in history, yet was fought with miniuscule forces compared to the millions deployed in France and Flanders. The campaign also showed that great advances can be made with extremely small casualties.

The Palestine campaign demonstrated that a commander—by audacity and mobility—could overcome the superiority of the defensive over the offensive that had marked warfare since the American Civil War and that turned the war on the western front into a stalemate that produced millions of casualties.

Between the end of the Civil War in 1865 and the outbreak of World War I in 1914, technology revolutionized the material factors of Western civilization and, with them, the weapons of warfare.

By the Civil War most countries possessed the railroad, which immensely increased the mobility of people and the delivery of goods, and the electric telegraph, which made communication between distant points almost instantaneous.

By World War I, Western civilization had developed the automobile powered by the internal-combustion engine, which permitted much greater mobility over roads; the airplane, which raised warfare from the surface dimensions of length and breadth to the third dimension of depth, and the radio telegraph, which by 1901 permitted communication between continents and virtually elevated warfare to the fourth dimension, since it destroyed time as well as space.

Other developments radically altered military weapons specifically. The Civil War had been largely fought with the single-shot muzzle-loaded rifle. By World War I, inventors had perfected the high-velocity bolt-action magazine rifle with brass cartridges and the machine gun. The magazine rifle increased the range of cartridges by several hundred yards, but its greatest impact was to triple or quadruple the rate of infantry fire. The machine gun did even more: a single weapon could produce as much fire as 1,000 riflemen.

The addition of smokeless powder permitted infantry for the first time to remain concealed when delivering fire. When these developments were added to the entrenchments and other field fortifications that had protected troops so effectively in the Civil War, the strength of the defense increased enormously at the expense of the offense.

A similar transformation occurred in field artillery. Although the long-range rifled cannon had been developed prior to the Civil War, its effectiveness was limited by often-imperfect fuses and gunpowder. By 1914, inventors had developed far better fuses, smokeless explosives much more powerful than gunpowder, and a method by which artillery could be fired from concealed positions.[1]

1. Indirect laying of artillery became possible with the development of the goniometric or panoramic sight, which permitted guns, wherever located, to be sighted accurately by aligning them on a known base point. A battery could be hidden at any place from which it could hit enemy positions. It could fire indirectly by calculating the azimuth, or clockwise angle of deflection measured from the north, from the

Firing cannon from concealed positions revolutionized the use of artillery, because infantry fire no longer could reach it. Now artillery could shatter a selected point on the enemy line before the enemy could halt the barrage with counterbattery fire. This turned artillery into the most powerful weapon on the battlefield and reversed the situation in the Civil War. In 1861–65 the most effective cannon were smoothbores deployed in the open close to the enemy and charged with canister or case, which riddled a wide swath of enemy infantry with deadly metal balls and fragments. Such smoothbores were vulnerable to enemy sharpshooters, who could kill or wound gunners and horses.

At the start of World War I the French were not impressed with the effectiveness of massed artillery, although it had been proved in the Russo-Japanese War of 1904–5, and they ignored the fact that the magazine rifle and the machine gun had vastly increased the power of the defense over the offense.

Their doctrine, soon to lead to disaster, was the *offensive à outrance* or headlong attack. They expected soldiers to advance in the open for the last 400 yards and to drive the enemy out of his entrenchments with the bayonet. They did not like howitzers, which have a high trajectory to drop shells directly on top of enemy troops and emplacements. Instead, they had developed a mobile, quick-firing 75-millimeter field gun with a flat trajectory, which they intended to bring along with their

---

battery to a hill, clump of trees, or other terrain feature in enemy territory that could be located on a map and the distance to it measured and that also could be seen by a forward observer. Using the bearing and distance as shown on the map, gunners could determine by triangulation the approximate range and deflection for a shell to reach this base point. Gunners could adjust range by elevating or depressing the barrel and increasing or decreasing the explosive charge. They could move fire horizontally by traversing the gun barrel left or right. When a gun dropped a shell on or near the base point, the forward observer, using field glasses or telescope, could observe the explosion, then send back orders to the gun to move fire right or left and add or drop range. Once the range and deflection to this base point had been established, the forward observer could shift fire to an actual enemy target by adding or subtracting range and by deflection left or right. Thereupon numerous cannon, using the same range and deflection, could bombard the target.

infantry to break up enemy field fortifications with direct fire. Although the Germans adopted the heavy howitzer, they did not initially see the advantages of keeping their artillery hidden in the rear. As the war progressed, however, they changed their minds, and the French followed suit, since both experienced immense losses when they deployed cannons in the open.

The French believed the Germans would advance through the difficult terrain of the Ardennes Forest of Luxembourg and southeastern Belgium, remaining east of the Meuse River, which runs northward some forty miles east of Brussels. The French placed two armies to strike this expected German advance in the flank and cut enemy communications, while two more French armies were to advance immediately into the German center in Lorraine, in the vicinity of Metz and Thionville.

The Germans had no intention of so conveniently playing into the hands of the French and had developed the Schlieffen Plan, named after Count Alfred von Schlieffen, German chief of staff from 1891 to 1906. Schlieffen conceived an enormous enveloping movement, concentrating the mass of the German army on the right wing and wheeling through the plains of Belgium and northern France, crossing the Seine River near Rouen, circling around south of Paris, and turning northward to destroy from the rear the French armies in Lorraine and against the Swiss frontier.

The greatness of this plan rested on Schlieffen's distribution of force. Of the seventy-two German divisions to be available, fifty-three were to be allocated to the wheeling movement, ten were to form a pivot facing Verdun, and only nine were to hold the left or eastern wing along the French frontier. The plan was to weaken the German left to such a degree that the French would attack in Lorraine and press the German left wing back toward the Rhine River. The farther the French advanced toward the Rhine, the more difficult it would be for them to extricate their armies when the German pincer swept around onto their rear.

Schlieffen's successor, Helmuth von Moltke, did not understand the plan and, by radically altering the distribution of forces, ultimately destroyed it. He increased the left wing disproportionately to the right, and when the French offensive developed into Lorraine in August 1914, he diverted six new divisions to the left wing, giving the commander there, Prince Rupprecht of Bavaria, sufficient strength to take the offensive instead of retreating, as the Schlieffen Plan called for.

The Germans quickly shattered with terrible losses the opening French offensive, and Rupprecht threw the French back on their fortified frontier. This, however, increased the power of resistance of the French and permitted them to transfer troops westward to counter the German wheeling movement.

Moltke also diverted seven divisions of the right wing to stand guard over Antwerp, Givet, and Maubeuge, which had not surrendered, and four to reinforce the East Prussian front against the Russians. These transfers reduced the extreme right wing, the 1st Army under Alexander von Kluck, to just thirteen divisions against twenty-seven French and British divisions on this decisive flank.

The final destruction of the Schlieffen Plan occurred when Moltke approved a decision by Kluck to move southeastward in aid the German 2d Army and to abandon the decisive southwestward march around Paris. Kluck now was driving east of Paris, with his right flank exposed to the French forces on the extreme west. This led to the French-British attack on his flank on September 5, 1914, and the battle of the Marne, which halted the offensive and threw the Germans onto the defensive.

Thereafter came the "race to the sea" as each side tried to go around the other's western flank. The result was a continuous line of entrenchments stretching from Switzerland to the coast of Belgium and the end of mobility on the western front. In the face of field fortificiations, rifles, machine guns, and massed artillery, neither side could open enough space to reinstitute a war of movement.

The French and British attempted to break the deadlock by direct attack. They generally gave away tactical surprise by prolonged "warning" artillery bombardments and their frontal assaults invariably failed, although the losses in dead and wounded were astronomical. The Germans remained on the defensive, except for an attempt in 1916 to take Verdun, another direct attack, which failed, and a final offensive in 1918, which also failed. A stalemate accordingly developed that lasted for four years.

Although British and French commanders in France and Flanders still believed they could reach a decision by direct attacks, more objective leaders realized this was not possible and looked for other means of victory.

They saw an opening in late October 1914, when Turkey entered the war on the German and Austrian side. Turkey hoped to regain much of its empire, especially Egypt, occupied by Britain in 1882 to protect the Suez Canal, and to guard against the Russian desire to seize the Dardanelles, the sea connection between the Black and Mediterranean seas.

Turkey retained Anatolia, Mesopotamia, Syria, Palestine, and the Hejaz, the western part of the Arabian peninsula, including the Islamic holy cities of Medina and Mecca. Turkey's belligerency served German interests by opening a front against Russia in the Caucasus and in threats to the Suez Canal from the Sinai desert.

The British minister of munitions, David Lloyd George, had lost faith in the possibility of breaking through the western front and proposed transferring most of the British army to the Balkans and advancing through the enemy's "back door."

A French general, J. S. Galliéni, advocated a landing at Salonika, Greece, and a march on Constantinople with an army strong enough to induce Greece and Bulgaria to join the Allies (Britain, France, Russia). Capture of Constantinople and the Dardanelles would open a supply line to Russia and offer an opportunity to advance up the Danube River into Austria-Hungary.

In early 1915, however, Allied generals in France successfully thwarted the proposals to focus on the Balkans. Nevertheless, Winston Churchill, first lord of the British Admiralty, helped to push through a plan to seize the Dardanelles. This campaign, beginning April 25, 1915, ultimately failed because commanders on the spot did not seize opportunities that initial Turkish unpreparedness offered them.

The Dardanelles failure ended any strategic effort to go around the stalemated lines of the western front. Though Allied forces ultimately occupied Salonika, Greece, and advanced on

Austria-Hungary in the last months of the war, the campaign came too late to be decisive.[2]

Until 1917, Britain's Egyptian Expeditionary Force under General Sir Archibald Murray had achieved little against a combined Turkish and German force, which had faced the British in the Sinai desert for two and a half years. The campaign settled into a stalemate along a line of entrenchments from Gaza on the Mediterranean to the water wells of Beersheba, at the foot of the mountains thirty air miles to the southeast.

Along this line, cut across the desert, conditions were terrible: high temperatures often reaching 110 degrees Fahrenheit, dust storms, little shade, difficulties of supply, and a great dearth of water. Murray alleviated the latter two conditions somewhat by building a railway and a water pipeline from the Suez Canal to Gaza. But the troops were disillusioned and angry because Murray had no idea how to break the deadlock, kept his headquarters in the comfort of the Savoy Hotel in Cairo, and gave awards for gallant services to members of his large headquarters staff, many of whom had never seen the front.

One of the few achievements during Murray's command was the British-instigated Arab Revolt against the Turks, which began June 10, 1916, under Hussein, Sharif of Mecca and leader of the Hejaz region of western Arabia. The Arabs, under three of Hussein's sons, Ali, Feisal, and Zeid, had some initial success, but a Turkish force repulsed them and the Arabs became annoyed at lack of support from the British.

Ronald Storrs, a British diplomat, was sent in October 1916 to discuss the matter with the Arabs, and T. E. Lawrence (1888–1935), a British intelligence officer in Cairo, received permission to go along. Thenceforward the revolt came to be associated more and more with him. Lawrence had received first-class honors at Oxford University in history in 1910 for a thesis on Crusader castles in Syria and Palestine and had been on a secret project mapping the Sinai peninsula for military purposes just prior to the war.

2. The war was actually won by the British naval blockade, which so reduced imports to Germany that the people were threatened with starvation.

T. E. LAWRENCE

UPI/Bettmann

Lawrence was impressed with Feisal and sized up the military situation with great acumen, recommending that money, weapons, and a few British officers be sent to Feisal but no Allied troops. He believed the proud Arabs would fight better on their own as guerrillas than with European troops, who would consider them second-class soldiers. Murray, who wanted to keep all his forces in Egypt and Palestine, favored this recommendation and sent Lawrence back to the Hejaz.

Lawrence worked on a joint expedition to capture the port of Wejh (Al Wagh) on the Red Sea, 400 air miles northwest of Mecca. A force under Feisal and Lawrence was to attack the port from the interior while six British warships with Arab infantry and British marines assaulted it from the sea. Despite an arduous march through the desert, Feisal's men arrived too late, after the seaborne attack had already seized Wejh. This seemed to confirm suspicions by professional army officers that the Arabs were unreliable, and Lawrence and a few attached British officers began training Feisal's men to carry out military duties more proficiently.

On advice of the British, the Arabs' attention now centered on breaking Turkish hold on the railway that ran down to Medina from Damascus, Syria, the sole means of supply for the Turkish army in the Hejaz. To establish a base from which to operate guerrilla teams against this railway, Lawrence conceived the idea of seizing the port of Aqaba, at the northern end of the Red Sea, 250 air miles northwest of Wejh. Instead of marching directly against Aqaba, however, Lawrence and Feisal undertook a long and extremely difficult roundabout 800-mile journey through deserts considered to be impassable and descended from the rear on July 6, 1917, achieving complete surprise and quickly capturing the port.

This superb strategic move gave the Arabs a firm base and transformed a liaison officer with the Arab army into Lawrence of Arabia, the active leader of the revolt.

The capture of Aqaba came only a few days after the general who was to develop and carry out the Palestine campaign, Sir Edmund Allenby, arrived at Cairo to replace Murray as supreme commander.

Allenby (1861–1936), a professional soldier who had com-

SIR EDMUND ALLENBY

Imperial War Museum

manded the British 3d Army in France, had given little evidence that he possessed strategic views radically different from those of the senior Allied generals on the western front. These officers were convinced the war could be won only by defeating the Germans in head-on battles in France and Flanders. But Allenby had seen the futility of direct assaults, and A. P. Wavell, a brilliant liaison officer who came to know the new Palestine commander well, wrote that Allenby was not wedded to the obsession, which dominated the War Office in London and headquarters in France, that the best place to attack the enemy was at his strongest point.

Lloyd George, who became British prime minister in late 1916, insisted that the military consider ways of getting around the barrier of the western front. He pushed for a campaign against Turkey to press against Germany's and Austria's back door. Although the army leadership considered Palestine a sideshow, they humored Lloyd George and put forward Allenby as commander.

Allenby walked into the ornate Savoy Hotel in Cairo on June 28, 1917, and began almost immediate changes. He sent home a large number of staff officers, a few elderly colonels, one division commander, and the chief of his general staff. Within days he visited the troops on the Gaza line, over 200 miles from Cairo. Soon thereafter he moved general headquarters from the Savoy to a point in the desert just behind the battle line.

Shortly after the capture of Aqaba, T. E. Lawrence rode across the Sinai desert to Cairo. Allenby, impressed with Lawrence's feat, received him, in his flowing Arab robes, and accepted Lawrence's proposals to turn Aqaba into an important base and to supply equipment and gold to bring about Arab advance northward into Syria. He promoted Lawrence to major and ordered Feisal's force to form the right wing of his own army, bringing Lawrence and Feisal directly under his control.

Lawrence and Allenby departed with one misunderstanding. Lawrence, as part of an effort to determine whether "a war might be won without fighting battles," intended to make hit-and-run attacks on the Hejaz railway, keeping it barely open so the Turkish troops at Medina could just survive. Allenby, more conventional, wanted the railway cut. Lawrence was correct.

The Turks were determined to keep the Hejaz railway open for reasons of prestige, politics, and religion and exerted a great deal of strength they could ill afford to maintain a large garrison in Medina and to guard track and bridges against Arab raids. Allenby's immediate task was to crack the Gaza line and force the Turks and Germans beyond Jerusalem. There were three possibilities. He could attack directly into the main enemy defensive position at Gaza along the Mediterranean; he could strike in the center; or he could advance on Beersheba, on the extreme right. Allenby quickly discarded a center attack because there was practically no water there. He also discarded an attack at Gaza because, being the most obvious point, it was where the Turks expected the British to advance, since their left or seaward flank could be guarded by the Allied ships, which controlled the sea, and their main line of communications with Egypt ended just behind the Gaza line.

This left Beersheba. But this deep into the desert and far from the pipeline from the Nile at Gaza, the need for water was imperative. There were ample wells at Beersheba, but if the British could not capture them in the first hours of the attack, the Turks might destroy them and force the British to retreat.

Allenby's solution was masterful: he made obvious preparations for an attack at Gaza, drawing enemy attention to the point where they expected the offensive anyway. But this was entirely sham.

Allenby also summoned Lawrence from Arabia and directed him to break the railway bridge over the Yarmuk River east of the Sea of Galilee (Lake Tiberias). This would cut the only railway line serving Palestine and might force withdrawal of the Turko-German armies into Syria. Lawrence made a determined effort, getting to the Yarmuk gorge on a moonless night and setting explosives. But one of the Arabs dropped his rifle and set of the alarm. Lawrence's party had to run without detonating the charges.

The German-Turkish force was under a senior German commander, General Erich von Falkenhayn, who had succeeded von Moltke as chief of the German general staff when his attack on France failed in 1914 and who himself had been succeeded by Erich von Ludendorff after Falkenhayn's attack on Verdun had collapsed in 1916. His chief lieutenant was

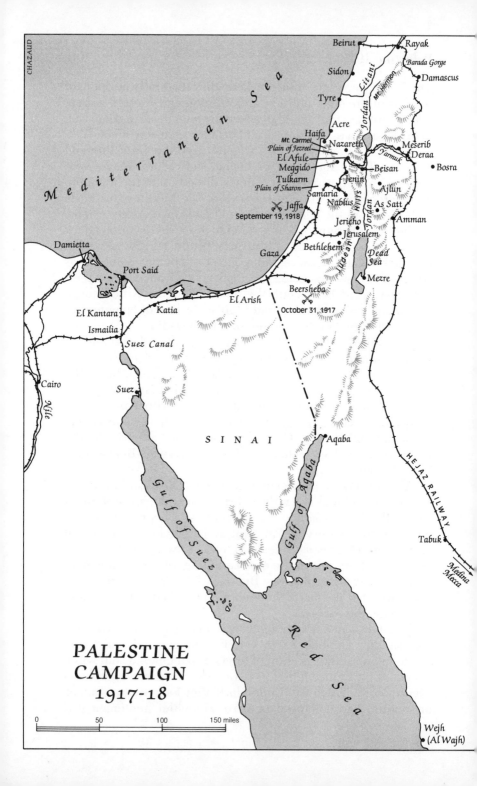

PALESTINE
CAMPAIGN
1917-18

General Kress von Kressenstein, who commanded the force facing Gaza.

To convince the enemy that the British were planning the main blow at Gaza, Colonel Richard Meinertzhagen, chief of military intelligence under Allenby, contrived a simple ruse: a staff officer, ostensibly on reconnaissance, was to get himself chased by Turkish outposts, pretend to be wounded, and drop a bloodstained haversack containing fake papers and maps. Most of the papers were innocent, but others, carefully prepared, suggested the attack on Beersheba was merely a subsidiary to the major push on Gaza. The British attempted this ruse twice and failed to get the Turks to pursue. Finally, on the third try, Meinertzhagen himself exposed himself with his haversack to Turkish outposts and succeeded. The Germans and Turks were completely deceived and girded themselves at Gaza.

Allenby opened the campaign with alternating blows both at Gaza and at Beersheba, keeping the enemy in doubt as to his intentions. Meanwhile he marched his 20th Corps by night from Gaza to the jumping-off point for Beersheba, leaving tents and dummies behind to make the enemy think that the corps was still poised to attack at Gaza. The 20th Corps joined the Desert Mounted Corps, a three-division cavalry force, which was to make the breakthrough at Beersheba.

In the last week of October 1917, Allenby delivered a strong artillery barrage and naval bombardment against the heavily fortified Gaza line, fixing the enemy's attention there. Kressenstein expected the British to use their sea power to force a landing behind Gaza. When the offensive opened against Beersheba four days later, Kressenstein believed it was a feint, having been taken in by the haversack ruse, and having made no effort to reinforce the garrison.

The Turks were hopelessly outnumbered when the 20th Corps stormed the defenses of Beersheba. While the garrison's attention was fixed to the front, the Desert Mounted Corps struck the enemy's left flank, broke through two defense systems into the streets of the town, and seized the vital wells just as they were being prepared for demolition.

The capture of Beersheba cracked the entire enemy line, forcing the Turks and Germans to retreat; they abandoned Jerusalem on December 9, 1917. But firm Turkish resistance prevented the British from encircling the enemy armies and destroying them, as Allenby had hoped to do, and Falkenhayn formed a strong new line north of Jerusalem, anchored on the Mediterranean and the Judean Hills. The loss of Jerusalem cost Falkenhayn his job. He was replaced by General Liman von Sanders, a German cavalryman who had been attached to the Turks since 1913 and had achieved fame for his defensive tenacity at Gallipoli.

In July 1918, Allenby attempted to cross the Jordan River east of Jerusalem by way of Jericho, aiming to cut the Hejaz railway in the vicinity of Amman. His purpose was to focus enemy attention on this sector, while he made his major attack on the west near the Mediterranean. However, the intense heat due to the whole region being well below sea-level, lack of cover, and dust in the Jordan Valley and around the Dead Sea made conditions virtually intolerable for the soldiers, and the offensive petered out against formidable Turkish defenses.

From this point on, the Turkish command was extremely sensitive of its left flank and kept about a third of its forces east of the Jordan. This preoccupation played into Allenby's hands when he developed a new strategy to win the war with Turkey in a single lightning campaign.

Allenby's plan was to be the Gaza-Beersheba campaign in reverse. He decided to feint into the Jordan Valley but attack on the west, along the Mediterranean, breaking through the formidable German and Turkish defensive line with infantry. This would open a breach through which the cavalry corps could ride northward through the ideal horse country of the Plain of Sharon, cross the uplands of the Mount Carmel range, then turn eastward, some forty miles behind the enemy front, and cut *all* the Turkish lines of communication and supply.

Such a strike would force capitulation or destruction of the two Turkish armies west of the Jordan and place British forces as close to Damascus as the Turkish army east of the Jordan. One cavalry force, in cooperation with Lawrence and his Arabs, would seize Deraa, a rail junction on the Hejaz railway about sixty air miles south of Damascus. This would ensure the retreat of the Turkish army east of the Jordan. Meanwhile the remainder of the cavalry corps would move on Damascus, cutting off the retreat of this army and ensuring its destruction as well. Thus, all of the enemy armies in Palestine and Syria would be eliminated and Turkey would have to sue for peace.

Allenby's plan followed Napoleon's maxim that "the whole secret of the art of war lies in making oneself master of the communications." Allenby saw this opportunity because the two Turko-German armies in Palestine were served by a single railway system running west from Deraa, over the Yarmuk River bridge that Lawrence had failed to break, across the Jordan River to Beisan (Beyt Shean), then northwest up the Valley of Jezreel to Afula (El Afule), some dozen miles south of Nazareth. From Afula a rail line branched south to serve the armies. Consequently, capture of Afula would sever the Turkish umbilical cord. Also placing of a cavalry corps at Afula and Beisan would establish a strategic barrage on the main Turkish line of retreat, leaving the Turks and Germans with only one avenue of escape east of Nablus down steep mountains into the Jordan Valley.

Nevertheless, there was great risk in Allenby's plan. Experience in the war had shown that cavalry could easily be stopped by a handful of infantry with machine guns. Therefore, even if the British infantry broke a hole in the enemy line and opened the Plain of Sharon to the cavalry, a few soldiers could halt the advance at one or two passes in the Mount Carmel massif. Allenby recognized this danger clearly and—to prevent the Turks and Germans from being able to react—resolved to use two weapons, his aircraft and Lawrence's Arabs, to make the enemy command deaf, dumb, and blind.

On September 16 and 17, 1918, a force of Arabs under Lawrence emerged out of the desert and blew up the railway north, south, and west of Deraa. This temporarily shut off the flow of supplies to the Turko-German armies and persuaded the command to send its few reserves toward Deraa. The British air force meanwhile had been strengthened until it was much superior to the German and Turkish air commands. This force commenced a sustained campaign to drive the enemy's aircraft out of the skies, at last leaving fighter planes "sitting" over the Turkish aerodrome at Jenin, ten miles south of Afula, preventing the enemy machines from taking off. When the time came to execute Allenby's plan, the air force bombed and destroyed the enemy's main telegraph and telephone exchange at Afula. It also bombed the enemy's two army headquarters west of the

Jordan, cutting wires to the divisions and to General Liman von Sanders at supreme headquarters at Nazareth. Consequently, Sanders and the army headquarters were without communications for the entire day of the attack.

To divert attention from the coast where the attack was coming, Allenby had set in motion a number of ruses to convince the enemy that the British were once more planning to attack through the Jordan Valley. He had been aided by the failures of the previous campaign in this forbidding region. Throughout the summer of 1918, Allenby kept cavalry forces, periodically relieved, in the Jordan Valley to hold the enemy's attention. When the cavalry were moved west to the coast for the offensive, Allenby ordered their camps to remain standing, for new ones to be built, and for 15,000 dummy canvas horses to be set up to deceive enemy aerial observers. Mule-drawn sleighs regularly created dust clouds, giving the impression that troops and guns were moving toward the Jordan. Infantry marched by day toward the valley, then marched back at night, repeating this process for days. Officers took over a hotel in Jerusalem and began elaborate preparations to establish "general headquarters" there.

While this was happening, the main British army was marching by night to the western flank along the sea, where troops and equipment were concealed in orange groves or doubled up in camps already in existence. Nothing appeared on the surface to reveal the enormous concentration of British force, which rose to a five-to-one superiority over the Turks and Germans on this flank.

Although General von Sanders feared an attack along the sea, Allenby's elaborate deceptions convinced him the main British effort was coming in the Jordan Valley.

On the night of September 18 the British 53d Division on Allenby's extreme right sprang forward into the hills on the edge of the Jordan Valley. This had the double effect of reinforcing Sanders's belief that the British attack was coming in this direction and of moving the division toward closing the enemy's only route of retreat, eastward across the Jordan.

At 4:30 A.M., September 19, 1918, on the coast, 385 British cannon opened a violent fifteen-minute bombardment on a selected frontage of the Turko-German main line of resistance.

Then the infantry assaulted under cover of a lifting or "rolling" barrage, in which artillery fire advanced only a few yards ahead of the leading infantry. The British and a few French infantry swept almost unchecked over the stunned defenders and broke through two trench systems. This cracked a huge hole in the Turko-German defenses.

Now the infantry wheeled inland, like a huge door swinging on its hinges. On the east, one British division and the French force formed the hinge. Five miles west, three British divisions formed the middle panel, and by the sea, another British division formed the outside panel. These pressed the shattered enemy forces eastward into the hills.

Meanwhile the three cavalry divisions of the Desert Mounted Corps burst through the great gap in the enemy line and—with no enemy now standing in their path—rushed northward across the Plain of Sharon. By evening they reached the Mount Carmel range, thirty-five miles away, and armored cars secured two vital passes.

At 8:00 A.M., September 20, British cavalry seized the strategic key of Afula, thus severing the enemy's rail communications. And at 4:30 P.M. the 4th Cavalry Division captured Beisan, having covered seventy miles in thirty-four hours, and sealed off any possibility of enemy retreat to the northeast. A little later the Australian Mounted Division turned south to Jenin, placing an even closer barrier across the enemy's line of retreat. During the morning of the 20th a British cavalry brigade also descended on supreme headquarters at Nazareth, but General von Sanders was able to escape.

The Turks and Germans now had only one route of retreat, down the steep gorge running from Nablus to the Jordan. While rear guards stubbornly held up the advancing Allied infantry in the hills, the survivors of the two Turkish armies formed a huge column on the morning of September 21 and began filing down the gorge. British aircraft spotted this column and—with the Turkish and German air force swept from the skies—commenced a merciless four-hour bombing and machine-gun attack that reduced the two enemy armies to chaos. Those who survived became scattered fugitives, easily rounded up and captured by cavalry.

Within three days two Turkish armies and the entire enemy

position in Palestine had been destroyed. Only the Turkish 4th Army, east of the Jordan, remained. Its commander made the mistake of waiting until September 22 to retire northward. Now a broken railway and the Arabs lay across its line of retreat, and on September 26 the 4th Cavalry Division moved eastward from Beisan to intercept it, while the remaining two cavalry divisions made directly for Damascus.

The Turkish 4th Army disappeared under rapid attrition by repeated small blows, delivered by the 4th Cavalry Division and the Arabs under Lawrence. The last survivors of the 4th Army were headed off and captured near Damascus, while this ancient city was occupied by the Allies on October 1.

All organized Turkish resistance had collapsed, and the 5th Cavalry Division advanced on Aleppo, 200 miles north, in conjunction with an Arab force. The cavalry's leading armored cars reached the city on October 23. Three days later, the British had planned an assault but during the previous night the Arabs had slipped into the town and captured it on their own.

With virtually no organized forces available to counter the British advance into the Turkish heartland of Anatolia, the Turkish government capitulated on October 31. In thirty-eight days the British had advanced 350 miles, seized all of Palestine, Lebanon, and Syria and isolated Mesopotamia, leaving the Turks there no option but retreat. During this period the British had captured 75,000 prisoners and had suffered fewer than 5,000 casualties.

General Allenby had won the campaign almost entirely with surprise and mobility—without a battle. The Turks and Germans had collapsed the moment they realized the British cavalry had established a strategic barrage across their major line of retreat at Afula and Beisan. This campaign proved that mobile warfare could be reinstituted once infantry and heavy artillery had broken the barrier of the existing trench system and field fortifications. It also proved that decisive results could be achieved on other fronts than in France and Flanders. Consequently, the four-year stalemate and the enormous casualties on the western front had not been necessary.

7

Mao Zedong

THE WINNING OF CHINA

ALTHOUGH THE COMMUNIST PARTY ousted the Nationalists and their leader, Chiang Kai-shek, from mainland China in 1949, the true victory of Chinese Communism occurred in 1934–35 when Mao Zedong saved the Red Chinese army from certain destruction.

As a result of this campaign, one of the longest and most arduous in the annals of warfare, the Red Army developed the myth of its invincibility, the Nationalists realized they were unable to destroy the Communist movement, and Mao Zedong emerged not only as one of the great captains of history but as the sole leader of the Chinese Reds.

Mao (1892–1976), the son of a peasant in Hunan province, was one of the founders of the Chinese Communist Party (CCP). But Mao played only a modest role in the movement until after Chiang Kai-shek ordered the massacre of every Communist he could reach in 1927. This bloodbath ended the alliance of the Nationalists and the Communists, which had begun in 1923 and had contributed greatly to Nationalist successes in reducing the power of warlords who had divided China into numerous semi-independent fiefdoms.

The 1927 slaughter convinced Mao Zedong that the Communist movement required a professionally trained and disciplined army if it was going to overcome the landlords, industrialists, and militarists within the Nationalist Party, or Kuomintang (KMT). These wanted no change in China's long policy of exploiting the peasants with excessive rents and taxes and the workers with low pay and atrocious factory conditions.

In contrast to Mao, the Communist leadership believed that China could be impelled to revolution by stirring up the workers and peasants. These, so ran the theory, could quickly overcome all opposition by their dedication and enthusiasm for reform. The theory originated with the Third Communist International or Comintern, the Soviet Union's foreign-subversion arm, which increasingly took over direction of the CCP after the 1927 debacle.

Mao disputed the Comintern's argument with a statement that became one of his most famous aphorisms: "We must be aware that political power grows out of the barrel of a gun."

To escape the KMT armies that were seeking to destroy the last vestiges of the Communist movement, Mao led about 1,000 followers to a famous bandit bastion, Jinggang Shan, in the Luoxiao Mountains dividing Hunan and Jiangxi provinces in southeastern China. In the spring of 1928, Zhu De, a Communist military leader, joined Mao with 600 men, and in July 1928, they moved 130 air miles eastward to the vicinity of Ruijin in the high Wuyi Mountains dividing Jiangxi province from Fujian province. Other Red leaders were creating smaller rural bases in other out-of-the-way places.

In the Wuyi heights, Mao and Zhu set up a tiny soviet republic and laid the foundations for a new kind of army with a new kind of soldier. Over time this army came to be as democratic as a hierarchical command structure can be. Unlike Western or KMT armies, it had no distinct officer corps separated by class and education from the men. There were no ranks, no insignia. Men (and often women) became leaders by demonstrating their ability. Men addressed commanders by their job titles, like "comrade platoon leader" or "comrade company commander." Officers did not beat or mistreat the men. Everyone lived together, ate the same food, dressed alike. The Red leadership teams or cadres forbade seizing food or property from peasants. They punished rape, robbery, and violence harshly. The Red soldier came to be seen by the people as a friend, not as a plague, as was the case with often poorly disciplined KMT soldiers or men in the armies of the numerous

MAO ZEDONG
Bettmann Archive

warlords, who had seized control of some Chinese provinces or regions in the chaotic years after the Chinese Revolution of 1911.

Communist leaders encouraged soldiers to solve various everyday problems and put much faith in the capacity of the individual soldier to understand his military task and carry it out. In a practice unheard of in other armies, leaders gave soldiers extensive precombat briefings about the tactical situation and battle plans and took pains to explain why orders they issued were important.

The Comintern cared little about Mao's new-model army and in August 1928 placed Li Lisan, a twenty-eight-year-old labor leader from Hunan in charge of the Chinese Reds with instructions to carry out a revolution based on the doctrinaire Marxist-Leninist belief that leadership had to come from the urban proletariat or worker. This implied seizure of China's cities and was wholly unrealistic, since the urban industrial proletariat represented less than 1 percent of China's work force and only a minuscule fraction of these workers had been organized by the Reds.

Mao Zedong turned Marxist-Leninist theory on its head, holding that the peasants, not the industrial proletariat, were the key to Communist victory, since 80 percent of China's people were peasants and landlords exploited them in every village. The gentry and landlords had been crushing the peasants for several thousand years, Mao wrote. There could be no improvement until the peasants overthrew the landlords' political power. Therefore the revolution had to arise among the peasants, not among the tiny urban industrial proletariat. However, Mao never deviated from the conviction that the struggle had to be waged by a Red army on behalf of the masses and not by the masses themselves.

The stage was set for a major conflict between Mao's concept of how to win the revolution and Li Lisan's. Mao wanted to use the few Red troops the movement possessed as guerrillas to attack vulnerable targets, then retreat to safe base areas. He wanted to expand the base areas or soviets outward methodically, capturing counties first and then provinces. But the Comintern had directed Li Lisan to create a strong labor movement in the cities and to lead the workers in revolt. This required him to capture some cities at almost any cost.

In 1930, Li Lisan ordered the Communists to seize several medium-sized cities before massing against the huge city of Wuhan on the Yangtze river. Although Mao and his forces briefly captured Changsha, capital of Hunan, Nationalist forces were too strong and the Reds had to retreat everywhere. Li Lisan's campaign failed miserably. But the Comintern blamed Li, not its policy, and turned the party's leadership over to the "Twenty-eight Bolsheviks," young Chinese students who had studied in the Soviet Union and could be relied upon to follow the Kremlin's line and Soviet interests, whichever way they might turn.

Chiang Kai-shek, thoroughly alarmed at the attempts on the cities, in December 1930 sent 100,000 warlord troops in his first "extermination campaign" or "bandit-suppression drive" to root the Communists out of Mao's "central soviet" in the Wuyi Mountains, by far the largest and most significant Red base. Mao and Zhu De could muster only 40,000 poorly equipped Red soldiers.

In this campaign Mao demonstrated his military genius and mastery of guerrilla warfare for the first time. He used friendly peasants to spy out the Nationalists' intentions and dispositions; moved to counter KMT forces rapidly and secretly, mostly at night; attacked only when he could achieve local superiority in numbers and weapons, and then swiftly dispersed. Mao lured the KMT troops deep into the territory of the soviet or into areas friendly to Red soldiers. There, with superior forces, he encircled and attempted to destroy isolated Nationalist units, thus momentarily reversing the general strategic advantage enjoyed by the Nationalists.

The climax of the campaign came when Mao and Zhu De concentrated much of their force against two brigades of one division and routed them, capturing 9,000 men. The victory caused two adjoining KMT divisions to flee. The Reds pursued one of them, catching it on the run and destroying most of it. The campaign petered out in early January 1931, with complete defeat for the Nationalists.

Chiang Kai-shek tried again in April 1931, doubling the number of warlord troops to 200,000 and placing command

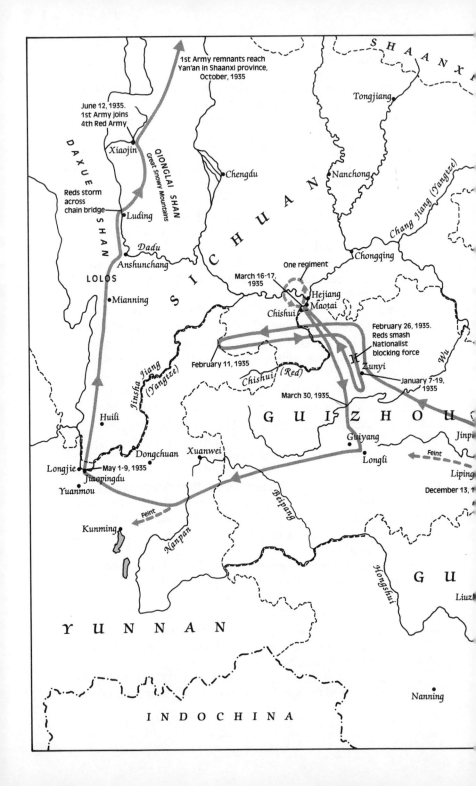

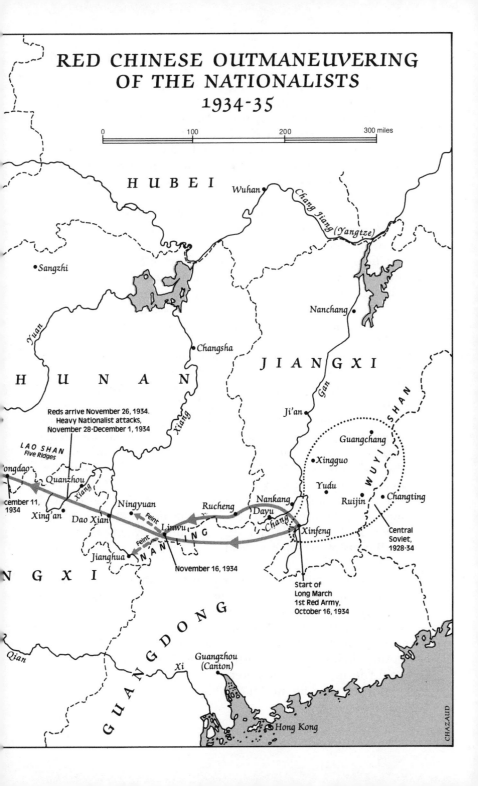

RED CHINESE OUTMANEUVERING
OF THE NATIONALISTS
1934-35

0   100   200   300 miles

H U B E I

Wuhan

Chang Jiang (Yangtze)

Sangzhi

Nanchang

Yuan

Changsha

J I A N G X I

H U N A N

Ji'an

Gan

Reds arrive November 26, 1934.
Heavy Nationalist attacks,
November 28-December 1, 1934

WUYI SHAN

Guangchang

LAO SHAN
Five Ridges

Xingguo

ongdao

Quanzhou

Xiang

Ningyuan

Rucheng

Nankang

Yudu

Ruijin

Changting

cember 11,
1934

Xing'an

Dao Xian

Feint

Linwu

Dayu

Chang

Xinfeng

Central
Soviet,
1928-34

Jianghua

Feint

N A N - L I N G

November 16, 1934

Start of
Long March
1st Red Army,
October 16, 1934

N G X I

G U A N G D O N G

Qian

Guangzhou
(Canton)

Xi

Hong Kong

CHAZAUD

under one of his most loyal generals, He Yingqin. However, He repeated the tactics of the first campaign, moving ponderously into the Red areas by seven columns. Mao had only 30,000 men to bring against the KMT forces but concentrated against one of the columns, defeated several regiments, and destroyed its offensive power. Immediately afterward, Mao attacked in quick succession three more columns, defeating each in turn, then partly destroyed a fifth column. The remaining two columns retreated without giving battle. Within fourteen days the Red Army had fought five battles and marched eight days, ending with a decisive victory.

Chiang at last realized he was dealing with a tough and wily enemy, and for the third extermination campaign, begun in July 1931, he took personal charge. He brought in 100,000 of his own well-equipped government troops and assigned 200,000 warlord troops to support roles.

Chiang believed his own troops would make short work of Mao's poorly equipped army. But Chiang had been preparing his soldiers for the wrong sort of war. Since 1927 he had employed some forty German army advisers to instruct his army. Although German skill produced a better soldier, the Germans were experts in orthodox methods developed in stand-up fights between European field armies. To defeat the semiguerrilla warfare of Mao Zedong, the Nationalists needed different tactics and training. The Reds advanced by stealth, combined quickly, struck hard, then as quickly dispersed. They relied heavily on ambush, used spies to detect enemy strength and movements, formed no battle lines, made no distinction between front lines and rear areas, and concentrated only against small units of the enemy, destroying each in turn before moving on.

Chiang's strategy was orthodox in the extreme. He decided to "drive straight in," taking the soviet by storm. He moved eight columns by fast marches of over twenty miles a day into the heart of the central soviet, hoping to squeeze the Reds into a corner and force them to stand and fight. In such a "set-piece" battle, Chiang's superior artillery, machine guns, and aircraft would destroy the Communists.

But Mao had no intention of fighting Chiang's kind of war.

His forces, still about 30,000 men, were exhausted and resting in the Wuyi Mountains about thirty miles northeast of Ruijin. To get in position to retaliate, Mao and Zhu moved the army by forced marches to Xingguo, about thirty-five miles northwest of Ruijin.

Mao's original plan was to march about fifteen miles northwest to Wan'an on the Gan River, drive north down the east bank, then sweep eastward across the Nationalists' lines of communication, cutting off supplies and striking any isolated units that appeared. But KMT observers spotted the movement, and Chiang rushed two divisions to the Gan river. To avoid being trapped, Mao withdrew about ten miles south of Wan'an.

Mao now moved northeast under cover of night, slipped undetected through a thirteen-mile gap between two KMT forces, and drove about thirty-five miles east of Wan'an, placing his army in the rear of the Nationalists. Here Mao struck an isolated Kuomintang force and threw it into retreat. The next day Mao smashed a KMT division, also isolated, and sent it reeling backward. The Red Army now took three days to move mostly by night fifteen miles eastward to Huangbei to surround and defeat another solitary enemy division.

Chiang Kai-shek ordered all KMT forces to close on Huangbei by forced marches to encircle the Reds and annihilate them. Mao's peasant spy network gave him warning, and he found a seven-mile gap in high mountains between the KMT forces converging from the west and slipped through to reassemble near Xingguo. There the Red soldiers collapsed in exhaustion.

It took Chiang several days to discover his quarry had flown. Weary, hungry, and demoralized, the KMT forces moved out of the soviet area in late September 1931 to reorganize. Mao now lunged after them, catching a brigade and an entire division separated from supporting forces and nearly wiping out both. That ended the third "bandit-suppression drive."

But Chiang's police had success elsewhere, seizing the Communist Party's secret service chief in Wuhan in June 1931 and forcing him to divulge names. This led to the moving of the Twenty-eight Bolsheviks and the party's ruling Politburo, including Zhou Enlai, from their secret hiding places in Shanghai and elsewhere to Mao's central soviet. This brought on an immediate move by the Twenty-eight Bolsheviks to curb Mao's authority.

They condemned Mao for his guerrilla tactics, even though they had been eminently successful, and for allowing rich peasants in the soviet area to keep land instead of giving it to poor peasants. They called for adoption of regular warfare instead of guerrilla tactics, expansion of the Red Army, and use of uneducated "proletarian" leaders instead of literate persons, since these were often rich peasants or former small landlords.

The doctrinaire Communists now running the CCP wanted to follow the strategy and tactics the Soviet Communists had employed in defeating the White forces after the Russian Revolution of 1917. The Soviet strategy had been essentially conventional open warfare employing large armies in stand-up fights. However, the Soviets had been generally superior to the White armies and had behind them the strength of Russian industry and people. The situation was the reverse in China. Chiang had almost unlimited manpower available and controlled most of the country and the ports where arms could be landed.

In August 1932, Zhou Enlai and other Politburo leaders criticized Mao for his conservative, defensive military views and demanded a "forward and offensive line" to counter the next KMT assault against the central soviet. The occasion marked the loss of most of Mao's influence in the army, with Zhou Enlai becoming leader of the army's political commissars.

On January 1, 1933, Chiang Kai-shek assembled 150,000 men and launched his fourth eradication campaign against the central soviet. But public anger at Chiang's inaction against the Japanese, who had occupied Manchuria in 1931, forced him to send 50,000 troops northward in March (which he did not use) and permitted the Reds to push back the remaining KMT forces.

Chiang at last worked out an uneasy truce with the Japanese and used the opportunity to organize what he hoped would be the final solution to the rural Communist soviets. For this fifth campaign, Chiang conceived a radically different strategy. It resembled the method the British finally devised to destroy resistance of the Boer guerrillas in the last stage of the South African War (1899–1902) by moving civilians in large numbers into concentration camps and building mutually supporting blockhouses that restricted the movement of Boer fighters.

Chiang built 700 miles of motor roads to give access to the rough Wuyi mountain highlands of the central soviet, and he set up radio and telephone nets to coordinate movements of his encircling forces, which totaled 750,000 men, while several hundred thousand other soldiers were closing in on the smaller soviets elsewhere.

In January 1934, the CCP held a conference in Ruijin to prepare for the blow about to descend. Here the leaders reemphasized the "forward and offensive policy" and instructed the Red Army not to let "the enemy occupy an inch of our soviet territory." They completely repudiated Mao's strategy of luring the enemy into the soviet areas in order to destroy them.

Chiang's offensive got unexpected assistance from the Comintern agent with the Reds, Otto Braun, an Austrian who had served in World War I and graduated from the Frunze Military Academy in the Soviet Union. Braun considered himself a great military expert. He deprecated Mao Zedong's guerrilla tactics and said the time had come for the Red Army to fight conventional warfare. He got the leadership to agree to concentrate forces for "fast and close sorties" against KMT troops while they were building new blockhouses. It was essentially a policy of direct frontal attacks and was bound to fail, in view of the Kuomintang's powerful artillery, machine guns, and 150 fighter-bomber aircraft and the Red Army's virtual lack of offensive weapons.

Chiang began a "walling in" of the soviet area. KMT troops uprooted several million people living around the soviet and forced them into concentration camps away from the battle zone. With every step the Nationalists took, they left a deserted region, barren of food and friends to the Reds. The blockhouses formed an interconnected cordon that limited Red troop movement. Shortage of food and salt affected the health and energy of the Red soldiers.

In April 1934, Chiang's soldiers pressed to the vicinity of Guangchang, about sixty miles north of Ruijin, gateway to the central soviet. The Red leadership, following Otto Braun's advice, decided it was crucial to hold Guangchang and moved up four corps and installed field fortifications. Kuomintang aircraft and artillery promptly flattened the fortifications, and the Red commander, Peng Dehuai, lost 1,000 men the first day. Peng fiercely opposed the tactics but got nowhere. The Reds attacked into the teeth of KMT artillery and machine guns and lost more than 4,000 dead and 20,000 wounded.

This crippled the Red Army, demonstrated the barrenness of Braun's tactics, and forced the party leadership to prepare for the worst: evacuation of the central soviet. The KMT forces did not resume their advance until July, but the Red Army continued to decline rapidly from malnutrition, casualties, and desertions.

In a desperate move, one corps split into small units in July and moved into Fujian and Zhejiang provinces, but it failed to divert KMT forces and the corps largely disintegrated. By October 1934, the KMT had pressed the Reds into a small pocket and the Communists completed plans to evacuate the central soviet.

Their objective was a measure of their desperation: a tiny soviet under He Long in northwest Hunan around Sangzhi, 440 air miles away. This soviet, too, was under pressure from Chiang Kai-shek's forces, and a move to it would only draw all KMT armies. If they failed to reach He Long, there was an even more remote soviet under Zhang Guotao that had been established in 1932 around Tongjiang in the huge interior province of Sichuan, 660 air miles to the northwest.

Mao Zedong played little role in the decision. Indeed, to reduce his influence further, the Red leadership wanted Mao to remain in the central soviet with about 6,000 troops under Mao's friend Chen Yi, with orders to maintain a strong guerrilla presence. But Mao's prestige was too high for anyone to challenge his decision to go with the main army. Chen Yi's force was reduced in a few months to remnants hiding in the mountains.

The remaining Communists, about 72,000 soldiers organized as the 1st Army and 14,500 officials, civilians, wives of important leaders, and government workers, broke out on October 16, 1934, through a thinly held KMT cordon about seventy-five miles southwest of Ruijin. The Long March had begun.

By moving mostly at night and along paths and trails, the 1st Army was able to get clean away from the encircling KMT forces. It took Chiang two weeks to realize the quarry had flown. But his aircraft and information network discovered the route of the Red retreat, and he was able to place roadblocks to slow the advance and to start movements of his armies, totaling over 400,000 men, to close in on the Reds from all sides.

The Reds could do little about the concentration of Chiang Kai-shek's armies, but they knew in advance of the ambushes and were able to break them, because Zhou Enlai years before had sent men to be trained in cryptology in the Soviet Union and they were able to decipher the Nationalist radio codes.

On November 16 the Red Army's columns reassembled at Linwu in Hunan just north of the Guangdong border in the shelter of the Nan Ling mountain system. They were 220 air miles west of the central soviet and were marching much lighter than when they started, having jettisoned nearly all of their heavy equipment, including artillery. The army kept only its 650 machine guns and its thirty-eight mortars. These weapons, plus rifles and hand grenades, gave the army the firepower it had to have to survive.

Chiang knew from the direction of the Red Army's travel that it probably was heading toward the small soviet in northwestern Hunan around Sangzhi. He kept his forces in two concentrations: one to the north to block this movement and the other to the rear under Zhou Hunyuan to pursue the Reds. Chiang also called on the warlords of Guangdong and Guangxi provinces to close the noose from the south.

Zhu De, the Red Army commander, realized he must get out of this developing trap and ordered the army to move by forced march for the Xiang River some one hundred air miles westward, knowing it had to cross this barrier before turning north toward the soviet at Sangzhi.

Although the fast and nimble leading elements of the Red Army, the 1st and 3d Corps, reached the Xiang on November 26, 1934, the civilians marching with the army and carrying much equipment and records were much slower, and Chiang Kai-shek had time to close in on the 8th Corps, forming the rear of the Red Army, and destroyed one of its divisions with about

2,500 men. While KMT forces advanced from north and south, Zhu De held up all combat elements still east of the river so the civilian column could get across. It took three days, beginning November 28, for all the noncombat elements to flee over the Xiang. During this period the Red troops east of the river endured air and artillery bombardment and infantry assaults by immensely superior KMT forces. The Communists suffered fearsome losses, including another entire division of 2,500 men.

The Red Army now was in a desperate situation. The leaders were extremely angry with Braun, Zhou Enlai, and Bo Gu, leader of the Twenty-eight Bolsheviks, for their poor military leadership, which had led to the nearly impossible position they faced. As a result of battle losses, sickness, and desertion, the army was down to fewer than half the number it possessed at breakout. A large KMT army blocked the way north to He Long's redoubt, while other KMT forces made it impossible to move back east. A drive south into Guangxi would lead to more enemy attacks from all sides and into a sack from which there was no escape. To the west the prospect was just as daunting: the incredibly steep and formidable heights of Laoshan ("Old Mountain") and the Five Ridges, a high, almost trackless extension of the Nan Ling system in northern Guangxi.

At this point Mao Zedong came forward with a plan to save the army and the Communist movement: scale Laoshan and the Five Ridges and break out north into Guizhou province, where the enemy was weak. From Guizhou the Red Army could march toward either He Long in northwest Hunan or Zhang Guotao in northeastern Sichuan.

The Red leaders realized Mao was right: any other direction spelled destruction. They turned the army toward the Old Mountain, and it began to climb. The path in places was no more than two feet wide; it was so steep climbers often could see the soles of the shoes of the people ahead. Only the most resolute got over Laoshan and the Five Ridges and came down on December 11, 1934, into the lower country of Guizhou.

There were perhaps 35,000 soldiers left in the 1st Army and about 5,000 civilians. Many brave men had fallen on the way, but all of the fainthearted had gone, too. The force that was left was the hard and determined core of the Communist movement. It had endured a trial by fire and had survived. The leadership was aware that the entire future of the movement hung on what was going to happen to this small, imperiled army.

The military council held a hasty meeting to discuss what to do. Mao Zedong was not a member but was invited to attend. It had become clear that his advice was needed. Mao immediately took a dominant role. Radio intercepts had shown that if the army turned north toward He Long it would be blocked by a quarter of a million Kuomintang troops, 100,000 of them already in Hunan. Mao proposed that the attempt to reach He Long be abandoned and that the army move northwest into Guizhou, where there were few troops and better prospects. The military leaders agreed and the other leaders joined in, including Zhou Enlai, Otto Braun, and Bo Gu.

Two days later the 1st Army captured Liping, a substantial county seat where everyone could rest and get much-needed food. Here Mao gained a de facto place on the party's ruling Politburo and got it to agree to head for Zunyi, a city of about 50,000 people in northern Guizhou about 150 miles northwest. There the army could form a new base or move northeast to join He Long or across the upper Yangtze River to Zhang Guotao in Sichuan. As a last resort, it could retreat southwest into Yunnan province.

Nevertheless, Chiang Kai-shek was not going to allow the Reds to march unopposed on Zunyi. His forces were approaching half a million men, and they could be brought to bear from any direction.

In this situation, Mao Zedong, now the effective leader of the march, ordered a series of maneuvers that rank among the most deceptive and successful in history.

To throw off KMT general Xue Yue, who was following behind the Reds with a force considerably stronger than the entire 1st Army, Mao ordered a Red column to make a feint straight west toward the Guizhou capital of Guiyang. As the main Communist army turned northwest, Xue obligingly sent his force west to relieve the city and thereby removed it from the strategic picture.

The Red Army did not march directly on Zunyi. Instead, it sped north, giving the impression it might turn northeast to join

He Long, now less than 200 miles away. This move held in place the strong bodies of KMT troops along the Hunan-Guizhou border. With nothing but weak Guizhou provincial troops now facing it, the Red Army switched northwest and struck for Zunyi, seizing the city on January 7, 1935.

Although the Red Army was momentarily safe, examination showed that the Zunyi region was not suitable for a new soviet area. It was poor, producing little surplus food. Moreover, Xue Yue's KMT army was now in Guiyang and had stimulated Guizhou's warlord, Wang Jialie, into attacking the Reds from the south while Chiang Kai-shek, now at Chongqing in Sichuan, was blocking passage across the Yangtze and junction with Zhang Guotao.

On January 15, 1935, twenty Red leaders sat down at Zunyi for a three-day conference. This meeting was one of the turning points of the twentieth century. Here the Communist movement abandoned the doctrinaire, Moscow-inspired leadership that had been destroying Marxism-Leninism in China. In its place it named Mao Zedong as its leader. Though a heretic to orthodox Marxists, Mao saw an indigenous route to domination of China through championing the cause of the peasants. But this was not the reason for his victory at Zunyi. Rather, it was the advice he had given that had saved the Red Army. This had convinced most Communist leaders that he should lead the movement. Thus his military sagacity, not his political arguments, ensured his dominance.

On January 19, the Red Army moved north out of Zunyi. It numbered about 35,000 men. Ranging in all directions were Kuomintang and warlord troops, 400,000 of them, all far better armed than the Communists. Chiang Kai-shek was confident the Reds would try to force the Yangtze River, and he had every possible crossing covered with troops, every ferry boat secured.

Mao did want to cross the river and hoped he could find a poorly guarded crossing upstream (southwest) from Chongqing. But he ran into a strong body of Sichuanese troops which mauled the Red Army. He continued another eighty miles upriver, but radio intercepts showed that Chiang was shifting troops to block him. To continue would lead the army into a cul-de-sac with KMT forces shielding the river and troops from Yunnan barring the way west.

Mao realized the only hope for the army was to confuse Chiang as to its whereabouts and intentions. For the next six weeks he carried out a campaign almost unparalleled in deception, speed of movement, and unexpected descent upon enemy forces.

On February 11, Mao abruptly turned the Red Army about-face and raced it back at forced march toward Zunyi. As soon as Chiang's aircraft detected the movement, Chiang began shifting his forces back eastward to cover once again the crossings of the Yangtze. He also ordered Wang Jialie to move up from the south to capture Loushan Pass about twelve miles north of Zunyi, the only opening south through the mountains. This would seal off the Red Army between the Yangtze and the pass and permit Chiang to destroy it at leisure.

The Red Army was about twelve miles north of the pass on February 26 when radio intercepts told Mao that Wang Jialie's troops had just left Zunyi. It became a race for the pass, with each army equidistant. The Reds won by five minutes, climbing onto the crest while Wang's vanguard was only 300 yards away. Red gunfire scattered the enemy and secured the pass. The next morning the Communists rushed down the pass, shattered the force Wang had drawn up, seized Zunyi, and struck two KMT divisions coming up behind, driving them against the Wu River and forcing 2,000 soldiers to surrender.

Mao now turned back toward the crossings of the Yangtze. He wanted Chiang to believe they were still his goal, although they no longer were. His only hope of escape was to hold the bulk of Chiang's forces along the river. Making no secret of his movements, Mao marched over the Chishui or Red River, a tributary to the Yangtze, giving the impression the whole army was heading for the Yangtze. But he ordered his men to hide just beyond the stream and sent a single regiment across the Yangtze into southern Sichuan, where it attracted as much attention as possible.

This convinced Chiang that the Reds were trapped. With his wife, Soong May-ling, he flew to the Guizhou capital of Guiyang on March 24 to set up headquarters for the final destruction of the Communists. He now had around 500,000 troops encircling the Red Army. But the bulk was positioned to the north, east, and west to prevent Mao from crossing the Yangtze or moving to join He Long in Hunan. There were few troops to the south around Guiyang. And this was precisely the direction Mao was marching.

On the night of March 21–22, Mao swiftly moved his army back across the Red River, ordered the regiment in Sichuan to return by forced march, and set off for Zunyi and points south. Within a few days, KMT aircraft and spies knew of the movement and guessed Mao's target was Guiyang. Chiang was shocked but wired the Yunnan commander, Sun Du, to hurry his best troops to defend the city. On March 30 the Red Army forced a crossing of the Wu River and marched straight toward Guiyang. But just as the Yunnanese troops arrived at Guiyang, reports showed the Reds were bypassing the city and were striking for Longli, about twenty-five miles to the east.

Chiang figured the Reds were heading back east toward their old soviet on the Hunan-Jiangxi border and ordered Sun Du to march toward Longli to pursue them. But the next morning Chiang realized he had been duped: the Reds had passed through Longli and, instead of turning east, were thrusting south and west toward Yunnan. They had broken clean through Chiang's ring and were in the open.

However, Chiang was not certain what the Reds were up to. Mao left one corps north of the Wu River to give the impression he might still move to join He Long. This once more held KMT troops in place to prevent a junction. The corps remained in the area until April before following secretly and by mountain trails a more direct route west to join the main army.

Chiang continued to believe the Reds were heading back toward Jiangxi. At last, when it was too late to catch them, he realized they were marching southwest into Yunnan and ordered his troops to pursue.

Mao still had to get over the Yangtze River. The only place left was somewhere along the upper portion, called the Jinsha Jiang or the River of the Golden Sands. The only feasible crossings were where the river comes out of the high mountains of western Yunnan and Sichuan and makes a huge bend about eighty miles north of Kunming. These sites were accessible to Yunnanese and KMT troops. But east of the bend the situation was worse: KMT forces were close to the few crossings. West of the bend, the river runs through enormous canyons, offering few safe fords. Mao knew the crossing had to be at the bend of the Golden Sands or nowhere.

Fortunately, Chiang still thought the Reds might turn back to Jiangxi, while Mao's movement into the west raised the possibility they might try to establish a soviet in Yunnan. To deceive Chiang, Mao made straight for Kunming, the Yunnanese capital. Chiang took the bait, withdrew his troops from the Golden Sands, and marched them toward Kunming. While a strong Red force under Lin Biao pressed noisily within eight miles of Kunming, raising a panic that it was about to be assaulted, the rest of the army turned abruptly north and raced for the Golden Sands. By May 1, 1935, one Red regiment was across at Jiaopingdu, a caravan crossing point for a thousand years, and in a few days all the rest of the army was across except the 5th Corps, which held open the passage for Lin Biao's force. Lin Biao, under Mao's urgent orders, made for the Golden Sands under forced march, covering a hundred miles in forty-eight hours. On May 8 and 9, Lin Biao's troops crossed the river and the 5th Corps, now holding off a large force of Yunnanese troops, also slipped across to safety, setting the ferry boats adrift and watching them smash on rocks in the river.

The Red Army had been reduced to fewer than 25,000 men but it had survived. And the incredible campaign that Mao had waged to get over the upper Yangtze already was becoming a legend.

Chiang Kai-shek was furious. He flew to Chengdu in Sichuan to mobilize new forces to block the Communists at one more river, some 200 miles north of the Golden Sands. This river, the Dadu, whirls fast and deep down a great canyon out of the high plateau of Qinghai province. Meanwhile the Red Army had a difficult march through rugged highlands passable only by narrow, rocky paths and inhabited by the Lolos, a tribe of Yi peoples, who had been ousted from lower, more fertile and temperate lands by the Han Chinese a millennium previously and had been enemies ever since.

The Red Army vanguard gained the ferry crossing at An-shunchang on the Dadu on May 24 and forced back Kuomin-tang forces on the opposite bank. However, it found only a few ferry boats and learned Chiang's troops were on the march for the crossing, while KMT aircraft quickly appeared to bomb it.

Mao made a startling decision: the main army would rush north upstream, fifty miles by air, to the famous bridge of iron chains at Luding. With huge KMT armies closing in, an attempt to retrace the army's steps into Lololand or Yunnan or to move west into the barren, nearly foodless wastes of western Sichuan and Tibet would ensure the army's destruction.

The bridge at Luding was the army's last hope. Swaying 370 feet across the Dadu, anchored by huge stone buttresses on each shore and guarded on the east by Luding's town gate-house, the bridge dated from 1701 and for many years had per-mitted caravans from Tibet and Nepal to connect with the emperor's palace in Beijing. Nine huge chains, upon which planks were laid, formed the floor of the bridge and two chains on either side made "rails" to steady man and cart.

While the 4th Regiment, under Yang Chengwu, moved up the western bank of the Dadu with the main army marching behind, the 1st Division, already across at Anshunchang, drove up the east bank. The 1st Division was slowed by a KMT force, but the 4th Regiment arrived opposite Yuding on May 29 and saw the town was occupied by several hundred Nationalists.

The KMT soldiers had removed the planks on two-thirds of the bridge, leaving the Red soldiers facing bare chains yawning high above the water rushing violently far below. Yang sent an assault unit of twenty-two men under Liao Dazhu over the bridge. The men inched across the chains toward the remain-ing boards. Once on the planks they were to rush the gatehouse on the eastern end. As they moved forward, huge flames erupted from kerosene-soaked wood in front of the gatehouse. The Na-tionalists were trying to block passage by fire. Flames licked fiercely around the planks on the eastern end of the bridge. Success or failure hung by a hair. The assault team charged through the flames into the town, driving back the KMT de-fenders, giving the men a chance to put out the flames and reinforcements time to get across the bridge in support. Eighteen of the twenty-two assaulters survived unhurt.

Within two hours the 4th Regiment secured the bridge and the town, and it stood waiting when the 1st Division came up from the south on the eastern side of the river. The men replaced the planks on the bridge, and the next day the main army arrived and began marching across in a carnival mood. The Red soldiers knew that now, at last, though dangers lay ahead, their army was going to survive. It was a pitifully small force now. The marching and fighting from Guizhou to the Luding bridge had taken a steady toll of killed, wounded, sick, and stragglers, reducing the 1st Army to perhaps 13,000 men. Nevertheless, from the moment the Red Army crossed the Dadu the belief in its invincibility was born.

On June 12, 1935, the vanguard of the 1st Army bumped into a scouting party of Zhang Guotao's army about seventy-five air miles north of the chain bridge. Zhang Guotao, with a force six times the size of the 1st Army's remaining 10,000 men, sought to seize leadership of the Communist Party from Mao Zedong and to keep the combined armies in northwestern Sichuan, threatening the rich Chengdu Plain of Sichuan's Red Basin. If Nationalist forces pressed too hard, he said, the Communists could move into Tibet or into Xinjiang province in far northwestern China.

To the Han Chinese leadership of the party, Zhang's ideas were absurd. Not only did they have no intention of handing over leadership of the party to Zhang Guotao, but to move the heart of the revolution into an inhospitable, largely barren region thinly populated with hostile non-Han Chinese tribes would be to lose its Han identity and turn it into a tiny minority-race protest movement with no significance for the future of China. The hope of the revolution lay in China proper and especially as a rallying point of Chinese nationalism against the Japanese, who had gobbled up Manchuria and were threatening the heartland of China around Beijing while the Nationalists were doing little to stop it.

On September 10, 1935, Mao and 6,000 men and women of the 1st Army slipped away to the north, leaving Zhang and the remaining Red forces, and struck for Yan'an in the great loess highlands of northern Shaanxi province in north-central China, where a tiny Communist soviet had been in operation since 1931.

When the 1st Army reached the soviet on October 21, 1935, it was a pitifully small remnant of the force that had retreated from Jiangxi a year before. But the survivors, most of them now trained cadres, formed a priceless treasure of leadership. Had they not endured this Long March, it is doubtful whether the Communist movement could have overcome the intense pressure of the Nationalists, who never faltered in their hatred and determination to eradicate the Reds. And it was due primarily to the military genius of Mao Zedong that the 1st Army survived and reached its final sanctuary at Yan'an.

This army, along with members of Zhang Guotao's force who belatedly arrived in Yan'an later, formed the nucleus of a soviet that held its own until it formed a united front in 1937 with the KMT when war against Japan broke out. During the war the Reds expanded into north China in regions ostensibly occupied by the Japanese. But the invaders actually dominated only the cities and narrow corridors along the major highways and railways, while the Communists took control nearly everywhere else, ruling ninety million Chinese people.

When the Japanese were defeated in 1945, the Chinese Communist movement was so powerful that Chiang Kai-shek was unable to defeat it, despite massive American assistance. In the Chinese civil war of 1947–49 the Communists occupied all of mainland China, forcing Chiang and the Nationalists into exile on the island of Taiwan.

8

France 1940

VICTORY BY SURPRISE

AFTER 1918, MOST GENERALS were haunted by memories of the incredible defensive power of the machine gun, massed artillery, trenches, and field fortifications that had produced the devastating stalemate on the western front in World War I.

These conditions dictated positional warfare that turned land attacks into exercises in self-massacre. Convinced that the next war would be a repetition of the last, numerous generals concluded offensive warfare was no longer possible and concentrated on making the defense even more foolproof. Out of this thinking grew the greatest defensive system in modern history: the French Maginot Line, a powerful series of deeply dug-in, interconnected concrete fortifications and pillboxes that spanned the entire Franco-German frontier and was virtually impervious to frontal assault.

But not all military theorists despaired of opening warfare once more to movement. Two Englishmen especially, Captain Basil H. Liddell Hart and General J. F. C. Fuller, had seen how the primitive tanks of World War I, despite inadequate range, low speed, inferior weapons, and thin armor, had been able to drive through defensive lines, though they had never been used in sufficient mass to bring victory. These officers and a few other thinkers were convinced that the tank could be developed into a weapon to break the deadlock of positional warfare. In 1925, Liddell Hart in his *Paris, Or the Future of War* described tanks as the modern form of heavy cavalry, which should be concentrated in as large masses as possible for a decisive blow against the Achilles' heel of the enemy, his communications and command centers.

Some other officers believed that the airplane could make decisive tactical strikes on the battlefield by destroying troops, field fortifications, trenches, transportation, and supplies. Another school of air power, led by the Italian Giulio Douhet, believed that successful ground offensives were no longer possible and that a nation must launch massive strategic bombing attacks against enemy centers of population, government, and industry. These, Douhet maintained, would open a new dimension in offensive warfare and, by destroying enemy morale and war production, achieve victory without campaigns by surface forces.

The victorious generals of World War I generally accepted the idea that the defense would remain stronger than the offense, while the losers searched hardest for new offensive solutions to reverse the verdict of 1914–18.

Both winners and losers investigated all types of military aircraft. However, German theorists gave greater attention to close-in strike weapons that could assist in tactical victories on or near the battlefield, while Americans and Britons gave more emphasis to strategic bombers. The Germans created the Junkers 87B Stuka[1] dive-bomber, which could drop bombs with pinpoint accuracy on battlefield targets, while the Americans and Britons built long-range four-engine aircraft like the B-17 and the Lancaster.

Douhet's theories of air power led to massive saturation bombing of cities by the Germans in 1940 and by the Allies thereafter. Although these aerial attacks produced staggering civilian casualties, they did not make ground warfare unnecessary. In fact, they did not destroy enemy morale or war production and were not decisive—until the Americans dropped the new atomic bomb on Hiroshima, Japan, on August 6, 1945.

The greatest distinction between the Germans and the French, British, and Americans was the differing emphases

---

1. German abbreviation for *Sturzkampfflugzeug* or dive-bomber.

they placed on the tank. There were some American designs for improved tanks after 1918 but little practical development. However, France and Britain, locked to the idea of a defensive war in the future, built substantial numbers of the "infantry tank," a slow, short-range, heavily armored weapon designed to assist foot soldiers in attacking prepared positions. British and French commanders parceled out most tanks among infantry divisions and expected them to advance with the infantry, not to operate on their own.

In Germany a radically different concept emerged, stimulated, oddly enough, by Liddell Hart and Fuller, whose ideas were largely ignored in England. The major German theorist on tanks, Heinz Guderian, became convinced by 1929 that tanks could never achieve decisive importance while working alone or with infantry. He was persuaded that tanks must have supporting artillery and infantry carried by motorized vehicles that would give them the speed and cross-country performance of tracked tanks, thereby permitting them to stay up with the armor and assist it in breaking enemy resistance. It was wrong, Guderian insisted, to place tanks in infantry divisions. Instead, tanks should be massed in armored divisions and these divisions should include all the supporting arms needed to allow the tanks to fight with full effect.

The basic concept of armored warfare was to concentrate tanks in a large mass, break through the enemy main line of resistance at one point, roll up and secure the flanks on either side, then penetrate at full speed into the rear before the enemy had time to react. Guderian maintained that following these tactics, armored or panzer divisions could open up warfare to wide-scale offensive movement. Any other use of tanks would waste the best means available for attack on land.

Guderian had a difficult time convincing the German army high command of this idea. But because of the enthusiasm for tanks of Adolf Hitler, who became chancellor in 1933, the German army in 1936 formed three panzer divisions, three "light divisions" with some armor, and four motorized infantry divisions. In the 1939 invasion of Poland, the Germans found the light divisions to be awkward and converted them to panzer divisions. By 1940, Germany had concentrated all of its armor into ten panzer divisions, supported by a number of motorized infantry divisions.

Unlike Britain and France, Germany chose a "fast runner" over a "thick skin" tank, concluding that speed was more desirable on balance than heavy armor plating. Consequently the Allied tanks were less vulnerable to enemy fire and generally mounted heavier guns but were slower and had shorter range.

The Mark I German tank was armed only with two machine guns, while the Mark II carried a machine gun and a light 20-millimeter cannon. However, the Mark III medium tank mounted a 37mm gun and the Mark IV medium a 75mm gun, and they had a maximum speed of 25 miles per hour, not appreciably slower than the Marks I and II. The panzer divisions carried enough fuel for 90 to 120 miles range, and aircraft were detailed to drop gasoline by parachute to spearheads whenever they ran short. The German tank, like its French and British counterparts, had all-around field of fire for the turret gun, but possessed more reliable radio communication between tanks and commanders and superior optical devices that permitted the gunner to fire on enemy targets with great accuracy. By contrast, French optics were poor and tanks did not have radios. Commanders could change direction only by stopping the tanks and signaling.

In 1937, Guderian outlined the new German theory of tank warfare: "If an army can in the first wave commit to the attack tanks which are invulnerable to the mass of the enemy's defensive weapons, then those tanks will inevitably overcome this their most dangerous adversary: and this must lead to the destruction of the enemy's infantry and engineers . . . since they can be mopped up by light tanks."[2] However, if the defense could produce a weapon that could penetrate armor and deployed it at the right time, in sufficient numbers and depth, and at the decisive place, then tanks might fail.

Although the struggle for mastery between missiles and armor has been going on for thousands of years, Guderian insisted tanks could win if they achieved superiority over missiles

2. Guderian, 40.

HEINZ GUDERIAN

Hulton Deutsch Collection Limited

at a single point on the enemy's line. A rapid tank attack in sufficient width and depth to penetrate all the way through an opposing defense system could destroy targets as they presented themselves and create a hole through which reserves—in the form of panzer or motorized divisions—could follow. The breakthrough would permit exploitation into the enemy's rear and destroy the effectiveness of the enemy's main line of resistance.

Since the British and French were disposed to spread out their tank strength piecemeal among their infantry divisions, Guderian pointed out that the Germans could achieve massive superiority by *concentrating* their armor at a single point.

The campaign in the West, which opened May 10, 1940, was one of the most rapid and decisive in history. Germany—with fewer troops and tanks than those deployed against them—defeated France and the British army in six weeks and forced the British to evacuate their forces so hurriedly from Dunkirk that they left practically all their weapons on the continent.

The victory was even more astonishing because it was essentially achieved with only a small fraction of German strength: ten armored divisions with 2,600 tanks (against 4,000 Allied armored vehicles), plus the German air force, especially the Stukas. Had it not been for the barrier of the English Channel and the Luftwaffe's failure to wrest control of the air over it from the Royal Air Force (RAF), Germany could rapidly have conquered Britain.

A final remarkable aspect of the German victory was that it owed its success to the ideas of two generals—Guderian and Erich von Manstein—who occupied subordinate positions and had to fight the German high command to get them accepted.

Manstein developed the strategy that made victory possible, and Guderian, stirred by the vision of deep strategic penetration by armored forces, conceived and largely carried out the long-range tank thrust behind four French and British armies. This drive cut them off and led to their destruction or defeat.

In 1940 the French deployed forty-one of their divisions along the Maginot Line, running from Switzerland to Mont-

ERICH VON MANSTEIN

UPI/Bettmann

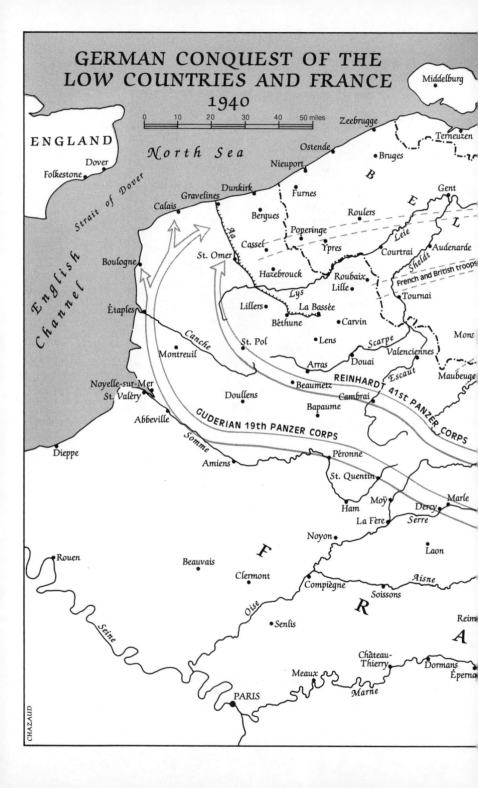

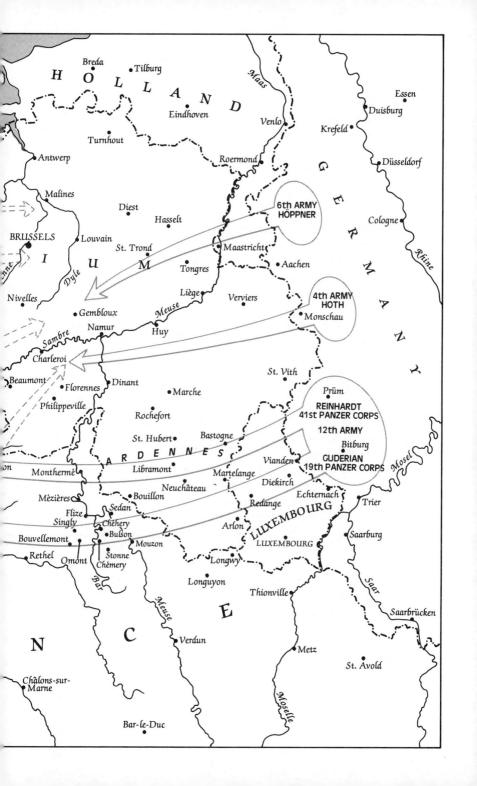

médy, near the Belgian frontier just south of the Ardennes. No one, German or Allied, believed this massive fortified line could be penetrated by a direct attack. Between Montmédy and the English Channel the Allies deployed thirty-nine French divisions, including France's three "light mechanized divisions" of converted cavalry with 200 tanks apiece, as well as the twelve divisions of the British Expeditionary Force (BEF).

The German high command planned to undertake a variation on the Schlieffen Plan of 1914, sending the vast bulk of its forces through Holland and Belgium in an attempt to get around the Maginot Line and into France on the west. The Allies accurately forecast this plan and were ready to counter it by rushing the three most modernly equipped French armies and the also-mobile BEF into Belgium to meet the German advance head-on.

To serve as a hinge in the vicinity of Sedan between the Maginot Line and this sweep northeastward, the French assigned two armies of four cavalry divisions and twelve infantry divisions composed mostly of older reservists. This Sedan sector, some twenty-five miles west of Montmédy, was the least-fortified stretch of the French frontier. Cavalry would be useless against tanks, while the infantry divisions possessed few antitank or antiaircraft guns. Even so, the French high command figured the forces would be sufficient because no German attack was likely in this area, since it would have to come through the Ardennes, a thick, mountainous forest with few roads covering eastern Belgium and northern Luxembourg.

The main German attack in the north was to be made by Army Group B under Colonel General Fedor von Bock. It was allotted forty-three divisions, the bulk of the German forces, including almost all of the panzer and motorized divisions. To protect Bock's flank on the south, the German high command allotted twenty-two nonmechanized divisions to Colonel General Gerd von Rundstedt's Army Group A. To face the Maginot Line and keep the French from diverting forces from it, Colonel General Wilhem von Leeb's Army Group C was allotted eighteen infantry divisions.

When Manstein, chief of staff of Army Group A, saw this plan, he immediately protested that it would fail. The enemy, he said, was bound to prepare fully against such a campaign, since the massing of German forces on the north could not be concealed. With the twenty Belgian and ten Dutch divisions, the Allies would be approximately as strong as the Germans in the north. Even if Bock's army group managed to fight its way into France by direct assaults, Manstein said, the Allies were likely to be able to form a strong new front along the lower Somme River and connect it with the Maginot Line. This might result in the same positional warfare that had resulted in the German defeat in World War I.

Manstein insisted that Germany's trump was the offensive capacity of its army and this should not be frittered away in a frontal attack against the massed strength of the Allies.

He proposed a radically different plan of great originality and subtlety. A major assault should still be made in Holland and northern Belgium, where the Allies expected it, using three panzer divisions plus all the airborne troops, to draw enemy attention and forces in that direction. It was almost certain the Allies would regard this advance as the main attack and move rapidly into Belgium to counter it. The more they committed themselves to this advance, the more certain would be their ruin.

Manstein insisted the main thrust should come through the Ardennes, where the Allies did not expect it. The Allied commanders were convinced the Ardennes was not suitable for tanks, but Manstein was certain that it was. In early November 1939, he asked Guderian whether the panzers could operate in the region, and Guderian, after a lengthy study, assured him that they could. Manstein proposed that the bulk of the panzer and motorized divisions should traverse the Ardennes and force a crossing of the Meuse River at Sedan before the French could organize a defense. This would put the German army *behind* the Allied lines and permit panzers to strike directly west toward the lower Somme and cut off all the enemy forces that had rushed into Belgium.

Both the commander in chief of the German army, Field Marshal Walter von Brauchitsch, and his chief of staff, Colonel General Franz Halder, opposed Manstein's alternative, and though they relented enough to allocate a panzer corps (the

19th) under Guderian to Army Group A, they dug in their heels to keep the original emphasis on a northern strike. When Manstein continued to object, army headquarters assigned him on January 27, 1940, to command an infantry corps, which was designed to play only a walk-on role in the campaign. The high command gave as its excuse that Manstein could no longer be passed over for promotion.

Meanwhile Guderian had become a devoted advocate of Manstein's strategy, and at a war game on February 7, 1940, he formally proposed that his corps force a crossing of the Meuse near Sedan on the fifth day of the attack and then immediately strike for Amiens on the Somme, 120 miles to the west. Halder pronounced the idea senseless and said the tanks might make a bridgehead over the Meuse but should wait for the infantry armies to catch up, on the ninth or tenth day, and then make a "unified attack."

Guderian was certain that in nine or ten days the French could easily assemble massive reinforcements along the Meuse and might halt the attack in its tracks. He contradicted Halder strongly and said that "the essential was that we use all the available limited offensive power of our army in one surprise blow at one decisive point; to drive a wedge so deep and wide that we need not worry about our flanks; and then immediately to exploit any successes gained without bothering to wait for the infantry."[3] Nevertheless, Halder repeated his objections at another war game on February 14, and even Rundstedt, also present, had no clear idea of the potential of tanks and declared himself in favor of a more cautious solution. "Now was the time we needed Manstein!" Guderian lamented.[4]

Manstein, however, had found a solution: going over the heads of the army chiefs to the German chancellor himself. Taking advantage of a meeting of Hitler with newly appointed corps commanders on February 17, 1940, Manstein outlined his views on the western offensive and found Hitler both quick to grasp the advantages of a strike through the Ardennes and in full agreement with Manstein's strategy.

3. Ibid., 90.
4. Ibid., 91.

Three days later, Hitler issued a change of plan. He added a third army (the 4th, under Günther Hans von Kluge) to Army Group A and, most significantly, two more armored corps. One of these, comprising the 6th and 8th Panzer Divisions under Georg Hans Reinhardt, was coupled with Guderian's corps of three panzer divisions (1st, 2d, and 10th) and Gustav von Wietersheim's corps of five motorized divisions into a panzer group under Ewald von Kleist. The five panzer divisions in Group Kleist were to traverse the Ardennes and strike the main blow of the campaign: cracking a wide hole in the French line around Sedan, then sweeping rapidly west and pushing behind the flank and rear of the Allied forces in Belgium. Meanwhile the second new corps of two panzer divisions (the 5th and 7th), under Hermann Hoth, was to lead the 4th Army across the Meuse around Dinant, some forty miles north of Sedan, and likewise strike west.

The offensive opened in the north with dramatic blows by the new German airborne forces, increased by the widespread menace of Luftwaffe strikes. These stunning actions riveted Allied attention on northern Belgium and Holland and distracted it for several days from the main thrust.

An airborne invasion of only 4,000 paratroops, backed up by a light division of 12,000 men carried by transport aircraft, was decisive in Holland. Under the leadership of Kurt Student, the airborne forces failed to capture the Dutch capital of The Hague by a *coup de main* but seized bridges at Rotterdam, Dordrecht, and Moerdijk and kept them open until the single panzer division (the 9th) allocated to the Holland campaign rushed from the German frontier and seized the heart of Holland. Stunned by these spectacular moves, the Dutch capitulated on the fifth day, although their main front was still unbroken.

The invasion of Belgium had an even more sensational opening. Walther von Reichenau's 6th Army was charged with crossing the Maas (Meuse) in the vicinity of Maastricht, Holland, then driving on the Belgian capital of Brussels with Erich Höppner's 16th Panzer Corps (3d and 4th Divisions) breaking the path. The great danger was that the Belgians would blow the bridges over the Maas and the parallel Albert Canal as soon as they learned of the advance. This could hold up the offensive for days and permit the British and French to build a powerful defensive line east of Brussels.

The Germans had only 500 paratroops left and used them to drop out of the night sky to seize two key bridges over the Maas, while a special detachment of only seventy-eight airborne soldiers landed on the roof of the powerful Belgian fortress Eben Emael, which dominated a long stretch of the Albert Canal and which, because of its powerful guns, could not be approached from any other direction. The bold paratroops quickly overcame Belgian antiaircraft gunners on the roof and blew up the armored cupolas and casemates of all the guns. This effectively neutralized the fortress and the 1,200-man garrison until German ground forces arrived and the fortress surrendered twenty-four hours later.

Höppner's panzers now burst across the undemolished bridges and spread out over the plains beyond, forcing the Belgians to retreat just as the French and British arrived to support them. The Allies remained confident Reichenau's attack was the main German thrust and, having sent their principal mobile forces to block it, were unable to switch them south to meet the greater menace that suddenly loomed on May 13 on the French frontier at Sedan.

Before dawn on May 10, 1940, the greatest mass of armor ever assembled in war was concentrated opposite the Belgian and Luxembourg frontiers: three panzer corps in three blocks or layers, the armored divisions making up the first two and the motorized infantry the third. Opposite northern Luxembourg and carrying the main burden of the campaign were Guderian's three panzer divisions with more than 300 tanks apiece, backed up by Reinhardt's two panzer divisions of about the same size. To the north were Hoth's two panzer divisions, the 5th and 7th (under Erwin Rommel, soon to be famous), with a total of 542 tanks and the secondary objective of getting across the Meuse at Dinant and keeping the Allies in Belgium from interfering with Guderian and Reinhardt in their thrust westward toward the English Channel.

Success depended entirely upon speed. Guderian's panzers had to get some sixty miles through the difficult, steep terrain of the Ardennes and over the Meuse at Sedan before the Allies woke up to the incredible danger they faced. If they did, they might assemble their armor and deliver a counterstroke against the German flank. Such a blow would probably paralyze the German advance—if for no other reason than its effect on the higher German commanders, who were extremely nervous and uncertain about Manstein's strategic plan and reacted in panic at any hint of a French move on the southern flank.

Guderian's panzers crossed the Luxembourg frontier at 5:30 A.M. on May 10 and, facing no opposition, drove into Belgium by nightfall. There they halted because Belgian troops had demolished some sections of road and laid some minefields. It took Guderian's engineers until the next morning to open passageways. The tanks rushed on, scattering the few Belgian troops and the French cavalry that had ridden forward but could do little against German armor. By evening, 1st Panzer reached Bouillon, eleven miles from Sedan, though French troops managed to hold the town until the next morning.

During the night of May 11–12 the German command exhibited its first case of jitters. General von Kleist, who had never commanded armor before taking over the panzer group just prior to the offensive, ordered the 10th Panzer on the south to change direction and drive on Longwy, just across the frontier, on the strength of reports that French cavalry were advancing from there. Guderian, knowing horsemen posed no threat to tanks, complained, and Kleist, after some hesitation, canceled his order. The French cavalry wisely did not appear.

Guderian's 1st and 10th Panzers captured Sedan and occupied the north bank of the Meuse on the evening of May 12, and Kleist ordered him to attack across the river with these formations the next day at 4:00 P.M.

However, Kleist altered the plan Guderian had worked out with the Luftwaffe prior to the campaign to assist his assault by continuous aerial attacks and threats of attack on enemy batteries and machine guns throughout the operation. Such a method of aerial attack, Guderian was certain, would force enemy gunners to take cover and permit his troops to get over the Meuse with little opposition. Kleist insisted on a massive bombing attack on the river line by bombers and dive-bombers. This might cause considerable damage, but the aircraft then would depart, leaving Guderian's troops to face the fire of the remaining French machine guns and artillery as they attempted to cross the river.

Guderian pointed out that most of the German artillery was being held back by congested roads and could not get into position in time to cover the river assault. The alternative Guderian saw was to use aircraft to pin down the French defenders until German troops could establish a firm bridgehead on the south bank and build a bridge to bring over guns and tanks. However, Kleist refused to change his orders.

When the river assault commenced, the Luftwaffe arrived punctually, and Guderian was astonished to see only a few squadrons of bombers and Stukas, operating under fighter cover, and they adopted the tactics of continuous actual and feigned strikes he had worked out with the air staff. Here, as throughout the campaign, the Stuka aroused unreasoning terror among defending troops by its wind-driven siren, which raised an eerie, high-pitched scream as the aircraft dived for the ground. Guderian found later that the Luftwaffe had gone on with the original plan because it had had no time to mount a massive bombing attack, as Kleist wanted.

The effects were remarkable. When the assault unit, 1st Rifle Regiment, had assembled on the Meuse just west of Sedan, French artillery was alert and the slightest movement attracted fire. But the unceasing attacks on French positions by Stukas and bombers almost paralyzed the enemy, forcing the artillerymen to abandon their weapons and machine gunners to keep down and unable to fire. As a consequence, 1st Rifle Regiment crossed the Meuse on collapsible rubber boats with little loss and quickly seized the commanding heights on the south bank, against feeble resistance. By midnight the regiment had pressed six miles farther south to establish a deep bridgehead, although neither artillery, armor, nor antitank guns had crossed the river, since the engineers did not finish building a bridge until May 14.

Meanwhile, Guderian's 10th Panzer Division had crossed the Meuse near Sedan and established a small bridgehead, while Reinhardt's panzer corps had got a narrow foothold across the river at Monthermé, about eighteen miles northwest of Sedan, but had a hard time holding it under strong French pressure. At the same time, Erwin Rommel's 7th Panzer Division had forced a large breach at Dinant, about forty miles north. The French recognized that Guderian's bridgehead south of Sedan threatened disaster. Once Guderian got his guns and panzers across—and this movement started immediately after the bridge was completed at daybreak on May 14—the French had only their 3d Armored Division in place to stop him from breaking entirely through the French line of resistance.

The 3d Armored had already been directed against Sedan, but some of its 150 tanks had been distributed to the infantry there. Nevertheless, most of the division launched an attack on the morning of the 14th with the support of low-flying French and British aircraft, which attempted valiantly to knock out the one functioning German bridge and the other spans under construction. The Luftwaffe gave Guderian's soldiers no help, having been called away to other tasks. But the corps' antiaircraft gunners did an outstanding job, knocking down a number of Allied airplanes and preventing any of the bridges from being broken.

In addition, the attacking French tanks moved slowly, and by the time they reached Bulson, about seven miles south of Sedan, 1st Panzer tanks and antitank guns were arriving. The French were at a disadvantage because of their poor signal arrangements, while the modern radio equipment of the German tanks gave them a clear edge in maneuver. Also, the slow-moving French aircraft supporting the tanks suffered heavily from 1st Rifle Regiment machine-gun fire and were unable to disrupt German positions.

In the fierce armored clash at Bulson, the Germans knocked out twenty French tanks. The French also tried to break through at Cheméry, about four miles northwest, and here the Germans left fifty French armored vehicles burning. The remnants of 3d Armored backed off, unwilling to hazard another assault.

The battle of Sedan brought about a major change in the conduct of armored warfare. Hitherto panzer leaders, including Guderian, had drawn a sharp line between rifle and armored units. Consequently, 1st Rifle Regiment had crossed the Meuse without tanks or heavy weapons and had gone forward unsupported during the night of May 13–14. If the French had counterattacked promptly, the regiment's position would have been precarious. Doctrine called for tanks to be kept massed in preparation for a decisive thrust, and commanders thought it unwise to attach tanks to infantry. The battle showed, however, that the infantry would have been safer and more effective if individual tanks had been ferried across the river with them. Thereafter, the Germans formed *Kampfgruppen* or mixed battle groups of armor, guns, and infantry, reestablishing an ancient principle that all arms should be concentrated in the same area at the same time.

Meanwhile in Belgium a violent tank battle developed on May 13 and 14 when Höppner's panzer corps ran into stronger French armor near Gembloux, twenty-eight miles southeast of Brussels. Superior German signals and unit training permitted the panzers to drive the French tanks across the Dyle River. Höppner, on orders from the high command, avoided Brussels and made his main effort along the line of the Sambre to keep in touch with Hoth's panzers advancing south of the river.

The principal task of Guderian's corps was to secure the dominating heights around Stonne, about seventeen miles south of Sedan, in order to deprive the enemy of any chance of breaking the bridgehead. The separate "Gross-Deutschland" infantry regiment and 10th Panzer assaulted these heights on May 14 and got into heavy fighting with defending French infantry and armor, the village of Stonne changing hands several times.

However, Wietersheim's motorized corps was coming up, and Guderian turned over to him responsibility for seizing Stonne and protecting the German southern flank, attaching the 10th Panzer to his corps until his own troops could take over. As a consequence, Guderian's advance was limited temporarily to the 1st and 2d Panzers.

After the French armor had been scattered on the morning of the 14th, Guderian met with senior panzer commanders and suggested that the corps should turn westward toward the English Channel. The armor chiefs eagerly concurred, repeating Guderian's slangy distillation of his armored doctrine that a strike should be concentrated, not dispersed: "Boot 'em, don't spatter 'em" *(Klotzen, nicht Kleckern).*

Consequently, Guderian ordered 1st and 2d Panzer immediately to change direction and to drive west with the objective of breaking clear through the French defenses. By evening of the 14th, elements of 1st Panzer had seized Singly, thirteen miles west of Cheméry.

The same evening, General André Corap, commander of the French 9th Army to the west of Sedan, made a fatal decision. Under the impact of Guderian's exploding pressure on the east and wild reports that "thousands" of tanks were pouring through the breach made by Rommel's penetration westward from Dinant, Corap ordered the abandonment of the Meuse and general withdrawal of 9th Army to a more westerly line, some fifteen or twenty miles behind the river. However, the 1st Panzer was nearly at this line as it was being established and the French withdrawal removed the block which had been holding up Reinhardt's corps. His forces were able to slip around the northern flank of 9th Army and drive westward along an open path.

The advance of Hoth's corps, led by Rommel, forestalled a planned counterattack toward Dinant by the French 1st Armored Division (150 tanks) and the 4th North African Division. The 1st Armored ran out of fuel and only a few of its tanks went into action, while the now-unprotected 4th North African collapsed in the face of the panzers and a stream of civilian refugees who clogged the roads and made movement difficult. The seemingly uncontrolled advance of Hoth, Reinhardt, and Guderian caused great confusion and a spreading disintegration among the French forces, quickly leading to chaos.

At this critical moment (May 15), Adolf Hitler himself developed a severe case of nerves. He had been frightened by his own boldness and told the equally anxious high command to stop the advance at once and allow the infantry divisions of 12th Army, trudging behind the panzers, to catch up and take over protection of the southern flank. General von Kleist told none of this to Guderian but simply ordered him to halt. However, Guderian—as well as the other panzer unit commanders—saw that a gigantic victory was within their grasp but could be assured only if the drive to the west continued at full fury and the distracted and increasingly desperate enemy was allowed no time to develop countermeasures.

After much argument, Guderian extracted from Kleist agreement to continue the advance for another twenty-four hours "so that sufficient space be acquired for the infantry corps that were following." Having thus received permission to "enlarge the bridgehead," Guderian drove to Bouvellemont, twenty-four miles southwest of Sedan, the farthest projection of 1st Panzer Division, where 1st Infantry Regiment had been engaged in heavy fighting.

In the burning village, Guderian found the regiment's soldiers exhausted. They had had no real rest since May 9. Ammunition was running low and the men were falling asleep in their slit trenches. The commander, Lieutenant Colonel Hermann Balck, told Guderian that his officers had complained against continuing the attack on the village. "In that case," Balck had told his officers, "I'll take the place on my own!" As he moved off to do so, his embarrassed troops followed and seized Bouvellemont.[5]

This cracked the last remaining French resistance, and the Germans broke through into open plains north of the Somme, with no substantial enemy forces ahead of them. By nightfall of May 16, Guderian's foremost units were at Marle and Dercy, fifty-five miles from Sedan.

That evening Guderian—assuming that his spectacular advance had eliminated any fears about continuation of the offensive—informed Kleist's headquarters that he intended to continue pursuit the next day, May 17. Early in the morning, Guderian received a message that Kleist would fly into his airstrip at 7:00 A.M. Kleist arrived promptly and without even wishing Guderian good morning began reprimanding him for having disobeyed orders. Guderian immediately asked to be relieved of his command, and Kleist, though taken aback, nodded and told him to hand his command over to the next-senior general.

5. Ibid., 108.

Back at his headquarters, Guderian radioed Rundstedt's army group that he had given up his command and was flying to group headquarters to report what had happened. Within minutes a message came back to stay where he was and await arrival of Colonel General Wilhelm List, commander of 12th Army, who had been instructed to clear up the matter. List arrived in a few hours and told Guderian the halt order had come from army headquarters and that he would not resign his command. List, however, was in full agreement with Guderian's desire to keep going and authorized him to make "reconnaissance in force."

Using this subterfuge, Guderian, immensely grateful, unleashed his panzers, and they burst forward, 10th Panzer seizing a bridgehead across the Oise River near Moy, seventy miles west of Sedan, by the night of the 17th. The next day, 2d Panzer reached St. Quentin, ten miles beyond Moy, while on the 19th, 1st Panzer forced a bridgehead over the Somme near Péronne, nearly twenty miles west of St. Quentin.

The incredible speed of Guderian's offensive would have posed grave risks to his exposed southern flank along the Aisne, Serre, and Somme rivers if the French army could have reacted. With the German foot soldiers slogging far behind the forward elements, 12th Army had to spread its few surplus motorized forces to protect this flank: individual panzer units at first, then Wietersheim's motorized corps, individual units leapfrogging on westward as soon as 12th Army infantry were able to relieve them at any point.

Yet it was the velocity of the offensive itself that made a powerful counterstroke nearly impossible. Guderian relied on the basic French formula: wait until the enemy's position could be ascertained exactly before doing anything. Although eight French divisions were concentrating near Paris, Guderian believed they would not advance against his flank so long as his armor kept moving.

Nevertheless, the newly formed French 4th Armored Division under General Charles de Gaulle had stayed with the panzers, and on May 19 a few of his tanks attacked near Laon but were severely repulsed.

Even after the breakthrough at Sedan, the French might

have stopped the German onrush if they had concentrated all their armor and delivered a single, powerful counteroffensive against the flank of the panzers' penetration. This not only would have terrified the already paranoid German high command but, if successful, would have cut the three leading panzer corps off from their fuel and ammunition supplies and left them vulnerable to converging blows from Belgium and the Somme flank.

However, neither the French nor the British grasped the revolutionary nature of the "blitzkrieg" or lightning warfare that Guderian and the panzers had introduced. The French had organized four armored divisions of only 150 tanks apiece in the winter past and had wasted them in isolated efforts like de Gaulle's 4th Armored at Laon. The 3d Armored had been shattered against Guderian's massed strength at Sedan, the 1st had run out of fuel and been overrun by Rommel's panzers, and the 2d had been spread along a twenty-five-mile stretch of the Oise River and Guderian's leading divisions had burst through them with little effort.

In Belgium, the three French mechanized divisions of 200 tanks apiece had been mauled in their fight with Höppner's panzers at Gembloux but remained a powerful force. Yet when they were ordered to strike south toward Cambrai and St. Quentin on May 19, the attack never came off, since many of the tanks had been detached to assist the infantry. Likewise, the ten British tank units in France had all been split among the infantry divisions, and the British 1st Armored Division did not embark for France until after the German offensive started.

On May 20, 1st Panzer captured Amiens and drove a bridgehead four miles deep across the Somme there. During the afternoon, 2d Panzer reached Abbéville, and that evening a battalion of the division passed through Noyelles and became the first German unit to reach the Atlantic coast. Only ten days after the start of the offensive, the Allied armies had been cut in two.

The Allied forces in Belgium had fallen back from Brussels to the line of the Scheldt River, with their southern flank resting at Arras only twenty-five miles from Péronne on the Somme. Through this narrow gap, supplies to the panzers were passing. Since most of the German armor was now west of Péronne, the Allies might still isolate the panzers if they could close the gap.

Lord Gort, commander of the BEF, ordered a counterattack southward from Arras on May 21. He sought to get the French to assist, but they said their forces could not attack until the 22d. With Guderian's panzers already at the English Channel, Lord Gort decided he could not wait and ordered forward the British 50th Division and the 1st Army Tank Brigade. Because of the hurry, the attack boiled down to a push by only fifty-eight small Mark I tanks and sixteen Mark II Matildas, supported by two infantry battalions. The attack got very little artillery and no air support. The Mark I tanks were armed only with machine guns, while the Matildas had a 40mm gun and three inches of armor. They were impervious to the standard 37mm German antitank gun, and even artillery shells often bounced off them.

Rommel's 7th Panzer had arrived south of Arras and commenced to swing northwest around Arras on the 21st, while the 5th Panzer pressed east of the city. Rommel's 25th Panzer Regiment—much diminished from its original strength of 218 tanks because of breakdowns and losses—had advanced ahead when, around 3:00 P.M., his infantry and artillery forces following came under intense fire from British tanks about five miles below Arras.

Rommel, with the artillery, ordered every gun he could locate into action, himself pointing out the targets. However, the British armor put the majority of the antitank guns and crews out of action, overran their positions, and were stopped only by the heavier artillery and 88mm high-velocity antiaircraft guns, which Rommel deployed as an antitank weapon, discovering that the large shell could easily penetrate the Matildas' thick armor. A devastating new weapon against Allied tanks had been found. The artillery and the "88s" destroyed thirty-six tanks and broke the back of the British attack.

Meanwhile the 25th Panzer Regiment had moved west of Arras but, on radioed orders from Rommel, turned southeast and took the British armor and accompanying artillery in flank and rear. In a horrendous clash of tank on tank, the panzer regiment destroyed seven Matildas and six antitank guns and broke through the enemy position, but lost three Panzer IVs, six Panzer IIIs, and a number of light tanks. The confused British fell back into Arras and attempted no further attack.

Even so, the British effort had widespread repercussions. Rommel's division lost 378 men at Arras, four times those suffered during the entire breakthrough into France. The attack also stunned General von Rundstedt, Army Group A commander, who feared for a short time that the panzers would be cut off before the infantry could come up to support them. As was to be seen, Rundstedt's anxiety fed Hitler's similar fears and led to momentous consequences within a few days.

On May 21, Guderian wheeled north from Abbéville and the sea, heading for the channel ports and the rear of the British, French, and Belgian armies, which were still facing the frontal advance of Bock's Army Group B. Reinhardt's panzer corps kept pace to Guderian's north. The next day, Guderian's panzers isolated Boulogne, and on May 23, Calais. This brought Guderian to Gravelines, barely ten miles from Dunkirk, the last port from which the Allied forces in Belgium could evacuate. Reinhardt also arrived at a point twenty miles from Dunkirk on the Aa (or Bassée) Canal, which ran westward past Douai, La Bassée, Béthune, and St. Omer to Gravelines. The panzers were now much nearer Dunkirk than most of the Allies were.

While the right flank of the BEF withdrew to La Bassée on the 23d under pressure of a northward thrust by Rommel from Arras toward Lille, the bulk of the British forces moved farther north to reinforce the line in Belgium where Bock's forces were exerting ever-increasing pressure, under which the Belgian army capitulated the following day.

Despite this, the failed British tank attack at Arras had affected Rundstedt, and on the morning of May 24, when Hitler visited his headquarters, Rundstedt gave a somewhat gloomy report, dwelling on the tanks the Germans had lost and the possibility of having still to meet attacks from the north and south. Rundstedt reinforced Hitler's own fears that the panzers might be bogged down in the marshes of Flanders, a senseless anxiety, since tank commanders could easily avoid wet areas. Hitler had been in a high-strung and nervous state ever since the breakthrough into France. He had become uneasy precisely because of the ease of the advance and the lack of resistance met, not realizing it was Manstein's strategy and Guderian's brilliant penetration into the rear of the French line at Sedan that was bringing about the most spectacular victory in modern military history. The Germans were entirely out of danger, but to Hitler, their success seemed too good to be true.

Hitler went back to his own headquarters and talked with Hermann Göring, one of his closest associates and chief of the Luftwaffe. Göring confidently told Hitler that his air force could easily prevent evacuation of Dunkirk. Hitler then called in the army commander in chief, Brauchitsch, and ordered a definite halt of the panzers on the line of the Bassée Canal. When Rundstedt got the news he protested but received a curt telegram saying: "The armored divisions are to remain at medium artillery range from Dunkirk [eight or nine miles]. Permission is only granted for reconnaissance and protective movements."[6]

Some observers saw a political motive in Hitler's stop order. At Rundstedt's headquarters, Hitler remarked that all he wanted from Britain was acknowledgment of Germany's position on the continent. This gave rise to a belief that Hitler deliberately prevented destruction of the BEF in order to make peace easier to reach. If so, Hitler failed.

To Kleist, panzer group commander, Hitler's halt order made no sense. He ignored it and pushed across the canal with the intention of cutting off the Allied line of retreat. However, Kleist received a more emphatic order to withdraw behind the canal. There the German tanks stayed for three days, while the BEF and remnants of the French 1st and 7th Armies streamed back toward Dunkirk in a race to evacuate before the German trap closed. They cemented a strong defensive position around the port, while panzer commanders had to watch the enemy slipping away under their noses.

The British hastily improvised a sea lift, using every vessel they could find, 860 all told, many of them civilian yachts, ferry craft, and small coasters. Although the troops had to leave nearly all their heavy equipment on the shore, between May 26 and June 4 the vessels evacuated to England 338,000 troops, including 120,000 French. Only a few thousand members of the French rear guard were captured.

One reason for the British success was that Göring was slow

6. Liddell Hart, *The German Generals Talk*, 132.

to mount a strong air assault. The first heavy attack came only on the evening of May 29. For the next three days the air attacks increased, and on June 2 daylight evacuation had to be suspended. RAF fighters valiantly tried to stop the bombing and strafing runs but were outnumbered and could not stay over the port long enough to maintain adequate air cover. However, the beach sand absorbed much of the blast effects of the German bombs, and though the Allied soldiers waiting on the beaches suffered, the Luftwaffe did most of its damage at sea, sinking six British destroyers, eight personnel ships, and more than 200 small craft.

On May 26, Hitler lifted his halt order and the panzer advance resumed, but against stiffening resistance. Soon thereafter, army headquarters ordered Panzer Group Kleist to move southward for the attack across the Somme, leaving to Bock's infantry the occupation of Dunkirk—after the British had gone.

The denouement in France now came quickly. In three weeks of lightning war the Germans had taken more than a million prisoners at a cost to themselves of only 60,000 men. The Belgian and Dutch armies had been eliminated and the French had lost thirty divisions, nearly a third of their total strength and the most mobile part of it. They had also lost the help of twelve British divisions, now back in England with practically no equipment. Only two British divisions remained in France south of the Somme, although the War Office sent over two more that were not fully trained.

French General Maxime Weygand, who had taken over command from General Maurice-Gustave Gamelin on May 20, was left with sixty-six divisions, most of them depleted, to hold a front along the Somme and Aisne longer than the original.

Weygand collected forty-nine divisions to hold the new front, leaving seventeen to defend the Maginot Line. But most of the mechanized divisions had been lost or badly beaten up. The Germans, however, brought their ten panzer divisions back up to strength, while they deployed 130 infantry divisions that had scarcely been engaged.

The Germans redistributed their forces, with Guderian getting command of two panzer corps to strike from Rethel on the

Aisne southeastward to the Swiss border. Kleist was left with two panzer corps to drive from bridgeheads over the Somme at Amiens and Péronne, while the remaining armored corps, under Hoth, was to advance between Amiens and the sea. The German offensive opened on June 5, and the collapse of France came quickly. Although not all of the breakthroughs were easy, panzer divisions soon were slashing almost unopposed through the French countryside against increasingly hopeless resistance. The Maginot Line collapsed quickly and almost without a shot: German forces approached it from the *rear*, cutting off its supplies. Its garrison had no choice but to withdraw.

The Germans entered Paris on June 14 and on the 16th reached the Rhône Valley. On the same night the French asked for an armistice. While discussions continued, German forces continued their advance, moving beyond the Loire River. On June 22 the French accepted the German terms, and on June 25 both sides ceased fire.

In six weeks France had been eliminated from the war. Britain had been thrown off the continent and, with scarcely an army, left only with the RAF, the Royal Navy, and the rough seas of the English Channel as its defense against destruction. The victory had been achieved by the military genius of two officers, Manstein and Guderian, over the objections and despite the timidity of their superiors.

9

The Desert Fox Rommel and Germany's Lost Chance

I N 1941–42, NAZI GERMANY possessed a unique opportunity to seize North Africa and the Suez Canal
with only four armored divisions. The conquest
would have ousted the British navy from the Mediterranean
Sea and delivered into German hands the entire Middle East
with its vast oil resources and an almost invincible strategic
position. Possession of Syria, Iraq, and the Arabian peninsula
would have forced Turkey and Iran to come to terms, split
Britain off from India and Australia, and rendered the Soviet
Union vulnerable to attack from both west and south.

Adolf Hitler and his high military advisers failed to see this
opportunity and turned instead to a futile attempt to destroy
the Soviet Union by main force and direct attack. This effort ate
up the resources of Germany and allowed the United States
and Britain time to build great military power. They then attacked Germany from the south through the Mediterranean and
later through France while Russia advanced from the east.
Weakened Germany could not sustain a war on two fronts and
collapsed in defeat.

Yet Germany need not have lost the war. After the surrender
of France in 1940, the Mediterranean, North Africa, Suez, and
the Middle East could have fallen like ripe plums. Britain possessed one incompletely equipped armored division and only
40,000 troops in Egypt. Even in 1941 and 1942, Britain had

immense difficulty maintaining forces in North Africa, because Italy barred the western Mediterranean and forced convoys to make long, time-consuming detours around the Cape of Good Hope.

In October 1940, the German high command sent one of its top armor experts, Major General Wilhelm von Thoma, to Libya to study whether German forces should help the Italians. Von Thoma reported back that four German armored divisions could be maintained in Africa and these would be necessary to drive the British out of Egypt and Suez and open the Middle East to conquest. At the time Germany possessed more than three times this many panzer divisions, none being used.

Hitler, army commander Walther von Brauchitsch, and chief of staff Franz Halder, however, already were eyeing an attack on Russia and did not see the immense strategic prizes that would fall to Germany if they seized Suez and the Middle East. Hitler and the top command exhibited a fixation on Europe and a fear of operations overseas that fatally compromised Germany's chance for victory. Hitler told Thoma he could spare only one armored division, whereupon Thoma responded that it would be better to give up the idea of sending any force at all. This angered Hitler, who revealed that his whole concept was narrowly political, since he feared the Italian dictator, Benito Mussolini, might change sides without German stiffening.

Hitler never committed himself to an African campaign and sent only the 15th Panzer Division and the small 5th Light Division to Libya in 1941 under Major General Erwin Rommel, who had achieved fame by his audacious handling of the 7th Panzer Division in France. Hitler dispatched these few Germans only because the Italians were on the verge of being ousted from Africa by a small British army that used its armor and mobility to encircle and destroy the ill-equipped and mostly foot-bound Italian infantry.

The consequence was that Rommel, one of the greatest generals of modern times, never was able to assemble the relatively modest power needed to achieve victory. With the inadequate forces he did scrape together, he conducted some of the most spectacular and successful military campaigns in

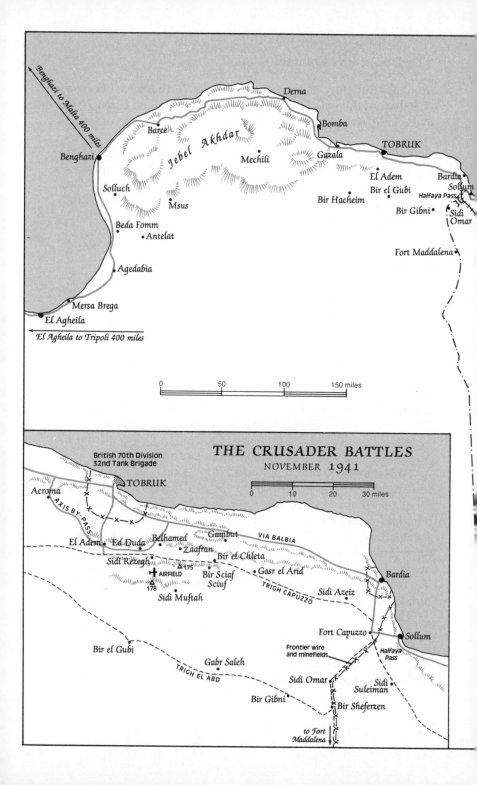

Benghazi to Malta 400 miles

Derna

Bomba

Barce

Jebel Akhdar

Benghazi

Mechili

Gazala

TOBRUK

El Adem

Bardia

Sollum

Solluch

Bir el Gubi

Halfaya Pass

Msus

Bir Hacheim

Bir Gibni

Sidi Omar

Beda Fomm

Antelat

Fort Maddalena

Agedabia

Mersa Brega

El Agheila

El Agheila to Tripoli 400 miles

0   50   100   150 miles

British 70th Division
32nd Tank Brigade

THE CRUSADER BATTLES

NOVEMBER 1941

0   10   20   30 miles

Acroma

TOBRUK

AXIS BY-PASS

VIA BALBIA

Gambut

El Adem

Ed Duda

Belhamed

Zaafran

Bir el Chleta

Bardia

Sidi Rezegh

175

AIRFIELD

Bir Sciaf
Sciuf

Gasr el Arid

178

Sidi Muftah

TRIGH CAPUZZO

Sidi Azeiz

Fort Capuzzo

Sollum

Bir el Gubi

Frontier wire
and minefields

Halfaya
Pass

Gabr Saleh

TRIGH EL ABD

Sidi Omar

Sidi
Suleiman

Bir Gibni

Bir Sheferzen

to Fort
Maddalena

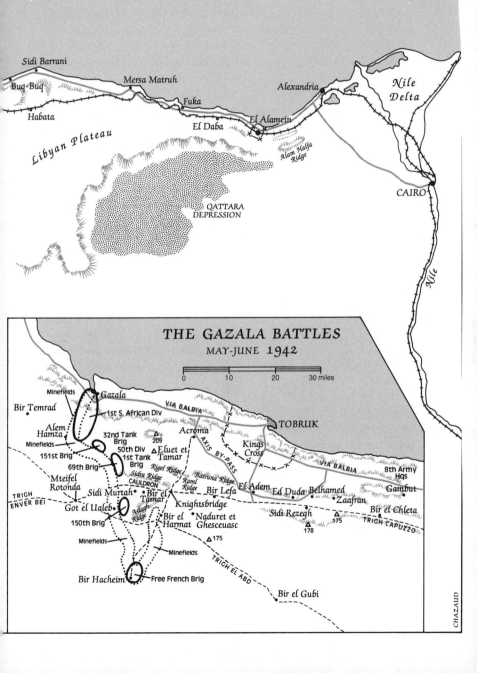

WAR IN THE DESERT
1941-42

Sidi Barrani

Buq-Buq

Mersa Matruh

Fuka

Alexandria

Nile Delta

Habata

Libyan Plateau

El Daba

El Alamein

Alam Halfa Ridge

CAIRO

Nile

QATTARA
DEPRESSION

THE GAZALA BATTLES
MAY-JUNE 1942

0   10   20   30 miles

Minefields

Gazala

VIA BALBIA

Bir Temrad

1st S. African Div

TOBRUK

Alem Hamza

32nd Tank Brig

△ 209

Acroma

AXIS BY-PASS

Kings Cross

VIA BALBIA

Minefields

△Eluet et Tamar

50th Div

151st Brig

1st Tank Brig

8th Army Hqs

69th Brig

Sidra Ridge

Rigel Ridge

Batruna Ridge

Raml Ridge

Bir Lefa

El Adem

Ed Duda

Belhamed

Gambut

CAULDRON

Mteifel Rotonda

Sidi Murtah

Bir el Tamar

Knightsbridge

Bir el Harmat

Naduret et Ghesceuasc

Sidi Rezegh

△ 175

Bir el Chleta

TRIGH ENVER BEI

Got el Ualeb

Asghi Ridge

Zaafran

178

TRIGH CAPUZZO

150th Brig

Minefields

△ 175

Minefields

TRIGH EL ABD

Bir Hacheim

Free French Brig

Bir el Gubi

CHAZAUD

history. But from the first, his efforts were doomed because his military superiors were blind to their opportunities and never adequately supported him.

This can be seen most cogently in the failure of the German high command to seize Malta, located directly on the vital line of ship communications between Italy and Libya. British air-craft and submarines based on Malta regularly sank Italian con-voys, choking delivery of supplies to Rommel. Yet Hitler did authorize seizure of the Greek island of Crete in the spring of 1941 by German airborne troops—although Crete possessed none of the strategic importance of Malta. Hitler entertained a plan to capture Malta in the summer of 1942 but called it off because he feared the Italian navy would abandon German and Italian airborne forces scheduled to land.

On February 6, 1941, when Adolf Hitler assigned Erwin Rommel to command Deutsches Afrika Korps (DAK) or the German Africa Corps, Rommel was forty-nine years old. He had risen spectacularly in recent years but was not a Junker, or member of the northern German military aristocracy that had dominated the Prussian army for centuries and the combined army since the unification of Germany in 1871. Rommel was a Swabian from southwestern Germany, son of a schoolmaster. In World War I, however, he had won the Pour le Mérite (the "Blue Max"), Germany's top decoration for valor, and later had written a best-selling book on military tactics (*Infantry Attacks*).

Hitler had named Rommel to command his personal body-guard, and from this position Rommel leveraged appointment as commander of the 7th Panzer Division. Rommel's move-ments were so fast, mysterious, and successful that the French called his force the "ghost division." He came out of the cam-paign almost as famous as Heinz Guderian, father of the pan-zers, and this high visibility made him the ideal general for Hitler to mask the fact that his commitment to Africa was mainly a public relations gesture to support Mussolini, not to reach a decision there.

Rommel, however much he suspected the limits of Hitler's interest in Africa, was not a general to rest on his laurels. He

ERWIN ROMMEL

Bettmann Archive

possessed a burning ambition to succeed and at once began planning a counteroffensive to regain Cyrenaica, or eastern Libya, which the British had occupied in a swift campaign that had commenced in December 1940.

The British offensive was under the overall supervision of General Sir Archibald Wavell, Middle East commander, and the direct command of Lieutenant General Sir Richard O'Connor. Its success was entirely unforeseen and occurred principally because the Italian army consisted largely of woefully ill-armed infantry without motor transport who could be surrounded and forced to surrender by the mobile British columns in the open, desert country of Libya and Egypt, where military formations could find little or no cover.

Desert warfare was strangely similar to war at sea, in that motorized equipment could move over it at will and usually in any direction, much as ships could move freely over oceans. Rommel himself described its similarity thus: "Whoever has the weapons with the greatest range has the longest arm, exactly as at sea. Whoever has the greater mobility . . . can by swift action compel his opponent to act according to his wishes."[1]

Warfare in north Africa was based on complete mobility, and it was the only theater where the belligerents fought pure tank battles. The campaigns demonstrated that infantry was unable to survive without vehicles and weapons that could destroy enemy tanks. They showed that the tank—because of its mobility and armor protection—was the key to victory and that infantry without an armored shield or reliable antitank guns was a liability and, in any case, had no influence beyond the range of its guns.

After capturing or destroying much of the Italian army in its retreat from Sidi Barrani in Egypt, the British virtually wiped out the remaining Italian forces on February 5 and 6, 1941, at Beda Fomm, some eighty miles south of Benghazi. There a motorized British infantry and artillery force formed a strategic barrage behind the Italians along the only paved highway in Libya, the Via Balbia, running near the coast. Meanwhile nineteen British tanks took up concealed positions on the inland

1. Schmidt, 77.

flank of the retreating columns and engaged the Italian armor, which came in packets, not concentrated. By nightfall the British tanks had been reduced to seven but had crippled sixty enemy tanks, and the next morning the British found forty more abandoned.

With their protecting armor gone, more than 20,000 Italian troops surrendered. The total British strength at Beda Fomm was only 3,000 men.

The British might have rushed on to Tripoli and ousted the Italians from Africa. But Winston Churchill, the British prime minister, diverted much of Wavell's strength, 50,000 men, to Greece in a foolish attempt to build a combination of Balkan nations against Germany. Greece had thrown back an Italian invasion from Albania, which it had occupied in 1940. But the primitive Balkan armies were no match for German panzers, and Hitler, with invasion of the Soviet Union scheduled, was determined to permit no enemy force on his rear. He got the support of Hungary, Romania, and Bulgaria, overran Yugoslavia and Greece, and forced the British to evacuate, leaving behind 12,000 men, all their tanks, and most of their equipment.

On May 20, 1941, German parachute troops landed on Crete, defended by 28,600 British, Australian, and New Zealand troops and about as many additional Greek forces. The Germans brought in 22,000 troops by air and suffered 4,000 men killed. But they destroyed or captured most of the enemy troops and drove 16,500 survivors, including 2,000 Greeks, from the island. German aircraft also sank three British cruisers and six destroyers and damaged thirteen other ships, including two battleships and an aircraft carrier.

Rommel asserted that the entire Balkan adventure was unnecessary. If the forces employed in subduing Yugoslavia and Greece had been used to support a German army in North Africa, he wrote, they "could then have taken the whole of the British-occupied Mediterranean coastline, which would have isolated southeastern Europe. Greece, Yugoslavia and Crete would have had no choice but to submit, for supplies and support from the British empire would have been impossible." Such a campaign, Rommel wrote, would have secured the

Mediterranean and the Middle East's oil and also accomplished German aims in southeast Europe. But his superiors had inhibitions about undertaking a major operation in a theater where supplies had to be brought up by sea and fought Rommel's proposals.[2]

When General Rommel arrived in the Libyan capital of Tripoli on February 12, 1941, the British were between El Agheila, some 380 air miles east of Tripoli, and Agedabia, sixty miles farther northeast. General O'Connor had gone back to Egypt, succeeded by Lieutenant General Sir Philip Neame, who was inexperienced in mechanized desert warfare. Also, General Wavell had replaced the experienced 7th Armored Division (whose men achieved fame as the "Desert Rats"), which had led the British offensive, with half of the raw 2d Armored Division, just arrived from England, while the other half had been sent to Greece. Also the seasoned 6th Australian Infantry Division had been replaced by the 9th Australian Division, but, because of difficulty in delivering supplies, part had been retained at Tobruk, 280 air miles northeast.

Wavell believed the few Italians in Tripolitania could be disregarded. And though intelligence reports showed that the Germans were sending "one armored brigade," Wavell concluded on March 2, 1941: "I do not think that with this force the enemy will attempt to recover Benghazi."[3] This was a logical conclusion, but Wavell did not reckon with the likes of a Rommel.

Preceded by reconnaissance and antitank battalions, Rommel's "armored brigade" arrived in Tripoli on March 11: 120 tanks of the 5th Panzer Regiment of the 5th Light Division. Half were light tanks useful only for scouting and sixty were medium tanks, either twenty-ton Panzer IIIs with maximum speed of 24 miles per hour or eighteen-ton Panzer IVs with maximum speed of 26 mph.

Despite the awesome reputation of the panzers, the German

2. Rommel, 120.
3. Ibid., 105.

tanks enjoyed no real superiority over British armor, while the fourteen-ton (M13) Italian tanks were decidedly inferior, being of obsolete design and mounting a low-power 47-millimeter gun; they were referred to by everyone as "self-propelled coffins."

Both German medium tanks at this time were armed with short-barreled weapons, the Mark IIIs with 50mm and the IVs with 75mm guns. Neither had the muzzle velocity to penetrate the heavy frontal armor (78mm) of the twenty-six-ton British Matilda "I" or infantry tank with a maximum speed of 15 mph and top cross-country speed of 6 mph, and they had difficulty stopping the faster (30 mph) British Mark V cruiser tanks with 40mm of frontal armor. Moreover, the 2-pounder (40mm) gun with which all British tanks were armed had higher velocity and slightly better penetration (44mm of armor at 1,000 yards) than the German tank guns. Since the German medium tanks originally had frontal armor only 30mm thick, the 2-pounder could often stop them.

Rommel had already sized up British armor in France the previous spring and in North Africa implemented new tactics that relied on maneuver to maximize his only advantages, the cross-country speed of the tanks (though later-model British cruiser tanks were slightly superior in this respect) and the high level of technical skill of the panzer troops.

Rommel realized that the greatest danger a motorized force could face in desert warfare was encirclement, since this subjected it to fire from all sides. However, a motorized force usually could break out by concentrating at a single point and bursting through. For that reason, attrition and destruction of the enemy's organic cohesion had to be the tactical aim.

To win a battle of attrition, Rommel wrote that a commander must (1) concentrate his forces, while trying to split the enemy's forces and destroy them at different times; (2) protect his supply lines, while cutting the enemy's; (3) attack enemy armor with antitank guns, reserving his own tanks for the final blow; (4) operate near the front so as to make immediate decisions when tactical conditions change; (5) achieve surprise, maintain great speed of movement, and overrun disorganized enemy formations without delay. Speed is everything, Rommel wrote, and, after dislocating the enemy, he must be pursued at once and never be allowed to reorganize.[4]

To minimize the vulnerability of his tanks, Rommel turned to two "secret" weapons: the 88mm antiaircraft (AA) gun and the 50mm antitank gun (which slowly replaced the poor 37mm gun developed before the war). The 50mm gun could penetrate 50mm of armor at 1,000 yards, thus could crack the Matilda's thick frontal protection only at point-blank range. But the 88 could blast through 83mm of armor at 2,000 yards, making it by far the most formidable antitank weapon on either side. Moreover, both guns could fire solid shot, to cut through armor, or high explosive, which could destroy or neutralize British antitank weapons or crews.

By comparison, the British 2-pounder antitank gun was ineffective. It fired solid shot and could destroy Axis (Italian and German) antitank weapons only with a direct hit; it could penetrate only the thinner side plates of enemy armor at ranges below 200 yards. The 25-pounder (105mm) howitzer had to be pressed into service as an antitank weapon, thereby being withdrawn from protecting British infantry, forcing British armor to take on the additional duty of guarding foot soldiers. It was not until spring 1942 that the British received the 6-pounder (57mm) antitank gun, which fired high-explosive as well as solid shot and had 30 percent greater penetration than the German 50mm antitank gun.

It took the British a long time to realize that Rommel's tactics rested on the concept of sending guns against tanks. In offensive operations, he leapfrogged the comparatively small and nimble 50mm guns from one shielded vantage point to another, while keeping his tanks stationary and hull down, if possible, to give them protective fire. Once the antitank guns were established, they in turn protected the tanks as they swept forward.

In defensive operations, Rommel tried to bait the British. His panzers, usually his faster, weakly armed light tanks, ad-

4. Ibid., 198–200.

vanced to contact the enemy, then retired. The typical British reaction was to mount a "cavalry" charge, though visibility was obscured by the dust and sand stirred up by the supposedly retreating enemy. Waiting in ambush in hollows and draws to the rear were 50mm antitank guns, while behind them was a "gun line" of 88s. The 50mms picked off British tanks if they got within range, while the 88s took on the advancing enemy armor at distances far beyond the capacity of the tanks' 2-pounder guns to respond. The British contributed to the success of Rommel's tactics by almost always committing their armor piecemeal, mostly single units instead of full brigades and never massed brigades.

The British played into Rommel's hands in three other respects: they persisted in distinguishing between "infantry" and "cruiser" or fast tanks, they formed motorized "support groups" of infantry and artillery, unprotected by armor, and they dispersed their armor widely instead of concentrating it.

While Heinz Guderian had been able to establish as German doctrine that all armored forces should be employed in panzer divisions, the British split their armor between armored divisions and brigades of "I" or infantry tanks. Thus they halved their effective strength by keeping with foot soldiers the heavily armored Matilda, which, though slow, was virtually impervious to anything except the 88mm AA gun.

The British came up with the idea of "support groups" because combined artillery and infantry units had been successful in harassing Italians and especially because such a force had blocked the retreat of the Italians at Beda Fomm. The British saw no need to combine tanks, infantry, and artillery into battle groups—which the Germans discovered to be so effective in the 1940 campaign in the west and which Rommel used extensively in Africa. Since support groups had to depend upon their few 25-pounder howitzers and 2-pounder antitank guns, they were vulnerable against the more resolute and better-armed Germans and German-backed Italian forces.

The idea of dispersing British units widely came about because it was impossible to conceal armor from the air in the desert. Rommel tried to practice an opposite policy: drawing every possible tank and gun together to work in concert against a single objective—which, because of British dispersion, often was only a small fragment of British armored strength.

Although transportation of 5th Light Division to Africa was not to be completed until mid-April and of 15th Panzer Division until the end of May, Rommel was determined to prevent the British from consolidating a defensive position at the Mersa el Brega defile, about twenty-five miles east of El Agheila. Here were commanding heights flanked by the sea on one side and salt marshes on the other, while beyond the marshes was the Wadi el Faregh, whose sand was difficult for tanks. Given time, the British might make this position almost impregnable.

The British were not expecting an attack. Rommel ordered forward the 5th Light Division elements on hand on March 31 and seized Mersa el Brega from the stunned defenders, then rushed his forces on to capture Agedabia. The British, confused by the swift German blow and magnifying Rommel's strength far beyond its reality, ordered the hurried evacuation of Benghazi and withdrawal to the east, creating chaos and disorder.

Rommel decided to make a bid for all of Cyrenaica in a single stroke, although the only support for his Germans was two weak Italian divisions. He ordered a double envelopment, sending the 3d Reconnaissance Battalion straight along the Via Balbia toward Benghazi, while directing the 5th Panzer Regiment and the Italian Ariete Armored Division (sixty tanks) across the chord of the Cyrenaican bulge to El Mechili, just south of the "Green Mountain" of Jebel el Akdar. If the panzers continued northward, they could block the British retreat along the coast. The effect was instantaneous: the British hurriedly evacuated Benghazi and fell back in confusion.

The 3d Reconnaissance Battalion entered Benghazi on the night of April 3 while the Italian Brescia Motorized Division moved forward to allow the battalion to turn against Mechili, toward which 5th Panzer and Ariete Division were racing. In the emergency, Wavell sent General O'Connor up to advise General Neame. Their unescorted car ran into a German spearhead, and both fell into German hands as prisoners.

Meanwhile the single British armored brigade lost nearly

all its tanks in the hasty retreat, while the commander of the 2d Armored Division with a newly arrived motorized brigade surrendered at Mechili. Rommel deceived the British there into believing his force was much larger by raising clouds of dust with trucks.

By April 11, the British had been swept entirely out of Cyrenaica and over the frontier into Egypt, except for a small force that shut itself up in the port of Tobruk, which the Italians had built into a fortress before the war and which the Royal Navy could supply by sea. Rommel had won largely by employing two principles that great captains have used down the centuries: he had deceived the enemy into believing his forces were stronger than they were and he had moved with great speed, thereby bewildering enemy troops and destroying their cohesion and order.

Although his forces were extremely weak and his supply problems were magnified by submarine and aircraft attacks on convoys, Rommel mounted several attacks against the resolute Australian and British garrison of Tobruk, but failed every time.

Meanwhile the British sought to relieve the siege of Tobruk. Unlike Hitler and the German high command, Winston Churchill recognized the importance of North Africa and was willing to run great risks to hold it. To increase Wavell's offensive power, he ordered a five-ship convoy with 295 tanks and forty-three Hurricane fighter planes to steam directly through the Mediterranean, instead of around the Cape of Good Hope. In a memo of April 20, 1941, to the chiefs of staff, Churchill wrote that the fate of the war in the Middle East and the loss of the Suez Canal "all may turn on a few hundred armored vehicles. They must if possible be carried there at all costs."[5] Helped by misty weather, the convoy got through to Alexandria on May 12 without air or sea attacks but lost one ship with fifty-seven tanks to a mine in the Sicilian Narrows.

Without waiting for the tanks to get to the front, Wavell launched his first effort, Operation Brevity, to relieve Tobruk

5. Winston Churchill, *The Second World War; The Grand Alliance* (Boston: Houghton Mifflin, 1951), p. 246.

on May 15, sending twenty-six Matildas in support of the 22d Guards Brigade in a direct assault against Axis forces guarding Sollum and Halfaya Pass along the coast, while twenty-nine cruiser tanks with a support group of motorized infantry and artillery moved around the desert flank and sought to get on the Axis rear. Sollum and Halfaya were the only places in the region where it was possible to cross the 600-foot escarpment that stretches from Sollum southeastward into Egypt.

Although the British lost seven Matildas, they seized Halfaya Pass. Threats of German flank counterattacks, however, induced the British to withdraw, but they left a small garrison at the pass. Rommel recaptured Halfaya with a sudden converging stroke from several directions on May 27 and dug in four 88mm guns, their barrels horizontal with little visible above ground. These 88s were to be of great importance in the next British effort, Operation Battleaxe.

The first stage of the Battleaxe plan was for an infantry force and half the British armor, a brigade of Matildas, to seize Halfaya, Sollum, and Fort Capuzzo, eight miles to the west, while the remaining armor covered the desert flank against the single panzer regiment Rommel had posted there. The plan contained the seeds of its own failure, because half of the British armor had little chance of destroying the panzer regiment before Rommel's second tank regiment could move up from Tobruk to assist.

Another problem was the 88s at Halfaya, which the British soldiers dubbed "Hellfire Pass." When the armor attacked on June 15, 1941, the commander radioed back his last message: "They are tearing my tanks to bits."[6] Of thirteen Matildas, one survived the tank trap of the four 88s, and the assault collapsed.

There were no 88s in the path of a column of infantry led by Matildas that captured Capuzzo, but the most southerly column, a brigade of cruiser tanks, ran into a German trap of antitank guns and four 88s on Hafid Ridge, a few miles southwest of Capuzzo, and suffered heavily. By now most of Rommel's forward panzer regiment had arrived and threatened an attack on the British flank, inducing the British to withdraw into Egypt.

6. Liddell Hart, *History of the Second World War*, 179.

By nightfall the British had lost more than half their tanks, most to fire from the 88s and 50mm antitank guns, while Rommel's tank strength was almost intact.

Fearing Rommel would attempt to cut them off, the British retreated back to their starting places.

Ever since the start of World War II and the unveiling of "blitzkrieg" with tanks and dive-bombers, the offensive had dominated the defensive. Battleaxe, as the Tobruk battles and Operation Brevity had foreshadowed, marked the end of this dominance. Rommel's success with 88s and his increasingly bold use of 50mm antitank guns in close combination with tanks showed that the defense could stop enemy armor, even in the open North African desert. Unfortunately the British commanders discounted reports of how 88s were being used as antitank guns, both in dug-in positions, as at Halfaya and Hafid Ridge, and in a mobile role, since four moved with the 15th Panzer Division. They also did not learn that their failure to concentrate armor had contributed greatly to their defeat in Battleaxe. Both these errors were to cost the British dearly.

Winston Churchill, disappointed with the failure of Battleaxe, was determined to renew the effort and poured additional troops and equipment into Egypt. In doing so, he slighted defense of the Far East and contributed to the fall of Singapore after the Japanese attacked the Americans, British, and Dutch in December 1941.

The campaign, code-named Operation Crusader by the British, opened on November 18, 1941, and turned into the most spectacular tank battle in history, a battle fought at extreme speed over a desert arena that allowed complete freedom of maneuver. From beginning to end, Rommel dominated the campaign, because he was prepared to throw in his last tank and last gun to achieve a decision.

The British possessed great advantage in the air, with nearly 700 aircraft against 120 German and 200 Italian. They had similar superiority in tanks, but again divided them between the infantry and armored divisions. Against Rommel's 414 tanks (including 154 Italian) and 50 tanks under repair, the British assembled 724 gun-armed tanks in five armored brigades, with

200 tanks in reserve. A brigade with the Tobruk garrison had 69 Matildas and 32 old cruisers, while the 1st Army Tank Brigade, attached to the infantry divisions, contained 132 Matildas or similarly slow and heavily armored Valentines. The other three armored brigades, 4th, 7th, and 22d, were equipped with cruisers, including 165 new American Stuart tanks, fastest in the field (36 mph) but with an inadequate 37mm gun and a tactical range of only forty miles, and 229 new Crusaders with maximum speed of 26 mph and heavy armor (49mm on the turret front), but armed with the same weak 2-pounder (40mm) gun as other British tanks.

The British also brought up three more motorized infantry divisions, making four, and sent in the British 70th Division to relieve the 9th Australian Division in Tobruk.

Although Hitler raised the status of Rommel's command from a corps to a panzer group, Rommel received few reinforcements and no additional tank units, keeping his original three (two German and one Italian). The 5th Light was renamed the 21st Panzer Division but given no increased tank scale, while Rommel formed the Africa Division (soon retitled 90th Light) out of independent units already in Libya. This division had no tanks and only four infantry battalions but had four artillery battalions, including a battalion of 88s. Rommel's Italian force consisted of the 20th Motorized Corps (Ariete Armored and Trieste Motorized Divisions) and four unmotorized infantry divisions, which could be used only in a static role and which handicapped Rommel's freedom of maneuver.

Rommel's problems were greatly accentuated by British possession of Malta. Warships, submarines, and aircraft based there sank 38 percent of all supplies shipped to Libya in September 1941, and of 50,000 tons sent in October, only 18,500 arrived.

Four days after the failure of Battleaxe, Churchill removed Wavell from command and replaced him with Sir Claude Auchinleck, commander in India. Meanwhile the British desert force was renamed 8th Army, placed under the command of Lieutenant General Sir Alan Cunningham, and divided into two corps, the 13th under Lieutenant General A. R. Godwin-Austen with the 2d New Zealand and 4th Indian Divisions and

"I" tanks, and the 30th under Lieutenant General C. W. M. Norrie with the "Desert Rats" of the 7th Armored Division (7th and 22d Armored Brigades, plus an infantry and artillery Support Group), 4th Armored Brigade, 22d Guards Brigade, and 1st South African Division. In reserve was the 2d South African Division.

The British strategy was fundamentally flawed because Auchinleck and Cunningham established "the destruction of the enemy forces" as the immediate objective of 8th Army. Armored forces are so fluid that they are unsuited to be an objective.[7] Rather the British should have sought to destroy Rommel's armor indirectly by establishing a strategic barrier across the Axis line of supply, requiring Rommel to commit his panzers under conditions favorable to the British.

Such a target was Acroma, on the Axis supply route twenty miles west of Tobruk. A concentrated attack on Acroma would have relieved the siege of Tobruk without a fight and forced Rommel to attack the barrier or retreat for lack of supplies. Yet the British never aimed for Acroma or any other strategic point astride the Axis supply line. Instead they crashed against Rommel's gun-lined traps in direct, costly assaults.

In addition, Rommel repeatedly caught their armor dispersed. As he remarked to a captured British officer after the battle: "What difference does it make if you have two tanks to my one, when you spread them out and let me smash them in detail?"[8]

The British plan was for the 13th Corps to pin down enemy troops holding the frontier from Sollum and Halfaya Pass to Sidi Omar, twenty-five miles inland, while the 30th Corps swept south of Sidi Omar, destroyed Rommel's armor, then linked up with the Tobruk garrison, seventy miles beyond the frontier.

Not only did the British divide their armor, but the three armored brigades that constituted their attacking force took on divergent objectives at the outset. The principal target they perceived was Sidi Rezegh airfield, atop an escarpment only twelve miles southeast of the Tobruk defensive perimeter. Pos-

7. Liddell Hart, *The Tanks,* vol. 2, p. 103.
8. Ibid.

session of it would threaten linkup with the Tobruk garrison and danger to the Axis position.

On the night of November 18, 30th Corps moved around Rommel's desert flank. The next day, General Cunningham sent two of the three regiments of the 7th Armored Brigade to capture Sidi Rezegh airfield. The third armored regiment and the division's Support Group did not come up until the next morning, November 20. By then Rommel had rushed up part of 90th Light and a large number of antitank guns to block the advance.

Meanwhile, the other two armored brigades were widely separated and ran into serious trouble. The 22d, newly arrived from England, launched a "charge of the Light Brigade" straight into the dug-in guns of Trieste Armored Division at Bir el Gubi, twenty-two miles south of Sidi Rezegh, promptly losing 40 of its 160 tanks. The attack bogged down.

The 4th Brigade stopped at Gabr Saleh, thirty miles southeast of Sidi Rezegh, in order to keep in touch with the left flank of 13th Corps, but one of its three regiments rushed off twenty-five miles in pursuit of a German reconnaissance unit. Rommel sent 21st Panzer Division's tank regiment, plus twelve field guns and four 88s, against the two remaining regiments of 4th Armored Brigade, destroying twenty-three Stuart tanks against a loss of three German tanks.

General Ludwig Cruewell, Africa Corps commander, led all his armor the next morning on a wild goose chase toward Fort Capuzzo, after receiving an erroneous report that a major British advance was coming from that direction. Although Cunningham knew of Africa Corps' departure, he made no immediate attempt to concentrate his armor. The 21st Panzer Division ran out of gasoline near Sidi Omar and didn't get refueled until after dark. The 15th Panzer Division swept back southwest and, in the afternoon, struck 4th Brigade, still at Gabr Saleh, and inflicted more heavy damage on it. Cunningham had ordered the 22d Brigade to assist, but it did not complete the twenty-eight-mile trek from Bir el Gubi until after the battle had ended. Yet the "I" tank brigade of 13th Corps was only seven miles to the east of 4th Brigade and eager to advance—

but, because it had "infantry" tanks, Cunningham did not call on it!

Rommel, realizing that the 7th Armored Brigade and the division Support Group were blocked by 90th Light at Sidi Rezegh airfield, ordered Africa Corps to advance on their rear next morning, November 21, in hopes of destroying them. General Norrie was planning to advance toward Tobruk in conjunction with a tank-led sortie from Tobruk. However, at 8:00 A.M. he saw German panzers approaching Sidi Rezegh from the south and east. Instead of concentrating his armor to meet the blow, Norrie left the 6th Royal Tanks to continue the Tobruk attack and diverted the 7th Hussars and the 2d Royal Tanks to challenge Rommel. The result was a disaster. The 6th Royal Tanks charged 90th Light's well-posted guns and was shattered, while Rommel himself directed 88mm fire that knocked out several "I" tanks and stopped the sortie from Tobruk.

To the southeast, 15th Panzer Division drove a wedge several miles wide between the 7th Hussars and the 2d Royal Tanks, allowing 21st Panzer Division to overrun and almost wipe out the isolated 7th Hussars. After refueling, Africa Corps came back in the afternoon and attacked 2d Royal Tanks, advancing antitank guns ahead of the tanks and around the flanks of the British armor and taking such a toll that the regiment was saved from annihilation only. by the belated arrival of 22d Armored Brigade from Gabr Saleh. The 4th Brigade did not come up until the next day.

Artillery of Support Group stopped an attempt by Africa Corps to overrun Sidi Rezegh airfield, but the panzer corps was now in the central position between Support Group and the 22d and 4th Armored Brigades coming up from the south. Rommel saw that it could destroy each in turn and ordered Cruewell to carry out the assaults the next day.

Cruewell, seeking "complete freedom of maneuver," had planned to take Africa Corps eastward during the night. Getting Rommel's order, however, he moved 15th Panzer toward Gambut, twenty miles northeast of Sidi Rezegh, while directing 21st Panzer to reassemble between Belhamed and Zaafran, some seven miles north of the airfield. Cruewell thus separated the two panzer divisions by eighteen miles and permitted 7th Armored Division to concentrate its remaining 180 tanks.

Rommel arrived around midday November 22 at 21st Panzer, discovered his armor had been split, but determined nevertheless to oust Support Group from the airfield. While the division's infantry and artillery attacked Sidi Rezegh from the north, locking Support Group in place, he wheeled the panzer regiment, plus a number of 88s and 50mm antitank guns, to the southwest, struck the western flank of the British position, overran the airfield, and overwhelmed part of Support Group. Again the British did not use their tanks in mass: 22d Armored Brigade came up to help, but 4th Armored Brigade inexplicably held back. German 88s and antitank guns destroyed half of the 22d's tanks before the brigade withdrew. When 4th Brigade at last intervened at dusk, it was unable to retrieve the situation.

The British now decided the airfield was untenable and withdrew to the south to await the 1st South African Division, ordered northward as reinforcement, although only the 5th Brigade arrived by the morning of November 23. Meanwhile Cruewell returned with the 15th Panzer and struck the 4th Armored Brigade from the east after it had drawn into a defensive perimeter. The Germans captured brigade headquarters and a large number of men and tanks, rendering the mutilated brigade unable to reassemble the next day.

Africa Corps was in command of the battlefield. The 15th Panzer was at Bir Sciaf Sciuf, fifteen miles east of Sidi Rezegh; 21st Panzer was defending the Sidi Rezegh area, and the Italian Ariete and Trieste Divisions were assembled about Bir el Gubi, twenty-two miles to the south.

Rommel believed the British were about twelve miles south of Sidi Rezegh and therefore ringed on three sides by Axis forces. He saw they might be destroyed by a concentric attack and directed the Italian divisions to advance northeastward and Africa Corps to "encircle the enemy and destroy them" on November 23. However, Cruewell had already put in motion his own plan by the time Rommel's order arrived.

Meanwhile, the 2d New Zealand Division had advanced the day before from the east, seized Fort Capuzzo, and sent its

6th Brigade westward along an Arab desert trail, the Trigh Capuzzo. Soon after daylight on November 23, after Cruewell had departed, the brigade bumped into Africa Corps headquarters at Gasr el Arid, twenty-five miles east of Sidi Rezegh, and seized it after bitter resistance. Loss of the corps staff and its radio links seriously handicapped Rommel in the days to follow.

Cruewell ordered 21st Panzer's infantry and artillery to hold the escarpment south of Sidi Rezegh airfield, while its panzer regiment joined with 15th Panzer for a wide sweep around the rear of 7th Armored Division and 5th South African Brigade, to join up with Ariete and Trieste Divisions moving up from Bir el Gubi. In this way, Cruewell planned to assemble all his armor, then strike the British a single, concentrated blow.

When Cruewell's forces rumbled southwestward through early-morning mist on November 23, they inadvertently surprised the center of the British position, which was farther east than the Germans had figured. The emergence of the panzers set off a wild stampede in all directions by British vehicles, tanks, guns, and men. Here was an opportunity for Cruewell to destroy the British forces in detail. But Cruewell, intent on linking up with the Italians, called off pursuit, and, swinging on an even wider outflanking movement, continued to the southwest. Cruewell thus missed one of the great chances of the war. This failure, and his earlier failure to abide by Rommel's order to encircle and attack the British, demonstrates how one subordinate's errors can wreck the plans of a great commander.

It was midafternoon before Cruewell joined with the Italians and launched a frontal attack from the southwest on the 22d Armored and the 5th South African Brigades, now isolated between German forces north and south of them. In the long respite that Cruewell had given them, the South Africans moved most of their artillery to their exposed flank and formed a formidable defensive barrier.

Cruewell now committed his third error of the day. Instead of following German tactical doctrine and advancing antitank guns forward and around the flanks to engage enemy armor and neutralize enemy artillery and tanks before committing his panzers, Cruewell formed up his tanks in long lines and, ordering his infantry to follow in trucks, launched a headlong charge. They met a curtain of fire. Tank after tank split. All of the German artillery had to be thrown in to silence the South African guns while British and German tanks and antitank guns fought tremendous duels, creating a sea of dust, haze, and smoke. By late afternoon the panzers finally punched a few holes in the front and the tank attack moved forward, destroyed 5th South African Brigade, and killed or captured 3,000 soldiers. As darkness fell, hundreds of burning vehicles, tanks, and guns lit up the battlefield.

Cruewell's attack had succeeded, but at a tremendous cost. Not only had the German infantry suffered extreme losses because of its exposure to heavy fire but Africa Corps lost 70 of its remaining 160 tanks. Although the British 30th Corps had only 70 tanks left fit for action—and these widely dispersed—out of 500 at the start, the British had large tank reserves, whereas Rommel did not.

The tank losses of this one direct attack on the strong South African defenses largely offset the gain from Rommel's skillful maneuvers over the previous days.

Although Rommel's offensive power had been crippled, he had lost none of his audacity and immediately ordered exploitation of his success by a strike deep into the British rear. His aim was to restore the situation on the Sollum–Halfaya Pass front, cut enemy supply lines, and force the British to give up the struggle. Given Axis weakness and British strength, this was the boldest decision Rommel ever made

Some critics have argued that Rommel should have finished off the remnants of 30th Corps or crushed the 2d New Zealand Division. But Rommel realized attacks against strong infantry defensive positions would eat up his strength, while the British cruiser tanks were faster than his own panzers and could avoid battle by escaping. His only hope of victory was to make a bold strike at the heart of enemy resistance to damage the morale of the British troops and, especially, to play on the fears of the British commander.

Leaving a weak force scraped together from various formations to maintain the Tobruk siege, Rommel struck out at midday on November 24 with 21st Panzer, ordering 15th Panzer,

Ariete, and Trieste Divisions to follow. Rommel scattered the 7th Armored and 1st South African Divisions and, in five hours, reached the frontier sixty miles away at Bir Sheferzen, twenty miles south of Halfaya Pass. He immediately sent a battle group through a gap in the frontier wire and belt of mines to Halfaya to dominate 8th Army's route of retreat and supply along the coast.

The move threw 30th Corps into wild disorder and caused its commander, Cunningham, to plan immediate withdrawal into Egypt—which had been Rommel's intention. The situation resembled that created in the American Civil War by Confederate General Stonewall Jackson when he descended on the rear of the Union forces at Manassas, Virginia, in the summer of 1862. Jackson's blow, like Rommel's, was aimed at the *mind* of the enemy commander: it was intended to raise the fear that he would be cut off and thereby induce him to withdraw. Jackson's move succeeded: Union General John Pope retreated quickly toward Washington. Rommel's move did not succeed, although Cunningham reacted precisely as did Pope. But General Auchinleck arrived at 30th Corps headquarters and ordered continuation of the campaign. Auchinleck realized that Rommel's strength was near its end while his was not, and he had the moral courage to stand when many a commander would have run. This decision ensured Rommel's defeat.

Auchinleck realized Cunningham must now be replaced, and on November 26 he named Lieutenant General Sir Neil Ritchie, his deputy chief of staff, to command 8th Army. This guaranteed that the battle would be continued irrespective of the risks.

Rommel's own vehicle was stranded east of the frontier fence because of engine trouble. Cruewell's command vehicle, a covered van captured from the British, happened by and picked him up. With darkness, the German commanders could not find the gap in the frontier wire, forcing them and their staffs to spend the night with Indian dispatch riders going back and forth and British tanks and trucks moving past. At daybreak they slipped away unchallenged and crossed back into Libya.

On returning after an absence of twelve hours, Rommel discovered that 15th Panzer still had not reached the frontier, while

Ariete and Trieste Divisions had stopped well to the west upon encountering a brigade of 1st South African Division. Also, supply columns bringing fuel and ammunition had failed to arrive. Consequently, Rommel could not carry out his plan to send a battle group to seize Habata, the British railhead thirty-five miles southeast of Halfaya Pass, or to block the British supply and escape route along the escarpment running southeast into Egypt from Halfaya. This meant that his bid to force the British into precipitate retreat had failed. Nevertheless, Rommel stubbornly held on, hoping for an opportunity to strike a decisive blow.

Because of Auchinleck's decision to continue the fight, 13th Corps—led by the 2d New Zealand Division and ninety "I" tanks—pushed westward toward Tobruk. The few Germans left to defend the Sidi Rezegh area were soon under great pressure. On November 25, New Zealanders seized Belhamed, only nine miles southeast of the Tobruk perimeter, and the next night the Tobruk garrison crashed through Axis besiegers and gained the top of the escarpment at Ed Duda, only a couple of miles from the New Zealanders.

Panzer Group headquarters sent frantic signals asking for return of the panzers, but Rommel was not willing to give up so easily and ordered Cruewell to drive north and clear the Sollum front by thrusts of 15th Panzer on the west and 21st Panzer, already at Halfaya, on the east. However, 15th Panzer had moved back to Bardia, fifteen miles north of Sollum, to refuel, while 21st Panzer was also headed toward Bardia because of a misinterpreted order. Realizing his hopes were dashed, Rommel ordered 21st Panzer back to defend Tobruk, but kept 15th Panzer south of Bardia. Early on November 27 the division's tanks overran headquarters of the 5th New Zealand Brigade at Sidi Azeiz, ten miles southwest of Bardia, and seized the commander, 800 men, and several guns. With this success Rommel ordered 15th Panzer likewise to move toward Tobruk.

Africa Corps had accomplished nothing decisive on the frontier. Now it possessed only a fraction of its original tank strength, while the British armored formations, left in control of the Sidi Rezegh battlefield, had repaired many tanks and received replacements from Egypt. Although British armor now outnumbered the panzers (130 British to 40 German tanks), Rommel used his tanks in concert while the British continued to scatter their armor and commit it piecemeal.

Rommel resolved to keep the Tobruk garrison isolated and to destroy the two brigades (2d and 4th) of the New Zealand Division in the Belhamed area. On November 29, 15th Panzer detoured to the south and west around Sidi Rezegh and, in a bitter battle, seized Ed Duda in an advance from the southwest. Ariete Division and 21st Panzer were to assault the New Zealanders from the east and south but made little headway because British armor attacked them on their southern flank.

Rommel's determination to continue to battle was a measure of his willpower. His men were exhausted, the weather cold, the country waterless, and the Axis supply system broken down. Although the New Zealanders were nearly encircled, strong British armor threatened to bowl over the light forces covering the southern flank, the 1st South African Brigade was coming up to help, and the Tobruk garrison was still powerful.

On the morning of November 30, 15th Panzer, in cooperation with battle groups from 90th Light, attacked southward from the escarpment north of Sidi Rezegh, and by evening it had captured some New Zealand positions, 600 prisoners, and twelve guns. Meanwhile, 21st Panzer and Ariete beat off a relieving attack by British armor from the south.

During the night most of the New Zealanders broke out, although the Germans captured more than 1,000 men and twenty-six guns. British armor and infantry moved south and east to regroup, once more isolating Tobruk.

The Axis seemed to have won. But the price had been too high. Rommel realized he had no offensive power left, while British tank strength was growing daily with shipments from the rear. Knowing he had to extricate his army if he hoped to fight another day, Rommel retreated westward in a masterful series of engagements, finally halting at Mersa el Brega, on the border of Tripolitania, on January 6, 1942.

Although the Axis garrison at Bardia surrendered on January 2, 1942, the starving force at Halfaya Pass held out until January 17. With the main travel routes blocked, the British found it difficult to bring up supplies and reduced their forces in the forward area about Agedabia to the 201st Guards Brigade and 1st Armored Division, newly arrived from England and replacing the worn 7th Armored Division.

Meanwhile the situation had improved greatly for Rommel. Adolf Hitler had transferred a large German air fleet to Sicily and Italy, and it successfully challenged British air superiority over the shipping lanes to Libya. On January 5, 1942, an Italian convoy reached Tripoli with fifty-five tanks and a number of antitank guns. These, plus repairs, brought Rommel's tank strength at the front on January 20 to 111 German and 89 Italian, with 28 more in the rear. The 1st Armored Division, in contrast, had 150 tanks manned by inexperienced crews.

Rommel decided on a counteroffensive. Keeping his plans from both the Italian and German high commands in order to avoid security leaks, Rommel lulled the British into complacency by forbidding all reconnaissance, camouflaging his tanks to look like trucks, and massing his forces by short night marches.

His blow, on the night of January 20–21, 1942, therefore, was a stunning surprise. Rommel sent a battle group of the 90th Light and some tanks northward along the Via Balbia, while Africa Corps advanced through the desert along the Wadi el Faregh, some forty miles inland, hoping to surround the British. But the panzers used up much fuel in the sand dunes and the enemy had time to escape encirclement, concentrating east of Agedabia. Africa Corps ran out of fuel, but Rommel took personal command of the 90th Light battle group and rushed directly on Agedabia, seizing the town on January 22, and continuing northward on the Via Balbia, throwing British supply columns into confusion.

Rommel now tried to surround 1st Armored, but the bulk of it escaped northward, although Africa Corps enveloped one combat group and destroyed seventy tanks near Saunnu, forty miles northeast of Agedabia. The remaining British armor broke for Msus, forty miles north, in one of the most extraordinary routs of the war. The panzers, in hot pursuit, sometimes at speeds of 15 mph, wrecked more than half the remainder of the British tanks.

Rommel now feinted with Africa Corps toward El Mechili, eighty miles northeast of Msus across the chord of the Cyrenaican bulge. Since Rommel had made such a move in his first offensive in April 1941, Ritchie fell for the bait and concentrated all his armor to meet it. Instead, Rommel rushed 90th Light along the coast to Benghazi. Again the British were surprised, losing mountains of supplies and 1,000 men from 4th Indian Division taken prisoner. The victory induced Hitler to promote Rommel to colonel general and redesignate the panzer group as a panzer army, though he sent no additional troops. Rommel's forces were exhausted and too weak for more offensive action. Ritchie withdrew all the way to Gazala, only forty miles west of Tobruk, and began to build a defensive line. Rommel came up to the line on February 6, 1942. He had achieved much with little, regaining most of Cyrenaica and a good position to attack again as soon as he could rebuild his strength.

Winston Churchill, who continued to pour men and equipment into Egypt, wanted Auchinleck to take the offensive as early as February 1942. But Auchinleck would not be hurried and insisted on building 8th Army's strength to ensure great superiority. In this regard, the British had something of an ally in Adolf Hitler. Rommel visited Hitler in March, but the Führer, preoccupied with the war against the Soviet Union, offered no major reinforcements. Rommel's one gain was increased flows of supplies, since the German Luftwaffe, in almost continuous bombing, was neutralizing Malta as an air and submarine base.

Seeing that the longer he waited the stronger the British would become, Rommel resolved to strike at the earliest possible moment. The date he chose was May 26, 1942, forestalling Auchinleck, who intended to commence his offensive nearly a month later.

By May 26 the Axis and the British were about equal in air power, but 8th Army had 850 tanks in five armored brigades, plus 420 more in the rear as replacements, compared to Rommel's 560, of which only 280 were gun-armed German Mark IIIs or IVs. The rest were 230 obsolete Italian tanks and 50 light tanks. Rommel's reserves consisted of thirty tanks under repair and twenty just landed at Tripoli. The British had a three-to-one superiority for the opening clash and a four-to-one edge if the campaign became a battle of attrition.

The great difference in armored strength, moreover, was not in numbers but in quality. The British now deployed 170 decidedly superior tanks: American Grants carrying a side-mounted 75mm and a turret-mounted 37mm gun and boasting 57mm of armor. They had 230 additional Grants in reserve. The tank's only major disadvantages were a high silhouette and a limited traverse for the 75mm gun. The closest German competitors were nineteen new Mark III Specials mounting a long-barreled, high-velocity 50mm gun and 50mm of armor. Older Mark IIIs, armed with a short-barreled 50mm gun, and Mark IVs, mounting a short-barreled 75mm gun, made up the bulk of Rommel's strength. They could be shattered by the Grant's gun at ranges beyond either tank's capacity to penetrate the Grant's armor.

The British also armed their motorized infantry with the new 6-pounder (57mm) antitank gun, with 30 percent more penetration than the German 50mm antitank gun. The German 88mm AA gun remained the most formidable tank killer on either side but Rommel had only forty-eight of these weapons.

The British line, defended by 13th Corps, now under Lieutenant General W.H.E. "Strafer" Gott, stretched from the sea at Gazala to Bir Hacheim, fifty miles south. In the north the 1st South African Division manned a firm ten-mile sector. Below it, however, the three brigades of the British 50th Division occupied widely separated defensive "boxes," flanked only by minefields. At Bir Hacheim, the 1st Free French Brigade of 4,000 men, plus 1,000 members of the Jewish Brigade, was especially isolated; its box was sixteen miles below the 150th Brigade box at Got el Ualeb. The boxes presented the danger that one or more might be bypassed or surrounded and forced to surrender. An added problem was that the British forward railhead and supply base was only forty-five miles east of the Gazala line at Belhamed. It was at once a point that had to be protected and a target for an enemy thrust.

As usual, the British divided their armor between three brigades of cruisers (including Grants) in the 1st and 7th Armored Divisions of 30th Corps, still under General Norrie, and two brigades of "I" or infantry tanks posted in support of the 1st South African and 50th Divisions.

General Rommel found the static, nonmobile defense at Gazala to be typical of British military thinking and based on their close association with infantry warfare in World War I. British commanders had failed to draw the correct conclusions from their defeats in the desert. "In any North African desert position with an open southern flank," Rommel wrote, "a rigid system of defense is bound to lead to disaster," since any such line could be turned and the forces manning it forced to retreat or surrender. Rommel held that defense must be conducted offensively to be successful.[9]

Generals Auchinleck and Ritchie planned to use the two armored divisions to operate offensively. Strangely, however, Auchinleck—while not discounting the possibility that Rommel might strike around the southern flank—believed he most likely would penetrate the center along the Trigh Capuzzo, the Arab desert trail. He gave Ritchie good advice: deploy both his armored divisions astride the trail, so that he could deal with either a thrust along it or a turning moving around the flank.

Ritchie, however, kept 1st Armored, with the 2d and 22d Armored Brigades, around the Trigh Capuzzo but sent 7th Armored, with its single 4th Armored Brigade, southward to support the French at Bir Hacheim and the 3d Indian Motorized Brigade in a guarding position a few miles east. Thus British armor, at the outset, was split into three segments: two "I" brigades (the 1st and 32d) in the north, 1st Armored in the center, and 7th Armored in the south.

Rommel all along planned to strike around the southern flank. But to draw the British toward the center, he ordered tanks and trucks driven in circles behind the Gazala line to give the impression that tanks were assembling. And, in daylight just before the attack, he sent all motorized forces toward the Italian infantry divisions detailed to demonstrate along the Gazala line, then brought them to their assembly points after nightfall.

9. Rommel, 194, 203–4.

Rommel's striking force consisted of Africa Corps (15th and 21st Panzer Divisions), the 20th Italian Motorized Corps (Ariete Armored and Trieste Motorized Divisions), and 90th Light Division. This entire force was to circle around Bir Hacheim. Then Africa Corps and the Italians were to strike directly for Acroma and the coast, cutting off and destroying the armor and troops along the Gazala line. Meanwhile 90th Light—equipped with trucks carrying aircraft engines to simulate the dust clouds raised by advancing tanks—was to push into the El Adem–Belhamed area, about fifteen miles southeast of Tobruk, and cut off the British from their supply dumps and reinforcements.

On the night of May 26, after Italian infantry under German General Cruewell made a diversionary frontal assault against the Gazala line, Rommel's mobile formations, 10,000 vehicles, struck out through a moonlit night and swirling clouds of sand and dust. They met no opposition, and after halting for a short rest just before daybreak a few miles southeast of Bir Hacheim, they thrust at full speed into the British rear.

By 10:00 A.M. on May 27, 90th Light seized El Adem and numerous supply dumps, soon stirring up a furious battle with British forces in the area.

Meanwhile, Africa Corps, now under General Walter Nehring, collided with 4th Armored Brigade some fifteen miles northeast of Bir Hacheim near Bir el Harmat, while, on the left flank, Ariete overwhelmed 3d Indian Motorized Brigade. Contrary to Rommel's orders, Nehring's panzers attacked without artillery support and also were stunned by the long-range penetrating power of the Grant 75mm gun. Fire destroyed tank after tank. The Germans only made headway when they brought up their antitank guns and 88s, while their tanks worked around the enemy flanks, finally inflicting a shattering defeat on the brigade and pushing the survivors northward.

In the late morning the British 22d Armored Brigade arrived from the north but was caught isolated, severely handled in a concentric attack by 15th and 21st Panzers, and forced to withdraw. Africa Corps advanced to the Trigh Capuzzo but there met uncoordinated attacks by 2d Armored Brigade on the west and 1st Army Tank Brigade of "I" tanks on the east, with Grants and Matildas charging recklessly. German antitank guns and

88s exacted a heavy toll, yet the assaults disrupted Africa Corps' advance, cut off German supply columns trying to move up, and forced the panzers, now low on ammunition and fuel, to form a "hedgehog," or defensive perimeter, at nightfall about three miles north of the Trigh Capuzzo.

The Axis forces were in a precarious position, isolated behind British lines. Yet Africa Corps had been able to stop all attacks because each enemy armored brigade had been sent in separately—while Ritchie had not even used the 32d Army Tank Brigade with a hundred heavy infantry Matildas and Valentines.

To Rommel the piecemeal commitment was incomprehensible. The sacrifice of 7th Armored south of Bir el Harmat especially served no purpose. "It was all the same to the British whether my armor was engaged there or on the Trigh Capuzzo," Rommel wrote. "The full motorization of their units would have enabled them to cross the battlefield at great speed to wherever danger threatened."[10]

Rommel's bid for quick victory had failed, victim of the great strength of the British armor and especially of the Grants. The Axis tanks were stalled, their supplies forced to be detoured around the southern flank and subject to attacks by British armored cars. Rommel, against his will, had been drawn into a battle of attrition. General Ritchie had a great opportunity to destroy Africa Corps on May 28 by a concentric attack, especially since the 32d Brigade was fresh and undamaged. However, Ritchie took no such action and gave Rommel time to reorganize.

On May 28, Rommel planned for 90th Light to join Africa Corps for an attack northward. But, harassed by the 4th Armored Brigade, the division was unable to extricate itself. Africa Corps and Ariete Division fought a confused series of engagements with British armored units committed piecemeal. At the end of the day, Africa Corps had 150 tanks left fit for action and the Italians 90, while the British still had 420.

During the night, 90th Light was able to withdraw to Bir el Harmat, and early on May 29, Rommel himself led a supply

10. Ibid., 208.

column to replenish Africa Corps' fuel and ammunition. Although British tanks attacked throughout the day, they again failed to coordinate their assaults and the Germans ended the day in a strong position.

Nevertheless, Rommel realized he could not continue northward until his supply line was secured, since columns circling around Bir Hacheim were being attacked by British motorized forces.

Rommel now made a dramatic decision that saved the campaign for him: he sent 90th Light westward while Italian infantry advanced eastward along the Trigh Capuzzo and broke a supply line directly through the Gazala-line minefields while the remainder of his force went over to the defensive on a shortened front. While defending this front, Rommel planned to destroy the now-isolated 150th Brigade box at Got el Ualeb and the Free French box at Bir Hacheim.

The plan presented an enormous danger. With Axis armor stymied deep in the British rear, Ritchie could have used his seasoned infantry and artillery to crash through the weak Italian divisions manning the Gazala line on the north and sever the Axis supply lines—leaving Rommel's panzers without fuel and endangering the very existence of Axis forces in Africa. However, Rommel knew British commanders would fear he might drive to the sea, although the 400 remaining British tanks, plus antitank guns, could have blocked his 130 remaining German gun-armed tanks and about 100 weak Italian tanks. Rommel was confident the British would fix their attention on the Axis armor and "continue to run their heads against our well-organized defensive front and use up their strength." [11]

This is precisely what happened. On May 30 the British made sporadic and uncoordinated attacks broken up by German 88s and antitank guns. By the end of the day the Axis forces had shot up fifty-seven tanks and established a firm front on the east-west Sidra Ridge, a mile north of the Trigh Capuzzo, and the Aslagh Ridge, about five miles south, enclosing an area the British named the Cauldron.

On May 31, Rommel personally led 90th Light, Trieste, and

11. Ibid., 211.

elements of Africa Corps against the 150th Brigade box. The British, aided by a regiment of Matildas, resisted stubbornly, but their position was hopeless. The next day, after suffering a heavy attack by Stuka dive-bombers and having expended all their ammunition, they gave up, surrendering 3,000 prisoners.

On June 2, 90th Light and Trieste assaulted the Bir Hacheim box. The battle turned into one of the fiercest in the war, lasting ten days, the defenders fighting skillfully from field positions, machine-gun and antitank-gun nests, and slit trenches. They resisted intense dive-bombing, 1,300 Stuka sorties in nine days.

On June 5 the British attempted to destroy Axis armor in the Cauldron, making direct, obvious, piecemeal attacks Rommel found easy to counter.

On the north, slow, heavy Matildas and Valentines of the 32d Tank Brigade lumbered forward in daylight, unsupported by artillery fire, providing perfect targets for antitank guns of 21st Panzer on Sidra Ridge. They ended in a minefield and were shot to pieces. The brigade lost fifty out of seventy tanks engaged.

On the east, 10th Indian Brigade drove Ariete Division off Aslagh Ridge. Then 22d Armored Brigade passed through, followed by the 9th Indian Brigade. The British tanks received terrific fire from German antitank guns and artillery and withdrew to Bir et Tamar, between Aslagh and Sidra Ridges. At midday, Rommel launched one of his most brilliant counterstrokes. While 21st Panzer thrust southeast toward Bir et Tamar, 15th Panzer emerged from a gap in the minefields south of Aslagh Ridge and struck the flank and rear of Indian troops holding the ridge. By nightfall the Axis had scattered the 9th Indian Brigade and formed a ring around the 10th Brigade on Aslagh, the Support Group of 22d Armored Brigade to the north and four field artillery regiments. The only hope for the British was a coordinated attack by their armor, but this never developed. By the end of the day on June 6, Africa Corps had destroyed a hundred tanks, wiped out 10th Brigade, and captured 3,100 men, ninety-six cannon, and thirty-seven antitank guns. Total British tank strength had fallen from 400 to 170.

Having stopped British attempts to destroy his armor, Rommel decided to eliminate Bir Hacheim before bursting out of the Cauldron. On June 8 strong elements of 15th Panzer joined other Axis forces for a coordinated attack of extreme violence from all directions against the Free French brigade, under the inspired leadership of Pierre Koenig. A German combat group finally cracked into the main enemy position on June 10. The greater part of the garrison broke out during the night and was picked up by a British motor brigade—showing how difficult it is to contain a determined force under a resolute commander. Only 500 Allied soldiers fell into German hands, most of them wounded.

The way was now clear for Rommel to thrust into the British vitals, though Ritchie had brought up reinforcements and had 330 tanks, twice the remaining strength of Africa Corps. But British confidence had been badly shaken, while the Axis forces, though sadly weakened, were smelling victory.

On June 11, 1942, 15th Panzer swung northeast toward El Adem, with 90th Light—now reduced to 1,000 men—on the right and Trieste Division on the left. By nightfall the divisions were south and west of El Adem, facing the 2d and 4th Armored Brigades. Rommel ordered 21st Panzer to swing around to the northeast the next day and take the enemy armor in the rear. The move cornered the two British armored brigades. German antitank guns moved forward and began a systematic execution. When 22d Armored Brigade advanced from the north to help, it suffered heavy losses from 21st Panzer and Trieste. The two trapped brigades attempted to flee, the 2d withdrawing in some order with 22d Brigade toward Knightsbridge box, a few miles north, but the 4th's retreat turning into a rout. The British lost 120 tanks. The next day, Rommel turned north and squeezed the British out of Knightsbridge box and continued to harry the fleeing armor. By nightfall Ritchie had barely a hundred tanks left. Rommel enjoyed tank superiority for the first time and was in possession of the battlefield, permitting him to recover many tanks.

The British along the Gazala line were in danger of being cut off, and Ritchie ordered them back on the morning of June 14. The same morning Rommel sent Africa Corps past Acroma with urgent instructions to seal off the Via Balbia during the night. But the German panzer troops were so exhausted they dropped down short of the road at nightfall. The next morning, 15th Panzer descended the escarpment and blocked the road, but by that time most of the South African infantry had escaped, moving quickly back to the Egyptian frontier. The British 50th Division found a different escape route, breaking out west through the Italian front, moving on a long circuit south, then east to the frontier.

The shattered British armored brigades now were no match for the panzers, and they retreated into Egypt. Africa Corps swept around the Tobruk perimeter, avoiding the large British garrison there, and seized airfields at Gambut, thirty-five miles east of Tobruk, thus forcing British aircraft eastward and beyond easy range of Tobruk. The panzers then turned back.

Tobruk was a symbol of British resistance, and Rommel was determined to seize it. The British, seeing the panzers go past, did not expect an attack, but Rommel mounted one quickly, cracking a hole in the southeast perimeter on June 20 with artillery and dive-bombers. Infantry widened the gap, then panzers poured through, overcoming the dazed defenders. Tobruk surrendered the next day, giving up 35,000 prisoners— second only to the capture of Singapore by the Japanese as the greatest British disaster of the war. Hitler was so impressed he promoted Rommel to field marshal. But Rommel wrote his wife, "I would rather he had given me one more division."[12]

The abrupt loss of Tobruk shocked General Ritchie to such a degree that he abandoned the potentially strong Sollum and Halfaya Gap positions on the frontier, although he had three times as many tanks as Rommel and three almost intact infantry divisions there, with a fourth on the way up. Ritchie planned to make a stand at Mersa Matruh, 130 miles east of the frontier. But Auchinleck—seeing Ritchie no longer had the confidence to lead 8th Army—took over direct command on June 25 and decided to withdraw all the way to El Alamein, 110 miles farther east and only 60 miles from Alexandria, the British navy's vital Mediterranean base.

12. Ibid., 232.

It was a difficult decision, certain to raise a terrible fright in London, for El Alamein was literally Britain's last-ditch defense of the Middle East. If Rommel threatened Alexandria, the British fleet would be forced to abandon the Mediterranean, severing the supply line to Malta, guaranteeing its surrender, and turning the sea into an Axis lake. Rommel then could have received ample supplies with which to seize the Egyptian Delta, Palestine, and Syria.

Nevertheless, Auchinleck's choice was shrewd and strategically brilliant. He knew Rommel was almost at the end of his tether, that he had only a few dozen tanks and the barest shadow of his former troop strength. Alamein could eliminate Rommel's only remaining advantage, his ability to maneuver, because the immense Qattara Depression was only thirty-five miles to the south and its salt marshes and soft sand formed an almost impassable barrier for tanks. With his tanks, infantry, and artillery deployed along the short Alamein front, Auchinleck could block Rommel's few remaining tanks and force him to fight the static, set-piece battle of attrition in which the British excelled.

If Auchinleck once stopped Rommel, the Axis position would rapidly become hopeless. For the British were close to their supply sources and had many more tanks, airplanes, guns, and troops to draw on in any case. Rommel, on the other hand, was dependent upon the weak Italian navy, which was certain to avoid sending convoys into Tobruk or Mersa Matruh for fear of challenging the Royal Navy and would ship supplies to Benghazi or Tripoli, requiring road transport of 750 or 1,400 miles to Alamein.

Rommel recognized the danger and pushed his vehicles and men mercilessly in hopes of getting past the Alamein barrier before the British could organize a defense. But he had only forty gun-armed German tanks and 2,500 motorized German infantry, while his 6,000 remaining Italian infantry were less mobile and slower coming forward.

Despite Auchinleck's decision, British forces attempted to defend Mersa Matruh. Rommel, knowing that everything now hinged on audacity, speed, and the moral effect of his previous triumphs, attacked with his three extremely weak German divisions on June 26. While 90th Light reached the coast road

east of Matruh the next evening, blocking the direct line of
retreat, 21st Panzer made a deep penetration farther south,
threatening the line of retreat of 13th Corps' mobile forces posted
in this area. The corps commander, General Gott, ordered withdrawal, but sent no word to the two divisions holding the Mersa
Matruh perimeter until the next morning. Nearly two-thirds of
the garrison escaped the following night in small groups, but
6,000 fell prisoner—a number larger than Rommel's entire
striking force.

Rommel now sent his panzers all out for Alamein. They
arrived on June 30. Auchinleck had established four boxes along
the thirty-five-mile stretch from the sea to the Qattara Depression, but the intervals between them were covered only by
small mobile columns. Rommel, however, believed Auchinleck had posted his tanks north of the depression, not realizing
they were still in the desert to the southwest, trying desperately
to get to Alamein. Consequently, Rommel halted to work out
an attack.

This halt, however inevitable, was fatal. Rommel did not
know it, but he had just one chance to break through at Alamein
before British armor came up. If he had done so at once he
could have rushed on to Alexandria and the Egyptian Delta.
He did not. This was the turning point of the war in North
Africa.

Rommel attacked the next day, Wednesday, July 1, 1942.
His reputation now was so awesome that, weak as he was, the
news terrified the British. The fleet immediately withdrew from
Alexandria and slipped through the Suez Canal to safety in the
Red Sea. In Cairo, chimneys smoked from sensitive files being
burned. Commanders frantically planned to evacuate the delta.

Africa Corps' attack went in about twelve miles south of the
sea at Deir el Shein and hit a box Rommel did not know was
there. Defended by the 18th Indian Brigade, the box held until
evening, when the Germans captured it with most of the defenders. British armor finally arrived, too late to save the box
but in time to check Rommel's efforts during the night to penetrate to the rear. From this point on, the Axis presence in Africa
was doomed.

Although Rommel renewed the attack the next day, the Germans had fewer than forty tanks and were forced to halt when they sighted British tanks in their path and others moving around their flank. Rommel, determined, tried again on July 3. By now he had only twenty-six tanks, but they advanced nine miles before British fire halted them. During the day a New Zealand battalion captured nearly all of Ariete Division's artillery in a flank attack, while the remaining Italians took to their heels, clear evidence of exhaustion and overstrain on the part of the Axis troops.

Rommel realized his troops were too tired and too few, and he broke off the attack to give them a rest. Auchinleck had at last gained the initiative, and he counterattacked on July 4. The Axis troops held, and both sides soon stopped out of sheer fatigue and slowly built their strength. In succeeding weeks they engaged in savage attempts to break through each other's lines. The tactical situation changed little, but the strategic situation worsened daily for the Axis, since Rommel had no hope of matching the immense buildup of British arms and troops.

On August 4, Churchill flew out to Cairo and decided to change Middle East commanders when he found Auchinleck strongly resisting his pressure to renew the offensive. Auchinleck wanted to wait until September in order for newly arrived forces to learn desert warfare. Churchill gave the command to General Sir Harold Alexander and brought out General Sir Bernard Montgomery from England to run 8th Army. Montgomery turned out to be even more insistent than Auchinleck on building up his strength, completing his preparations, and training his troops in his painstaking, deliberate methods of operation. Churchill was forced to give way.

Rommel launched an offensive on August 30, but, despite some gains, the panzers could not break through the strong British defenses. From this point on the Axis forces simply hung on, waiting for the British blow to fall.

Montgomery launched his offensive on October 23, 1942, a move designed to precede the joint American and British landings in Morocco and Algeria (French North Africa) on November 8. By this time Montgomery had 230,000 men and 1,440 tanks, with 1,000 more in the rear. Rommel had fewer than 80,000 men (27,000 German) and 210 gun-armed German and

280 obsolete Italian tanks. In the air, the Allies had 1,500 first-line aircraft, the Germans and Italians only 350. More important, the Royal Navy's submarines were strangling the Axis forces, sinking a third of all deliveries in September and half in October.

Rommel himself had become sick and was recovering in Austria when the attack opened. He flew back to Africa the next day, but there was nothing he could do to save the situation. However, he showed his greatness as a general by conducting a brilliant retreat into Tripolitania, never allowing his forces to become trapped.[13]

Although Rommel dealt American forces a stunning blow at Kasserine Pass in Tunisia on February 19–20, 1943, his remaining forces were drawn into Hitler's impossible effort to maintain a foothold in Tunisia and block both 8th Army and the huge Anglo-American armies advancing from Algeria. This effort consumed many times more forces than Rommel would have needed to seize all of North Africa and the Middle East in 1941–42. When the final Axis defeat came, however, Rommel had been withdrawn to Europe, where he fought an equally hopeless battle as commander of the German forces opposing the Allied landings in Normandy on June 6, 1944.

13. Montgomery's counterattack at El Alamein was widely viewed among the British as the figurative turning point of the war, since this marked the first time that a German army was defeated and forced permanently to abandon large segments of territory.

10

MacArthur

A JEKYLL AND HYDE IN KOREA

AFTER WORLD WAR II, American leaders believed that Joseph Stalin, premier of the Soviet Union, was leading an enormous conspiracy aimed at world conquest and that all Communists everywhere served as willing tools of Soviet aggression. They were unable to see that Communist states sought to advance their own interests, just as non-Communist states, and that no conspiracy existed.

The greatest collision point between the two superpowers occurred in Korea, a peninsula jutting out from East Asia. To facilitate the surrender of Japanese troops occupying the country, Russia and the United States had divided Korea along the 38th parallel in 1945. This temporary division quickly solidified into a bristling barrier between East and West, with the United States creating a right-wing government under Syngman Rhee in South Korea and the Soviets establishing a Communist state under Kim Il Sung in North Korea.

The Korean people as a whole were deeply disturbed by the division of their country, and on June 25, 1950, the North Koreans invaded South Korea with the intention of forcibly reuniting the country. Long afterward it became clear that Stalin, though he had armed the North Koreans, merely had gone along with Kim Il Sung's view that he could seize South Korea in a swift campaign. However, the U.S. president, Harry Truman, and his advisers were unanimous in the belief that the attack signaled Stalin's first overt move to conquer the world— and he had to be stopped at all costs.

The United States took advantage of the Soviet Union's boycott of the United Nations Security Council (because the United States was blocking admission of Communist China) and got the UN to endorse a campaign to drive North Korea back across the 38th parallel. Truman authorized General of the Army Douglas MacArthur, Far East commander, to employ the only American troops immediately available, the four understrength divisions occupying Japan, while the Pentagon commenced a frantic effort to remobilize large segments of the American military establishment.

The North Korean (NK) forces meanwhile shattered the much weaker Republic of Korea (ROK) army primarily by advancing heavily armored Soviet T34 tanks. These were virtually impervious to the fire of the South Koreans' few American 2.36-inch rocket launchers (bazookas) and 105-millimeter howitzers, which had no armor-piercing shells.

The first American troops committed also possessed nothing to stop the T34 and likewise fell back until, by August 1950, at last armed with tanks of their own and effective antitank weapons, they formed a small "Pusan perimeter" around the southern port city of Pusan. The North Koreans launched attack after attack against the perimeter in an attempt to force the Americans to evacuate. The Americans held on grimly, because they understood that if they once abandoned the peninsula, it would be difficult to get support from other UN members to reconquer South Korea.

Anyway, General MacArthur, only days after the invasion, had devised a method to destroy the NK army along with the North Korean state. To achieve his goals, the bulk of the North Korean army had to be kept pressing with all its strength against the Pusan perimeter.

While the world watched breathlessly as the thin American and ROK forces slowed and finally held the North Koreans, an intense undercover drama unfolded between the Joint Chiefs of Staff (JCS) in the Pentagon and MacArthur in his headquarters in Tokyo. The major issue, over which the Joint Chiefs and MacArthur differed most heatedly, was whether MacArthur's recipe would achieve a great victory or threaten a huge defeat.

MacArthur, already highly respected because of his successful campaigns against the Japanese in the southwestern Pacific and the Philippines in World War II, got his way over the opposition of the Joint Chiefs. And since his venture turned out to be hugely successful, he became a larger-than-life figure with a reputation for omniscience. This increased MacArthur's already elevated sense of his own brilliance while silencing the Joint Chiefs, who had proved to be so wrong. The consequence was that MacArthur, only weeks after pulling off one of the most spectacular victories in American history, led the United States into one of its most devastating defeats. MacArthur thus proved to be a military Dr. Jekyll and Mr. Hyde, capable of both brilliant strategic insights and desolating error.

MacArthur realized that the farther the North Koreans advanced southward, the deeper they fell into a sack that the United States could close at will behind them. This was because the United States possessed complete control of the sea and could place an amphibious force anywhere it chose behind the North Korean army. MacArthur also saw the perfect place to land the blow: the port of Inchon, only about twenty miles west of the Korean capital of Seoul.

Not only was Seoul of great political and symbolic importance, but through it ran the only double-tracked railway in Korea and the only roads sufficient to supply the North Korean forces around the Pusan perimeter. If American forces could seize Seoul, they would cut the North Korean umbilical cord, for the few north-south dirt roads east of the capital were inadequate as supply routes for the NK forces.

Consequently, a landing at Inchon and capture of Seoul would mean destruction of the North Korean army along the Pusan perimeter without a shot being fired. A modern army cannot exist long without food, oil, and ammunition. More important, it disintegrates when it is cut off from the rear because the men begin to consider how they, personally, can get out of the trap they're in. An army in this frame of mind soon turns into a mob seeking safety.

Almost immediately after the war started, MacArthur began making plans for a landing at Inchon. The JCS opposed the location because of the extremely high tides there and the narrow approach channel, approachable only from the south. At

DOUGLAS MACARTHUR
Imperial War Museum

Inchon, high tides and mud flats are produced by waters funneling through the narrow Yellow Sea between the Korean peninsula on the east and Chinese Shandong peninsula on the west. The situation is much like that in Canada's Bay of Fundy, closed in by New Brunswick and Nova Scotia.

Naval experts believed small landing craft would need twenty-three-foot minimum tides to operate safely over the Inchon mud flats and a twenty-nine-foot tide before Landing Ship Tanks (LSTs) could come in. Thus the navy could land men and equipment only from the time the incoming tide reached twenty-three feet until the outgoing tide dropped to twenty-three feet, about three hours. Troops ashore would be stranded until the next tide, about twelve hours later. The tide tables dictated September 15 as the earliest date the tide surges would be high enough. To wait longer would invite bad weather and an indefinite postponement of the invasion.

Given these constraints, the Joint Chiefs supported instead an invasion at Kunsan, a small port about a hundred miles south of Inchon and only about seventy air miles west of the Pusan perimeter line.

MacArthur pointed out that a landing at Kunsan would not sever the NK supply lines, while the North Koreans could shift forces quickly to form a new line across South Korea. Any U.S. attack thereafter would have to be a direct assault on defended emplacements, driving the North Koreans back on their reserves and supplies, not severing the NK army from them.

MacArthur's Inchon plan was a version of Napoleon's *manœuvre sur les derrières,* in which he sought to establish a strategic barrage or barrier between the enemy army and its sources of supply and to block its avenues of retreat (see page 107). It exploited the line of least resistance, because it was a line of least expectation of the North Korean leadership. The NK commanders saw little need to worry about Inchon or to post many troops there, because they knew of the high tides and believed an invasion virtually impossible.

MacArthur, on the other hand, recognized that physical impediments, however formidable, are inherently less dangerous and uncertain than the hazards of combat. Physical problems can be calculated and overcome, but human resistance is unpredictable.

The conflict between MacArthur and the Joint Chiefs is one of the most revealing cases in modern times of how one military leader sees opportunity while other leaders see danger in a given situation. This case is all the more remarkable because the Joint Chiefs did not recognize that MacArthur's proposal closely resembled the winning "island-hopping" strategy of the Pacific campaign in World War II. The Americans bypassed islands or positions heavily garrisoned by the Japanese and struck at targets beyond, leaving the bypassed Japanese useless for further military purposes. By landing at Inchon, the Americans likewise would bypass the NK forces along the Pusan perimeter, forcing them to surrender or disintegrate in attempting to flee back into North Korea.

MacArthur presented his first argument for the Inchon landing at a meeting on July 13, 1950, in Toyko with Generals J. Lawton Collins, army chief of staff, and Hoyt S. Vandenberg, air force chief of staff. During the talks he announced his intention to destroy the North Korean army, not merely to drive it back beyond the 38th parallel. This goal could not possibly be achieved without destroying the North Korean state.

Collins was skeptical of Inchon as a site, and when he reported to Omar Bradley, the chief of staff, Bradley responded: "I had to agree that it was the riskiest military proposal I had ever heard of." He called it a "blue-sky" scheme and said, "Inchon was probably the worst possible place ever selected for an amphibious landing."[1]

The Joint Chiefs focused on their opposition to Inchon as a landing site and—along with President Truman and Dean Acheson, secretary of state—did not face up to the implications of MacArthur's aim to destroy North Korea. This would present an enormous challenge to Red China, because it would eliminate the strategic buffer separating Communist China from the United States.

1. Bradley and Blair, 544.

Such a move would be even more provocative because Truman, at the outbreak of the Korean War, had established a protectorate over the Chinese island of Taiwan, to which the Chinese Communists' enemies, the Nationalists, had fled in 1949. Truman, believing the conspiracy theory, was convinced that the Red Chinese were in league with Stalin and helping the North Koreans, although the Chinese Communists were innocent and were seeking only to reunite their country.

Thus the presence of powerful U.S. forces on the Yalu River, the Chinese-Korean border, could only be interpreted by the Reds as a preliminary to an American or American-backed Nationalist invasion of the Chinese mainland.

MacArthur made a formal presentation for the Inchon invasion on August 23 in Tokyo to General Collins, Admiral Forrest P. Sherman, chief of naval operations, and several other high officers. The Joint Chiefs inclined toward postponing Inchon until they were sure the American forces (8th Army) could hold the Pusan perimeter, now under renewed attack. But President Truman, Secretary of Defense Louis Johnson, and Truman's roving ambassador W. Averell Harriman were convinced, Truman calling it a daring strategic conception. Thus civilians supported MacArthur's plan, while the top military men, the Joint Chiefs, were hesitant.

At this moment the NK command launched a last, desperate attempt to crack through the Pusan perimeter and drive the Americans and ROKs into the sea. They had assembled about 98,000 men, one-third recruits conscripted in South Korea and rushed into battle without training. Against them the UN command had assembled 120,000 combat troops, plus 60,000 support personnel. UN firepower was several times what the North Koreans could bring to bear. Consequently, the NK assaults, though carried out with great determination, failed all across the line and the NK army suffered 28,000 casualties within a couple of weeks.

The Joint Chiefs were frightened by the North Korean attacks and implied in a message on September 7 that the invasion might best be postponed, since "all available trained army units in the United States have been allocated to you except the 82d Airborne Division." The invasion, MacArthur replied

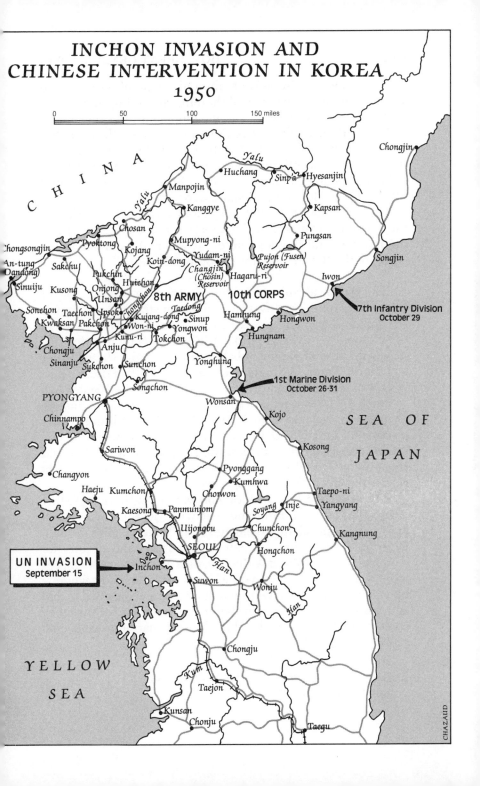

with vehemence, "represents the only hope of wresting the initiative from the enemy and thereby presenting an opportunity for a decisive blow." The envelopment from Inchon, he added, "will instantly relieve pressure on the south perimeter.
. . . The seizure of the heart of the enemy distributing system in the Seoul area will completely dislocate the logistical supply of his forces now operating in South Korea and therefore will ultimately result in their disintegration."[2]

On September 8 the JCS at last told Truman they endorsed the Inchon invasion. But the approval remained grudging to the last. General Bradley wrote: "It was really too late in the game for the JCS to formally disapprove Inchon."[3]

The Inchon assault, on September 15, 1950, was the world's last great amphibious invasion and demonstrated the immense strength and tremendous capability of the U.S. Navy. Unlike the more nearly even ground battles, the Inchon invasion displayed the overwhelming imbalance between the United States and North Korea. A single example: the North Koreans possessed nineteen piston-driven aircraft; the United States had so much air power, jet and piston, that there was not enough airspace to accommodate it over the battlefield and its approaches. The UN had assembled 230 vessels, including two escort carriers and two attack carriers, with a third attack carrier steaming at forced speed from California and a British light carrier serving in the covering force.

The key to the assault on Inchon was neutralization of a tiny island, Wolmi-do, a thousand feet wide, just off Inchon and known to conceal high-velocity 75-millimeter guns camouflaged in deep revetments. Although the navy and air force for days had been bombing Wolmi-do, plus numerous other places around the coast to deceive the North Koreans as to where a blow might land, the naval commanders knew they had to find and destroy the reveted guns before the invasion because they could wreak havoc on the thin-skinned marine assault craft scheduled to land at Inchon.

2. Alexander, *Korea: The First War We Lost*, 189.
3. Bradley and Blair, 556.

On September 13, therefore, Rear Admiral J. M. Higgins with two heavy U.S. cruisers, two light British cruisers, and six U.S. destroyers sailed up the narrow Flying Fish Channel and commenced shelling Wolmi-do, five of the destroyers anchoring just off the island, deliberately inviting fire from the 75s in order to find where they were hidden. The North Korean gun commander waited three minutes, knowing it was his duty to fire but also knowing it would bring down destruction on himself and his men. At last his high-velocity 75s opened fire, hitting three destroyers, inflicting some damage and a few casualties, but revealing the five guns' positions. The destroyers' gunners laid elevations and azimuths with sharpshooters' precision, then let go with salvo after salvo aimed directly into the deep revetments and upon the guns. The Wolmi-do 75s fell silent.

At 6:33 A.M. on September 15, landing craft carrying the 3d Battalion, 5th Marine Regiment, and nine M26 Pershing tanks landed on Wolmi-do and quickly seized the island, killing 108 men, capturing 136, and sealing 100 more in caves when they refused to surrender.

The way had been cleared for the main assaults, the 5th Marines on Red Beach, over a fifteen-foot stone seawall directly into the heart of the city, and the 1st Marines on Blue Beach southeast of the city. Both assaults went in around 5:30 P.M. against minimal resistance. Within a few hours the marines had gained commanding elevations with few casualties. Only a few North Korean forces were in Inchon, and these were largely ill-trained recruits.

At 7:30 A.M. on September 16 the two marine regiments made contact, sealing off the city. Major General Edward M. (Ned) Almond, commanding 10th Corps, which was running the operation, ordered a regiment of ROK marines to mop up the city. They made Inchon unsafe for friend or foe until they completed the task.

Meantime the 7th Marine Regiment and the 7th Infantry Division landed, while the two leading marine regiments struck out for Seoul.

The North Korean command was virtually paralyzed by MacArthur's stunning invasion. Only meager forces—and these

almost wholly green outfits never before committed to action—
were on hand to counter the UN blow. By chance the new 18th
NK Division was moving through Seoul on the way to the Pusan
perimeter when the Inchon assault came. The NK command
ordered it to retake Inchon, and advance elements checked
marines on September 17 halfway between Inchon and Yongdungpo, an industrial suburb immediately south of the Han
River at Seoul. There also was an NK regiment (the 70th) at
Suwon, twenty miles south of Seoul, and it moved up to join
the battle.

The North Koreans faced almost insuperable difficulties in
getting reinforcements to Inchon-Seoul. The 87th Regiment of
the 9th NK Division, on the Pusan perimeter front about 150
miles south of Seoul, departed by rail on September 16 but took
four days to get there, the train having to hide in tunnels during
the day to avoid American aircraft. Likewise, the just-formed
2,500-man 25th NK Brigade at Chorwon, fifty-five miles north
of Seoul, also took four days to arrive by rail.

The NK command made one wise decision: it did not inform
the troops on the Pusan perimeter that UN troops had landed
in their rear. As a consequence, the North Korean soldiers there
continued to look forward, not over their shoulders, and held
up an effort by 8th Army to break out of the perimeter on September 16. It was nearly a week before news of the landing
filtered through. And then the North Korean army disintegrated.

Only about 30,000 of the 70,000 soldiers facing 8th Army
eventually got back to North Korea, most of them walking through
mountains and nearly all leaving their weapons behind. There
had been no chance to retrieve the situation, because Mac-
Arthur had placed the North Koreans in an impossible position.
Their defeat was inevitable and their only solution was to retreat back into North Korea.

Although the marine and army advance severed the rail and
road links with the south, thereby achieving the purpose of the
invasion in the first couple of days, the NK command knew as
well as MacArthur the tremendous symbolic importance of Seoul
and attempted desperately to hold the capital. The commander

of the 1st Marine Division, Major General Oliver P. Smith, played into the North Koreans' hands.

Smith ignored a brilliant *coup de main* by a marine company commander, Captain Robert Barrow, which gave the marines a superb tactical position at Yongdungpo. North Koreans held up 1st Marines forces attempting to move on the suburb from the north and south but failed to guard a swampy area of rice paddies in the center. Barrow led his company undetected through the inundated land directly into the center of the city and firmly defended a barricade on the main exit routes out of Yongdungpo to the north.

This forced the North Koreans to evacuate the suburb and gave the marines the opportunity to cross the Han River directly south of Seoul, thereby flanking a strong three-mile-long defensive line the North Koreans established just north of the Han and just west of Seoul.

General Smith, however, refused to undertake an envelopment from the south and insisted on throwing the 5th Marines directly against the dug-in NK positions north of the river. Although Smith used air strikes and artillery liberally, the battle degenerated into a bloodbath. The marines at last destroyed the weak NK forces defending the line, but it took three days (September 22–25).

The North Korean commander ordered evacuation of Seoul only after General Almond—exasperated by Smith's extremely costly frontal assaults—sent the army 7th Division's 32d Regiment across the Han on September 25 and made the NK position in Seoul untenable.

Although the North Koreans withdrew their mobile forces northward, they left small parties in the streets of Seoul at numerous chest-high barricades of earth-filled bags with antitank mines in front. Behind the barricades the North Koreans manned antitank and machine guns, while other NK soldiers hid in nearby buildings and fired from windows and doors. This forced the marines and soldiers into a series of nasty little fights that caused casualties on both sides and destroyed large parts of the city.

When they encountered a barricade, U.S. troops ordered in

marine or navy aircraft to rocket and strafe the positions. Then mortars and artillery fired to keep the North Koreans down while engineers exploded the mines. Then two or three medium tanks advanced against the barricade, destroying the guns and breaching the barrier, followed by infantry. It sometimes took an hour to break a barricade, leaving behind a twisted, burning section of Seoul.

Throughout the entire Inchon-Seoul operation, the North Koreans were unable to concentrate enough strength at any point to achieve parity of numbers, much less superiority. The NK command was so dislocated and surprised that it had to commit troops in piecemeal blocking actions against UN forces that at each point were greatly superior. In an attempt to retrieve a hopeless situation, the NK commanders repeatedly ordered suicidal counterattacks and tenaciously held their troops on the western approaches to Seoul against murderous U.S. air strikes and artillery barrages. MacArthur's forces defeated the North Koreans consecutively in detail, and they could never concentrate for a decisive counterstroke.

MacArthur had accurately predicted the outcome. Thus it is surprising that Omar Bradley still called Inchon "the luckiest military operation in history." Hardly any operation involved less luck and more elimination of chance. At least Bradley owned up: "In hindsight the JCS seemed like a bunch of nervous Nellies to have doubted."[4]

The Inchon invasion was a spectacular success. It was this stunning victory that precipitated the United States into an invasion of North Korea. MacArthur's reputation after Inchon soared, and the Truman administration now paid more attention than ever to his admonitions to destroy the North Korean army and create a unified Korea.

While listening to MacArthur, the administration ignored Red Chinese troop buildups next to the Yalu River, the boundary between Chinese Manchuria and North Korea. Instead it concluded that Joseph Stalin would not risk world war over Korea. Since Truman, Acheson, and other top U.S. leaders were

4. Ibid., 557.

convinced that Red China was an obedient satellite of the Soviet Union, they decided that the Chinese Communists would make no independent move.

This wildly inaccurate appraisal of Red China was the most flagrant example of the Truman administration's misunderstanding of the Chinese revolution. This upheaval, led by Mao Zedong, son of a peasant, had resulted in a great civil war from 1947 to 1949, the flight of diehard Nationalists to Taiwan in 1949, and the establishment of the People's Republic of China on October 1, 1949, with the capital in Beijing.

The Chinese revolution grew out of oppression of the Chinese peasants and workers by landlords, industrialists, and merchants. Red China was never a Soviet satellite. There was plenty of evidence by State Department experts on China to confirm this, but administration leaders refused to acknowledge their findings, continued to view Red China as part of a great Communist conspiracy of world conquest ruled from the Kremlin, and were moving rapidly toward a de facto alliance with Chiang Kai-shek's Nationalists.

Consequently, the administration disregarded the implications of a united Korea from the point of view of Beijing. For a millennium, China had sought to maintain Korea as a shield in front of the North China plain against invasions by the Japanese. It had been grateful for the reestablishment of this buffer in the creation of North Korea. It could only view as a direct challenge a strong military presence on the Yalu by the successor to the Japanese as the danger from the sea, the United States—especially as any UN-sponsored Korea would be dominated by the United States, which had already shown itself an enemy of Red China by its quarantine of Taiwan.

Yet seizure of North Korea would not have improved the American strategic position appreciably. The great threat to the United States was the Soviet Union, which in 1949 had acquired nuclear weapons and which possessed the only military force capable of challenging the United States.

The Truman administration did not consider Red China in its decision to invade North Korea, but listened to Douglas MacArthur, whose mind was focused on driving back the Chinese Communists, and to public opinion in the United States, which after the Inchon success swung toward its traditional desire for total victory.

On September 27, Truman approved a JCS directive authorizing MacArthur to march north of the 38th parallel. Only after this order did the United States seek authority through the UN General Assembly for the invasion and for unification of the country. On October 7, 1950, the UN approved, 47–5, occupation of North Korea and UN elections to create a single Korea. Truman instructed MacArthur to clear operations north of the 38th with him and, in his only nod toward Soviet and Red Chinese anxieties, told MacArthur to employ ROK forces close to the northern Korean borders, yet did not prohibit using American forces there.

Unlike the superb strategic plan for Inchon, MacArthur's preparations to invade North Korea were astonishingly bad and ill-thought-out. As was to be seen, MacArthur exposed his forces to enormous military dangers, most of which could have been avoided.

These decisions show that MacArthur was not, like Napoleon, Stonewall Jackson, or Rommel, a great captain. While Inchon had demonstrated he was capable of brilliant strategy, his plans for conquering North Korea show erratic judgment and inattention to the challenges facing him. Great captains, like any leaders, can make mistakes. But a characteristic of great generals is an ability to see the strategic situation clearly, overcome dangers, and seize opportunities.

MacArthur did not possess this vision. He saw some opportunities, like the chance to cut the North Korean umbilical cord by seizing Seoul. But MacArthur did not look beyond this, his greatest victory. Although he had already told Washington he wanted to destroy North Korea, he made no plans for such a move—either by getting Truman's approval, by weighing the chances of Chinese or Soviet intervention, or by developing a battle plan. Yet, in the chaos that ensued after he seized Seoul, he would have his greatest opportunity to overrun most of North Korea before any significant enemy forces could assemble to oppose him. Likewise, when Truman approved the drive into North Korea, MacArthur did not take precautions to avoid a possible counterstroke—and allowed his army to be divided into two wings, neither of which could support the other. Inchon provides perhaps the best modern example of how one great victory can create in the public mind the conviction that the author of such a victory is virtually incapable of error. Since MacArthur also was convinced of his military sagacity, he labored under few internal restraints. This combination of public adulation and personal arrogance brought on one of the most severe military defeats in United States history.

The best plan to eliminate North Korea's military power would have been to send mobile forces from Seoul northeast to the port of Wonsan on the Sea of Japan to seal off the remnants of the NK army assembled around Chorwon and Kumwha in the middle of the peninsula just north of the 38th parallel. Thereafter the entire UN force could have assembled for a drive northward on Pyongyang, the North Korean capital. Instead, MacArthur withdrew his only fresh force, 10th Corps, already concentrated at Seoul, and sent it on a long sea voyage to an amphibious landing at Wonsan, while 8th Army, exhausted after having driven up from the Pusan perimeter, attacked north toward Pyongyang.

MacArthur's original idea was for 10th Corps to strike west from Wonsan and 8th Army from Seoul in a huge pincers movement to isolate the NK elements around Chorwon and Kumwha. But 10th Corps' amphibious movement took so much time to mount that South Korean infantry had already arrived at Wonsan by foot on October 10 before 10th Corps troops even got into their ships. Thus the last few trained NK troops were able to get away and reform the North Korean army.

Omar Bradley said afterward that MacArthur's plan would have been laughed out of the classroom at the army's Command and General Staff School. Yet such was MacArthur's reputation that the Joint Chiefs approved it without comment.

Since Inchon, the United States had ignored protests by Beijing and heavy Red Chinese troop buildups in Manchuria, just across the Yalu from Korea. Early on October 3, 1950, Zhou Enlai, the Chinese Communist premier and foreign minister, delivered his strongest warning. He informed the Indian ambassador—since the United States had no diplomatic relations with Beijing—that the People's Republic would intervene in

Korea if American troops crossed the 38th parallel, but not if ROK forces did so alone. Washington got the news hours later, but President Truman and Secretary Acheson discounted it and allowed MacArthur's invasion to go forward on October 9.

On October 6, the Red Chinese Politburo held an emergency session and made an astute decision to send "volunteers" to Korea. Although the troops were regular Chinese Communist forces in Chinese uniforms, as volunteers they preserved the fiction that the war was limited to Korea.

Red China consequently did not challenge the United States directly, a decision that prevented American attacks on China and suited U.S. interests, since the Truman administration feared the Soviet Union might intervene if it felt Red China was directly threatened. As a result, Washington preserved the Chinese "sanctuary," as MacArthur called it, saving Chinese cities from bombardment.

By limiting the war to mountainous Korea, the Chinese were able to exploit their military advantages—manpower, digging and tunneling, and light weapons—while partially neutralizing American superiority in heavy weapons and air power.

Under General Peng Dehuai, the Chinese assembled 120,000 men (twelve divisions) along the Yalu, followed by 60,000 reserve troops, and on October 18 sent them into Korea in one of the most remarkable undetected movements in history. Troops moved only from dusk to 4:00 A.M. and were concealed by 5:00 A.M. every day. Consequently, American air observers saw no activity, and in a few days the entire force was concealed in high mountains some forty to fifty miles south of the river.

Meanwhile President Truman, hoping to convince MacArthur of his foreign-policy views and also trying to reflect some of the general's glory to help fellow Democrats in the November congressional elections, flew out to Wake Island, 2,000 miles southeast of Tokyo, and met MacArthur on October 15. During this meeting MacArthur told Truman and General Bradley that the Chinese would not intervene in Korea and that if they did they would be slaughtered. Although Chinese threats had been made plainly and war preparations along the Yalu little hidden, MacArthur's reputation was so awesome that Truman and Bradley did not dispute his judgment.

The 8th Army sliced through weak North Korean resistance and soon captured Pyongyang and pressed on northward, while 10th Corps turned up the eastern coast after landing at Wonsan and sought to seize northeastern Korea. In allowing these two operations to go on simultaneously and separately, MacArthur divided his two major military formations. This fundamental failure to concentrate in the face of the enemy was accentuated by the high mountainous spine running the length of Korea. These mountains kept the two wings divided and unable to cooperate with each other. Had the American divisions been kept together, the disasters about to befall them could have been prevented or at least mitigated.

MacArthur made one additional military error: he allowed Lieutenant General Walton H. Walker, 8th Army commander, to split his advance into a number of disconnected columns moving independently up various roads toward the Yalu. These uncoordinated tactics were suitable only for mopping up demoralized enemy remnants, not advancing toward a possible confrontation with a major opposing force.

Peng Dehuai saw the "wildly arrogant, dispersed, rash advance of the enemy" as a great opportunity and revised the cautious defensive strategy he had planned. Peng concentrated 90,000 men against 8th Army and prepared to deliver a shattering warning blow.[5]

On October 23, 1950, leading elements of 8th Army reached the Chongchon River, a large stream about sixty miles south of the Yalu. There was no evidence of Chinese forces, but Truman's order to employ only ROK troops was in operation this close to the frontier. MacArthur, however, removed all restrictions and ordered American troops to press to the Yalu as well.

On October 25, Chinese Communist forces emerged from the mountains just beyond the Chongchon, shredded a three-division ROK corps into small, frightened fragments, and wiped an additional ROK regiment from the order of battle. General Walker called up a regiment of the U.S. 1st Cavalry Division (actually an infantry unit), but in a series of severe engagements

5. *Peng Dehaui* (Beijing: Liberation Army Publishing House, 1986), ch. 6, translated by Ellis L. Melvin, Tamaroa, Illinois.

over the next several days the Chinese destroyed one of its battalions and drove the remainder across the Chongchon in disorder.

Walker, stunned, withdrew all his forces south of the river. On November 6 the Chinese abruptly marched off the battle-field back into the mountains to the north. The Chinese never disclosed why they did so, but it's likely Beijing hoped the warning blow would stop the advance and both sides could agree on a mutual cease-fire line somewhere south of the Yalu, which would keep American forces away from the Chinese frontier.

MacArthur learned nothing from the experience. When the Joint Chiefs timidly proposed caution, MacArthur responded fiercely that the only way to keep the Chinese from entering the war was to advance to the Yalu. Yet they were already em-placed south of the river and had already attacked UN forces! Ignoring the facts and bowing to MacArthur, the Joint Chiefs went ahead with the offensive.

In the lull between November 6 and the new UN offensive on November 24, Peng gathered more than 300,000 Chinese troops, 180,000 in the west and 120,000 in the east facing 10th Corps. The UN command had assembled 247,000 men, not counting air combat personnel, and they had several times as much firepower as the Chinese.

The Chinese possessed little artillery and relied on small arms, machine guns, and mortars. They had few vehicles and walked into battle, carrying their weapons, ammunition, and food on their backs. Although this severely limited their mobil-ity, they did not have to rely on roads and could march over mountains and emerge at wholly unexpected places. This flex-ibility permitted the Chinese to exploit their highly effective tactics: night infiltration, attacks to the front, envelopments to the sides, and roadblocks in the rear.

The 8th Army offensive made deep penetrations in the first couple of days. But the Chinese knew the three-division South Korean corps on the right or eastern flank, less well armed and trained than the Americans, was the weak link in the UN chain. On the night of November 24–25, Chinese forces attacked the ROK 8th Division at Tokchon, on the corps' extreme right in the high Taebaek Mountains twenty-five miles east of the main U.S. positions along the Chongchon River. Strategically, this was a flanking move against the entire UN position on the Chongchon, and it achieved instant success.

Using their tactics of infiltration, envelopment, and road-blocks, the Chinese shattered the ROK corps and by November 27 had penetrated as far back as the supporting artillery units behind 9th Corps, which comprised the American 25th and 2d Infantry Divisions and the newly arrived 5,200-man Turkish Brigade and held the center of the UN line. These penetrations threatened to unhinge the entire 8th Army position.

Shortly thereafter on the 10th Corps front, Chinese forces encircled a large part of the 1st Marine Division and nearly destroyed three battalions of the 7th Infantry Division around the southern end of Changjin (Chosin) Reservoir.

On the night of November 25–26, Chinese troops attacked the 25th and 2d Divisions. The 25th, on and across the Chongchon, was able to withdraw across the river and retreat southward and miss the heaviest Chinese blows. However, the 15,000-man 2d Division, on the right, caught the full tide of the Chinese attack.

The 2d Division's positions centered about Kujang-dong, on the Chongchon about fifteen miles northwest of Tokchon. The Chinese hit the division's left-hand regiment, the 9th, on the front, flanks, and rear, and the outfit staggered under the blows.

Although reserves temporarily halted the Chinese penetrations, the division was in extreme danger. The ROK collapse on the right flank had eliminated any possibility of retreat southeastward. There were no north-south roads leading away from the river around Kujang-dong. This left only one line of withdrawal: a road leading southwest fifteen miles along the river valley to Kunu-ri, where another road led southward eighteen miles to Suchon. There the 1st Cavalry Division and the British 27th Brigade had emplaced to block any Chinese move farther southward.

It was imperative to keep open the road to Kunu-ri. Otherwise, the 2d Division would be blocked about Kujang-dong and forced to surrender. On the night of November 26–27 the Chinese attacked the 2d Division with the ferocity of the night before. At daylight, with his right flank in danger of collapse, the 9th Corps commander, John B. Coulter, sent the Turkish Brigade eastward on the Kunu-ri–Tokchon road in hopes of slowing the Chinese. The Turks got only eight miles east of Kunu-ri when they collided with a Chinese force, which quickly surrounded them.

Facing this severe threat, General Walker ordered withdrawal of the entire 8th Army. Most elements did so quickly, but 2d Division and the Turks remained in great jeopardy. However, the Turks broke out of their encirclement and pulled back toward Kunu-ri. They had suffered severely, but had kept the Chinese from sealing off 2d Division's retreat.

Units of 2d Division formed blocking positions in the mountains above the Chongchon Valley long enough for the main elements to withdraw to Kunu-ri. Then they fell back to the village as well. The division, with the Turks attached, prepared to move southward to Sunchon.

On the morning of November 29, however, the 2d Division commander, Laurence B. Keiser, got shocking news: a Chinese roadblock had been set up ten miles south of Kunu-ri on the lifeline to Sunchon. Keiser sent a reconnaissance and infantry company to crack the roadblock, but it failed. Although the British 27th Brigade moved northward from Sunchon, it needed time to reach the block.

General Keiser, realizing his division and the Turks were in danger of disintegration, ordered his 9th Regiment—now down to 400 men, an eighth its normal strength—to attack astride the Kunu-ri–Sunchon road at 7:30 A.M. the next day, while the remainder of the division followed behind.

The retreat of 2d Division and the Turks was gruesome. The 9th Regiment slowly cracked open the roadblock against fanatical Chinese resistance. Meanwhile other Chinese forces assembled in the hills on either side of the road and fired on everything that moved. The Americans and Turks soon realized they had to traverse an avenue of death and mayhem.

Whenever firing commenced from hidden Chinese soldiers, the men hit the ditches and their abandoned vehicles stalled the column. Although antiaircraft halftracks armed with twin 40mm cannon sometimes sprayed the roadsides with fire, the biggest reason the column was able to run the bloody gauntlet was that U.S. aircraft constantly ranged up and down the road, firing at anything on the sides that looked suspicious.

When the aircraft were on their runs, the Chinese mortars and guns fell silent. But as soon as the nose of an attacking plane turned up after a strafing run, the Chinese opened fire again. Progress accordingly came in short spurts, followed by halts caused by enemy fire or disabled or burning vehicles. These vehicles had to be bypassed or pushed aside. The remaining trucks and carriers soon became loaded with wounded. The dead were left strewn along the road.

By 9:30 P.M. the lead battalion had cleared the last blockade and the Turks and Americans pressed into Sunchon. Most of the Turkish Brigade had been killed or captured, while 2d Division had suffered 5,000 casualties and had been rendered combat-ineffective.

Although total disaster had been averted, morale collapsed in the United Nations forces. The entire 8th Army began a frantic retreat southward. By the middle of December it was nervously in place below the 38th parallel, having fallen back 120 miles in the longest retreat in American history and having completely lost the initiative.

Meanwhile in the 10th Corps sector the 25,000 Americans with a few attached ROKs and Britons began an agonizing retreat in extremely cold weather, losing 6,000 men before reaching the sea at Hungnam and evacuating to South Korea on December 24. The great effort to conquer North Korea had failed.

The Truman administration could have avoided the immense casualties and the humiliation of defeat if it had ignored General MacArthur's pressure and examined American national interests coldly. MacArthur himself lost much prestige because of his bad judgment and because the United States suffered severe additional defeats, including the loss of Seoul and a retreat into South Korea early in 1951. Only by taking advantage of the primitive Chinese logistical system were the Americans able to advance back toward the 38th parallel in the spring of 1951.

MacArthur remained intransigent to the end. In March 1951, he deliberately torpedoed an attempt by Washington to arrange a cease-fire. This treachery was so flagrant that Truman at last relieved him. Although this ended the general's influence on military decisions, the Truman administration was so angered by Beijing's intervention and so convinced of Chinese aggressive intentions that it spurned a Chinese offer for a cease-fire in June 1951 and allowed the war to go on. Republican President Dwight Eisenhower at last ended hostilities in July 1953, on basically the same terms the Chinese had offered two years previously—a cease-fire along the battle line.

11

The Enduring Unity of War

I N THIS VOLUME, we have marched alongside warriors through more than two thousand years of history. Our comrades have included Roman legionaries, Mongol horsemen, Napoleonic soldiery, American Civil War Rebels and Yankees, World War I Tommies, Lawrence of Arabia's Bedouins, Chinese revolutionaries, British Desert Rats, Rommel's Afrika Korps, and Douglas MacArthur's Inchon invaders.

However varied the weapons they wielded, however disparate their mobility, the soldiers of all these eras followed commanders who had to overcome virtually identical obstacles.

Now perhaps it is appropriate to summarize the lessons learned in the campaigns we have examined and to demonstrate how the principles of strategy have remained unchanged through the two millennia of warfare we have surveyed. This will show us there is a unity in war that transcends eras and technology, a unity that makes the tasks of Scipio Africanus in 210 B.C. practically the same as those of Norman Schwarzkopf, who commanded Desert Storm in 1991.

War remains an art rather than a science, despite the immense amount of invention, industry, and technology lavished on war since the beginning of organized society. We have seen that although the principles of war are simple and can be learned by anyone, the application of each principle requires much care, skill, and caution. We have seen that great captains recognize when one principle applied in a specific situation can bring victory, while another principle, equally valid, can bring disaster. A single example: faced with the destruction of the Confederate army if it remained united and inactive, Robert E. Lee and Stonewall Jackson violated the principle of concentration of force and divided the army in order to exercise another principle, the unexpected descent of part of the army upon the rear of the enemy. This permitted them to win a victory at Second Manassas in the summer of 1862.

Let us illustrate from examples in preceding chapters how great captains in different eras applied some of the salient principles of war and demonstrate that the principles don't change, although the circumstances under which they can be employed vary profoundly.

Operating on the Line of Least Expectation
and Least Resistance

Hannibal took his army through the formidable swamps of the Arnus River in Tuscany in 217 B.C. rather than face the Roman army directly. Not expecting such a move, the Romans left the route open, permitting Hannibal to emerge behind the Roman army with a clear road to Rome. This forced the Romans to abandon their strong position and rush after the Carthaginians. Hannibal ambushed the dislocated Romans at Lake Trasimene and destroyed nearly their entire army. (See page 41.)

The Carthaginians in Spain believed Scipio Africanus would strike at their armies and left unguarded their capital and principal port, New Carthage. Scipio seized this city in 209 B.C., cut off the main sea connection with Carthage, caused several Spanish tribes to come over to the Romans, and abruptly threw the Carthaginians on the strategic defensive. (See page 50.)

Genghis Khan focused the attention of the Khwarezmian army by fierce attacks on cities along the Syr Darya in Turkestan in 1220. He then led a Mongol army across the supposedly impassable Kyzyl Kum to seize Bokhara, far in the enemy rear, isolating the Khwarezmian capital of Samarkand and blocking reinforcements from the south. In a single quick campaign, the Mongols captured Samarkand and destroyed the Khwarezmian empire. (See page 82.)

In 1862, two Union armies were advancing on Staunton in Virginia's Shenandoah valley, while a third Union force under Irvin McDowell was marching from Fredericksburg to reinforce George McClellan, who was waiting on it to assault Richmond. Stonewall Jackson, instead of marching against any of the three armies, crossed to a rail junction east of the Blue Ridge Mountains. Federal leaders, believing he might attack northward, stopped McDowell in place. Jackson, without firing a shot, had neutralized McDowell and delayed McClellan's attack on Richmond. He now moved back into the Shenandoah Valley and forced one Union army to retreat into the Appalachian Mountains, leaving the other army isolated and vulnerable to his attack. (See page 131.)

When strong German forces attacked Holland and Belgium in 1940, British and French mobile forces rushed northward to block the advance. Erich von Manstein, knowing this would happen, had convinced Adolf Hitler to send most of his armored or panzer strength through the supposedly impassable Ardennes to seize Sedan, which was defended only by second-rate troops. When this occurred, the German panzers had a nearly clear path westward to the English Channel, trapping the Allied armies that had rushed into Belgium and ensuring the defeat of France. (See page 219.)

Maneuvering onto the Rear of the Enemy

By demonstrating with part of his army at Valenza on the Po River in northern Italy in 1796, Napoleon convinced the Austrian commander this was the sole French target, drawing Austrian defenders to that point. Napoleon then marched the majority of his forces downstream to Piacenza, thereby turning all possible enemy lines of defense, and forcing the Austrians to abandon all of northern Italy except the fortress of Mantua. (See page 107.)

Stonewall Jackson in 1862 convinced the Federal commander Nathaniel Banks he was driving directly on Strasburg in the Shenandoah Valley, where Banks had concentrated most of his army. Instead, Jackson crossed Massanutten Mountain, seized Front Royal in the enemy rear, cut the direct rail link with Washington, and forced the Union forces into disorderly retreat. (See page 133.)

In September 1918, Britain's General Allenby feinted against the eastern front of the Turkish and German army in Palestine but struck unexpectedly against the western flank near the Mediterranean, breaking a large gap in the enemy line. Cavalry and armored cars now rushed through, quickly traversed the Plain of Sharon, seized the passes in the Mount Carmel massif, and blocked all Turkish rail lines and routes of retreat northward. The Turkish-German army disintegrated as it tried to flee eastward into the Jordan Valley. British and Arab forces advanced on Damascus, Syria, and beyond, inducing Turkey's surrender on October 31. (See page 184.)

In early 1941 a British force led by nineteen tanks got around the Italian army retreating along the coastal highway in Libya and formed a strategic barrage at Beda Fomm. There the British armor destroyed most Italian tanks attempting to withdraw. Without tank support and cut off from their retreat route, the remainder of the Italian army surrendered. (See page 242.)

While almost the entire North Korean army was pressing United Nations forces into a narrow perimeter around Pusan in southern Korea in 1950, General Douglas MacArthur invaded Inchon far to the north by sea, severed the main highways and only double-tracked railway in Korea, and, by cutting off supplies and reinforcements, caused the North Korean army to disintegrate. (See page 284.)

Occupying the Central Position

In the opening act of the Italian campaign in 1796, Napoleon drove his army between the Piedmontese and Austrian armies in the Apennines west of Genoa, thereby permitting him to defeat one enemy force before having to deal with the other. (See page 104.) Later at Castiglione he got his army between two major Austrian attacking columns, driving back one, then defeating the other. (See page 110.)

Stonewall Jackson marched to Port Republic in the Shenandoah Valley in 1862, where his army kept the two Union armies pursuing him from uniting. Jackson then attacked one of the armies and forced it to retreat, causing the other Union army to withdraw as well. (See page 138.)

Following a "Plan with Branches"

Although an eighteenth-century French officer, Pierre de Bourcet, coined this phrase, Subedei Bahudur used the principle in 1241 in the Mongol invasion of Europe. One column of Mongol horsemen rushed westward into Poland and Germany north of the Carpathian Mountains, drawing off all forces in this region. Meanwhile, Subedei sent three columns toward Budapest, on the Danube River, one by a wide northern circuit, another through Transylvania to the south, and the third directly on the city. These widely separated penetrations kept Austrian and other forces from uniting with the Hungarians. Even if one column had been stopped, the others could have reached Budapest. The Mongols destroyed the now-unsupported Hungarian army a few days later. (See page 87.)

Napoleon, at the start of his Italian campaign in 1796, advanced several columns at wide points along the front, knowing that the enemy could not be at all places at once and that if one French column was blocked, the others could continue to seize key enemy positions. (See page 104.) Once the main resistance had been broken, Napoleon used a variation of the principle by sending three columns, each within a day's march of the other, against the Piedmontese capital of Turin. Each column, like an octopus's waving tentacle, could grip any opponent in its path, while the other columns could close up on it. This threat caused the Piedmontese government to capitulate (see page 106).

The Union's General Sherman, after capturing Atlanta in 1864, advanced through Georgia in several columns. Confederate defenders did not know whether the columns were aiming at Augusta to the northeast or Macon to the southeast and divided their forces between both. Sherman burst between them and seized Savannah. When Sherman turned northward into South Carolina, the Confederates could not tell whether he was targeting Charleston or Augusta. Sherman went between both and captured Columbia, forcing the Rebels to abandon Augusta and Charleston. Again, the Confederates did not know whether

Sherman was marching toward Charlotte or Wilmington, North Carolina. Instead he seized Fayetteville between the two, then marched on Goldsboro, having virtually eliminated the Confederate rear and forced the end of the war. (See page 159).

Early in 1935, the Chinese Communist army was being pressed front and rear by far superior Nationalist forces under Chiang Kai-shek in Guizhou province in south-central China. The Communist leader, Mao Zedong, ordered a column to feint directly west toward the Guizhou capital of Guiyang. This drew off the entire Nationalist force pressing on his rear. Mao then marched rapidly northeast, making Chiang believe he was planning to invade Hunan province and holding in place a huge Nationalist army on the Hunan border. Mao now turned northwest and struck for his real target, Zunyi, in northern Guizhou, which he seized almost without opposition. Although Mao was unable to set up a base at Zunyi or cross the upper Yangtze river into China's western province of Sichuan as he had hoped, he had so distracted Chiang that Nationalist forces were unable to combine against Mao when he retraced his steps and marched into the southwestern province of Yunnan. (See page 201.)

Making Convergent Tactical Blows

This is the essential formula for actual battle, achieved by dividing the attacking force into two or more segments and attacking the target simultaneously. One of the greatest examples of this formula was at Cannae in 216 B.C. Hannibal advanced his less dependable Gauls and Spanish soldiers in the center, while holding back his more reliable African infantry on each flank. When the Romans pressed this convex line backward, Hannibal launched his Africans against both Roman flanks. Meanwhile the Carthaginian cavalry, having driven away the Roman horse, fell on the Roman rear, cutting off retreat. It was the greatest battle of annihilation in history: 70,000 of the 76,000 Romans died. (See page 46.)

At Ilipa in Spain in 206 B.C., Scipio Africanus unexpectedly formed his army, half as wide and strong as the Carthaginian line opposing him, with his undependable Spanish levies in the center and his solid Roman legionaries on each wing. Hasdrubal Gisgo had lined up his best Carthaginian regulars in the center and his weaker Spanish infantry on the wings. Scipio ordered his Spaniards to advance on the regulars, but slowly, holding them in place, while sending his Roman legionaries forward at a fast pace. When close to the opposing line, the legionaries wheeled obliquely half left and half right and fell on the front and flanks of the Spaniards, shattering them and forcing the Carthaginian regulars in the center—who had not been engaged at all—to fall back in defeat. (See page 55.)

At Castiglione in northern Italy in 1796, Napoleon unveiled his "strategic battle," using "envelopment, breakthrough, and exploitation," by which he won numerous victories. First he pinned the enemy down with a frontal attack designed to draw all enemy reserves forward. Then he sent a strong force around the flank onto the enemy line of supply and retreat. The enemy commander, obliged to get troops quickly to defend against this thrust, thinned a part of his line closest to the flank threat. Napoleon could locate this point prior to the battle and assembled a strong *masse de rupture* opposite it in advance. This force cracked a hole in the weakened point. Cavalry and infantry then poured through, breaking the enemy's equilibrium and causing defeat or disintegration. (See page 110.)

Conclusion

Great captains, either consciously or unconsciously, have sought to follow an axiom that Sun Tzu enunciated nearly 2,400 years ago: "Supreme excellence consists of breaking the enemy's resistance without fighting." This, of course, is an ideal, seldom attained in practice. Yet great captains nearly always have sought ways to reduce the opposition they will face by striking at undefended or ill-defended targets of vital importance to the enemy, trying to pit their strength against enemy weakness.

Sometimes they do this by advancing on the rear of the enemy, a practice that Genghis Khan, Napoleon, and Stonewall Jackson made famous. Sometimes they attack the weak flanks of the enemy, as Scipio Africanus did at Ilipa. Sometimes they send out numerous columns, which confuse the enemy as to their intentions. Subedei and Sherman conquered vast stretches of territory by this formula.

A great captain must make his opponent believe he's aiming at a point different from his actual target or must force his opponent to cede one point to save another. Since no commander will willingly uncover his Achilles' heel, great captains must deceive to win. Thus, great generals throughout history have practiced the policy that Stonewall Jackson put into words in 1862: to "mystify, mislead, and surprise" the enemy.

Selected Bibliography

Alexander, Bevin. *Korea: The First War We Lost*. New York: Hippo-
    crene, 1986, 1993.
———. *Lost Victories: The Military Genius of Stonewall Jackson*.
    New York: Henry Holt, 1992.
Alexander, E. Porter. *Military Memoirs of a Confederate: A Critical
    Narrative*. New York: Scribner's, 1907.
Allan, William. *History of the Campaign of Gen. T. J. (Stonewall)
    Jackson in the Shenandoah Valley of Virginia*. Philadelphia:
    Lippincott, 1880.
Appleman, Roy. *South to the Naktong, North to the Yalu: The United
    States Army in the Korean War*. Washington: U.S. Govern-
    ment Printing Office, 1961, 1975.
Aron, Raymond. *Clausewitz: Philosopher of War*. Englewood Cliffs,
    N.J.: Prentice-Hall, 1985.
Barnett, Corelli, ed. *Hitler's Generals*. New York: Grove Weidenfeld,
    1989.
Barrett, John G. *Sherman's March Through the Carolinas*. Chapel
    Hill: University of North Carolina Press, 1956.
de Beer, Sir Gavin. *Hannibal: Challenging Rome's Supremacy*. New
    York: Viking, 1969.
Bradford, Ernle. *Hannibal*. New York: Dorset, 1990. Reprint of 1981
    original edition.
Bradley, Omar, and Clay Blair. *A General's Life: An Autobiography*.
    New York: Simon & Schuster, 1983.
Carver, Michael. *Dilemmas of the Desert War*. Bloomington: Indiana
    University Press, 1986.
Chambers, James. *The Devil's Horsemen: The Mongol Invasion of
    Europe*. London: Cassell, 1988.
Chandler, David G. *The Campaigns of Napoleon*. New York: Macmil-
    lan, 1966.
von Clausewitz, Karl. *On War*. Ed. Anatol Rapaport. Harmondsworth,
    England: Penguin Books, 1968.

Colin, Commandant J. *The Transformations of War.* Translated by
    L. H. R. Pope-Hennessy. London: Hugh Rees, 1912.
Collins, J. Lawton. *War in Peacetime: The History and Lessons of
    Korea.* Boston: Houghton Mifflin, 1969.
Cooke, John Esten. *Stonewall Jackson: A Military Biography.* New
    York: D. Appleton, 1876.
Dabney, Robert Lewis. *Life and Campaigns of Lieut.-Gen. Thomas J.
    (Stonewall) Jackson.* New York: Blelock, 1866.
Delbrück, Hans. *Geschichte der Kriegskunst im Rahmen der poli-
    tischen Geschichte.* Bände 1, 3, 4. Berlin: Verlag von George
    Stilke, 1900, 1907, 1920. Reprint, Berlin: Walter de Gruyter,
    1964. English translation by Walter J. Renfroe, Jr. *History of
    the Art of War Within the Framework of Political History.*
    Vols. 1, 3, 4. Westport, Conn.: Greenwood, 1975, 1982, 1985.
    Reprint, Lincoln: University of Nebraska Press, 1990.
Dorey, T. A., and D. R. Dudley. *Rome Against Carthage.* Garden City,
    N.Y.: Doubleday, 1972.
Douglas, Henry Kyd. *I Rode with Stonewall.* Chapel Hill: University
    of North Carolina Press, 1940, 1968.
Dupuy, R. Ernest, and Trevor Dupuy. *The Encyclopedia of Military
    History.* 2nd ed. New York: Harper & Row, 1986.
Flanagan, Lt. Gen. Edward M., Jr. "The 100-Hour War." *Army,* April
    1991, pp. 18–26.
Freeman, Douglas Southall. *R. E. Lee: A Biography.* 4 vols. New York
    and London: Scribner's, 1934–35.
————. *Lee's Lieutenants: A Study in Command.* 3 vols. New York:
    Scribner's, 1942–46.
Friedman, Norman. *Desert Victory: The War for Kuwait.* Annapolis,
    Md.: Naval Institute Press, 1991.
Fuller, J. F. C. *A Military History of the Western World.* 3 vols. New
    York: Da Capo, no date. Reprint of 1957 original edition.
————. *The Conduct of War, 1789–1961.* New Brunswick, N.J.: Rut-
    gers University Press, 1961.
Gardner, Brian. *Allenby of Arabia.* New York: Coward-McMann, 1966.
Griffith, Samuel B., II. *The Chinese People's Liberation Army.* New
    York: McGraw-Hill, 1967.
Guderian, Heinz. *Panzer Leader.* New York: E. P. Dutton, 1952.
Harrison, James Pinckney. *The Long March to Power: A History of
    the Chinese Communist Party, 1921–72.* New York: Praeger,
    1972.
Henderson, G. F. R. *Stonewall Jackson and the American Civil War.*
    New York: Longmans, Green, 1936.
Hsü, Immanuel C. Y. *The Rise of Modern China.* 3rd ed. New York:
    Oxford University Press, 1983.
Irving, David. *The Trail of the Fox: The Search for the True Field
    Marshal Rommel.* New York: E. P. Dutton, 1977.
Johnson, Robert U., and C. C. Buel, eds. *Battles and Leaders of the*

Civil War. 4 vols. New York: Century Magazine, 1887–88. Reprinted, Secaucus, N.J.: Castle, no date.

Kahn, Paul, adapter. *The Secret History of the Mongols.* San Francisco: North Point, 1984.

Kataoka, Tetsuya. *Resistance and Revolution in China: The Communists and the Second United Front.* Berkeley: University of California Press, 1974.

Kuo, Warren. *Analytical History of the Chinese Communist Party.* Books 2, 3. Taipei, Taiwan: Institute of International Relations, 1968.

Lawrence, T. E. *Revolt in the Desert.* New York: George H. Doran, 1927.

Legg, Stuart. *The Barbarians of Asia.* New York: Dorset, 1990. Originally published 1970 as *The Heartland.*

Lewis, Lloyd. *Sherman: Fighting Prophet.* New York: Harcourt, Brace, 1932, 1958.

Liddell Hart, Sir Basil H. *Paris, Or the Future of War.* New York: E. P. Dutton, 1925.

————. *A Greater Than Napoleon: Scipio Africanus.* Boston: Little, Brown, 1927.

————. *Great Captains Unveiled.* Boston: Little, Brown, 1928.

————. *Sherman: Soldier, Realist, American.* New York: Dodd, Mead, 1929.

————. *The Real War 1914–1918.* Boston: Little, Brown, 1930, 1964.

————. *The Ghost of Napoleon.* New Haven: Yale University Press, 1933.

————. *The German Generals Talk.* New York: William Morrow, 1948.

————. *Strategy.* New York: Frederick A. Praeger, 1954.

————. *The Tanks.* New York: Praeger, 1959.

————. *History of the Second World War.* New York: Putnam's, 1971.

Lister, R. P. *Genghis Khan.* New York: Dorset, 1989 (originally published 1969).

Liu, F. F. *A Military History of Modern China, 1924–1949.* Princeton, N.J.: Princeton University Press, 1956.

Livy. *The War with Hannibal.* Translated by Aubrey de Sélincourt. Harmondsworth, England: Penguin Books, 1981.

Lucas, James. *Panzer Army Africa.* San Rafael, Calif.: Presidio, 1977.

von Manstein, Erich. *Lost Victories.* Chicago: Henry Regnery, 1958.

Mao Tse-tung. *On Guerrilla Warfare.* Translated by Samuel B. Griffith II. New York: Praeger, 1961.

Marshall-Cornwall, Sir James. *Napoleon as Military Commander.* London: B. T. Batsford; Princeton, N.J.: Van Nostrand, 1967.

von Mellenthin, F. W. *Panzer Battles.* Norman: University of Oklahoma Press, 1956.

Miers, Earl Schenck. *The General Who Marched to Hell.* New York: Dorset, 1990.

Military Review, the Professional Journal of the United States Army,
Vol. 71, no. 9 (September 1991).
The Memoirs of Field-Marshal the Viscount Montgomery of Alamein.
Cleveland: World Publishing, 1958.
Paret, Peter, ed. *Makers of Modern Strategy.* Princeton, N.J.: Princeton University Press, 1986.
Polybius. *The Histories.* Book 3. Loeb Classical Library. New York: Putnam's, 1922.
Ratchnevsky, Paul. *Genghis Khan: His Life and Legacy.* Oxford: Basil Blackwell, 1991.
Rommel, Erwin. *The Rommel Papers.* Ed. B. H. Liddell Hart. New York: Harcourt, Brace, 1953.
Salisbury, Harrison. *The Long March: The Untold Story.* New York: Harper & Row, 1985.
Schmidt, Heinz Werner. *With Rommel in the Desert.* London: George G. Harrap, 1951.
Schnabel, James F., and Robert J. Watson. *The History of the Joint Chiefs of Staff, The Joint Chiefs of Staff and National Policy,* vol. 3, *The Korean War,* part 1 (1978), part 2 (1979). Washington: Historical Division, Joint Secretariat, Joint Chiefs of Staff.
Schram, Stuart. *Mao Tse-tung.* New York: Simon & Schuster, 1966.
Scullard, Howard Hayes. *Scipio Africanus: Soldier and Politician.* Ithaca, N.Y.: Cornell University Press, 1970.
Selden, Mark. *The Yenan Way in Revolutionary China.* Cambridge, Mass.: Harvard University Press, 1971.
Sherman, William Tecumseh. *The Memoirs of General William T. Sherman.* Bloomington: Indiana University Press, 1977.
Soren, David, Aicha Ben Abed Ben Khader, and Hedi Slim. *Carthage.* New York: Simon & Schuster / Touchstone, 1991.
Special Report: The U.S. Army in Operation Desert Storm. Arlington, Va.: Association of the U.S. Army, 1991.
Sun Tzu. *The Art of War.* Ed. James Clavell. New York: Delacorte, 1983.
Savage, Raymond. *Allenby of Armageddon.* Indianapolis: Bobbs-Merrill, 1926.
Tanner, Robert G. *Stonewall in the Valley.* Garden City, N.Y.: Doubleday, 1976.
Twitchett, Denis, and John K. Fairbank, eds. *Cambridge History of China.* Vol. 13. Cambridge: Cambridge University Press, 1986.
Wilkinson, Spenser. *The Rise of General Bonaparte.* Oxford: Clarendon, 1930.
Wilson, Dick. *The Long March.* New York: Viking, 1971.
―――. *The People's Emperor.* Garden City, N.Y.: Doubleday, 1980.
Young, Desmond. *The Desert Fox.* New York: Harper, 1950.

Index

Italicized page numbers refer to photographs.